D0152568

EUROPEAN WOMEN ON THE LEFT

Recent Titles in
Contributions in Women's Studies

Women in Irish Society: The Historical Dimension
Margaret MacCurtain and Donncha O'Corrain

Margaret Fuller's **Woman in the Nineteenth Century**
A Literary Study of Form and Content, of Sources and Influence
Marie Mitchell Olesen Urbanski

To Work and to Wed: Female Employment, Feminism,
and the Great Depression
Lois Scharf

Eve's Orphans: Mothers and Daughters in Medieval Literature
Nikki Stiller

Women, War, and Work: The Impact of World War I
on Women Workers in the United States
Maurine Weiner Greenwald

Self, Society, and Womankind: The Dialectic of Liberation
Kathy E. Ferguson

Women as Interpreters of the Visual Arts, 1820-1979
Claire Richter Sherman, editor, with Adele M. Holcomb

Flawed Liberation: Socialism and Feminism
Sally M. Miller, editor

Wartime Women: Sex Roles, Family Relations, and the Status
of Women During World War II
Karen Anderson

Women Writers in Black Africa
Lloyd W. Brown

The Paradise of Women: Writings by Englishwomen
of the Renaissance
Betty Travitsky, compiler and editor

The Origins of the Equal Rights Amendment: American Feminism
Between the Wars
Susan D. Becker

EUROPEAN WOMEN ON THE LEFT

Socialism, Feminism, and the Problems Faced by Political Women, 1880 to the Present

Edited by *Jane Slaughter* and *Robert Kern*

Contributions in Women's Studies, Number 24

GREENWOOD PRESS
WESTPORT, CONNECTICUT • LONDON, ENGLAND

Library of Congress Cataloging in Publication Data

Main entry under title:

European women on the left.

(Contributions in women's studies ; no. 24 ISSN 0147-104X)
   Bibliography: p.
   Includes index.
   CONTENTS: Springer, B. Anna Kuliscioff.--Honeycut, K.
Clara Zetkin.--Boxer, M. When radical and Socialist
feminism were joined. [etc.]
   1. Women and socialism--Europe--History--Addresses,
essays, lectures. 2. Feminism--Europe--History--
Addresses, essays, lectures. I. Slaughter, Jane,
1941-   II. Kern, Robert, 1934-   III. Series.

HX546.E9   335'.0094   80-23553
ISBN 0-313-22543-5 (lib. bdg.)

Copyright © 1981 by Jane Slaughter and Robert Kern

All rights reserved. No portion of this book may be
reproduced, by any process or technique, without the
express written consent of the publisher.

Library of Congress Catalog Card Number: 80-23553
ISBN: 0-313-22543-5
ISSN: 0147-104X

First published in 1981

Greenwood Press
A division of Congressional Information Service, Inc.
88 Post Road West, Westport, Connecticut 06881

Printed in the United States of America

10 9 8 7 6 5 4 3 2 1

Contents

EUROPEAN
WOMEN
ON
THE LEFT

Introduction

JANE SLAUGHTER AND ROBERT KERN

Women have fought, demonstrated, and served as leaders whenever radical political or social movements emerged in the past
centuries of European history. They participated in the religious and
political sects of the English Civil War, the tumultuous events of the
French Revolution, the collective but sporadic working-class actions
of the early nineteenth century, and the militancy of the 1870 Paris
Commune. Radical political movements clearly appeal to women
as well as to men, although perhaps for different reasons. Since the
late nineteenth century, however, when popular protest evolved
toward large-scale socialist organizations with clear objectives,
programs, and demands, it has become easier to measure what
radical politics have meant for women, and how women influenced
these movements.[1]

The socialist and communist parties of Europe and Russia,
because of their size and influence, provide the most extensive
material through which women's relationship to radical politics can
be analyzed. Well-defined socialist revolutionary organizations
appeared by the 1890s in France, England, Germany, Italy, and
Russia. By comparison with other contemporary political groups,
more women responded to the recruitment efforts of and became
involved in socialist politics. Socialist theory held out the promise
of a brighter future, but it also contained a systematic analysis of
women's oppression and the preconditions for women's emancipation.

The clearest picture of socialist ideology concerning women is
evident in the mainstream writings of Karl Marx, Friedrich Engels,

August Bebel, and V. I. Lenin. All accepted the fact of women's subordination in society and found the origin of this inequality at that point in prehistory when private property and the monogamous family appeared and mother right ended. Engels referred to this process as "the world historic defeat of the female sex."[2] The first class in the history of humanity to be oppressed was women in monogamous marriages. This pattern unfolded historically in the family, where "the wife became the head servant, excluded from all participation in social production, . . . remain[ing] excluded from public production and unable to earn."[3] Modern bourgeois marriage added the concept of individual sex love, a romantic notion that was in direct contradiction with the reality of the relationship between husband and wife. Given the analysis of the origins of inequality, the emancipation of women will occur only with the socialist revolution, the destruction of private property, and the disappearance of traditional marriage and the family. Lenin believed this change would come about automatically: "Real freedom for women is possible only through communism."[4]

Of course, theoretical statements are not always borne out in practice; and in fact, women's involvement in radical politics from the beginnings of socialist organizing has been marked by contradictions and frequent change. The essays in this volume, by examining a diverse group of radical women, illustrate the complexity of this relationship.

The First International of Socialist Parties, which existed from 1864 to 1876, at first produced a minimal linkage of women's concerns and socialism. The all-consuming struggle between Bakunists and Marxists over the strategies of revolution from above or below blocked all but a brief debate over reform legislation for protection of women and children employed in factories. Many artisans in the International strenuously objected to any special consideration for women, since they saw them as undesirable competitors for scarce jobs.[5] A minority wished to bar women from the workplace altogether.

The demise of the First International after the Paris Commune and the subsequent period of antisocialist legislation split the anarchists and socialists permanently and led to an improvement of socialist policy toward women. Even though the German Social

Democratic party refused to acknowledge equal rights for women in their Gotha program of 1875, the publication of August Bebel's *Woman Under Socialism* in 1883 opened the way for the creation of a separate women's organization among German socialists.

Delegates to the Second International of Socialist Parties, begun in 1889 and destroyed by World War I, ultimately recognized the creation of the International Socialist Women's Secretariat. As many as sixty female delegates attended the 1907 meeting at Stuttgart where support for universal suffrage finally was adopted. However, almost simultaneously, Rosa Luxemburg and Lenin began agitating for militant socialist action in case of a European war, and the issue of an international working-class strike to stop militarism paralyzed the socialist movement thereafter. Most socialist women, in their disappointment, nevertheless expected that war would create a revolutionary situation, and that in the process the consciousness of proletarian women was bound to rise. Almost all the women discussed in this collection found at least part of their inspiration and opportunity for activism during World War I and the Russian Revolution.

After the war and revolution, during the interwar years, the rise of fascism and authoritarian regimes in Italy, Spain, Portugal, and Germany competed for attention with any sort of women's rights activities. Once again, feminist content within socialism suffered enormously; antifascism allowed no place for other ideas, particularly in a Europe "manfully" preparing for a second war within a generation. World War II did little to liberate women in any revolutionary sense, although large numbers of women did participate in left-wing resistance activity. In fact, destruction of fascist totalitarianism, while removing active oppression and even perhaps generally discrediting conservatism for the next thirty years, was followed by only a slight revival of feminism. The returned soldier, determined to live normally and in utter convention, frowned upon any redevelopment of the movement, while the Eastern European socialist governments followed a strict form of Stalinist orthodoxy. Not until the 1960s did children of the war generation begin to appreciate the radicalism of the past and the work of earlier leaders, and ultimately move beyond them.

There are some important themes behind these events that mark the major chronological divisions of women's participation in radical politics. The most important one, certainly, is the relationship between feminist consciousness and revolutionary politics on both theoretical and practical levels.

> Feminism simultaneously complements and conflicts with the ideology of the primacy of class consciousness. It is complementary in that it implies equal rights for women within sexually mixed, class based settings; it is conflicting in that it also implies that the sexual identification creates a solidarity among women that transcends class divisions.[6]

Socialist leadership continued to be less than precise on the relationship between class and sex. Most socialists, male and female, rejected association with the bourgeois movement for women's rights that developed in the late nineteenth century. As Bebel wrote, "the class antagonism turns up likewise on the surface of the woman's movement." He went on, however, to indicate that "hostile sisters have, to a far greater extent than the male population, . . . a number of points on which they can, although marching separately, strike jointly."[7] Socialists themselves remained ambiguous as to whether working-class women should organize separately and work for goals common to their sex. Marx had proposed in 1868 the "formation of women's branches," or "female branches of the working class without, however, interfering with the formation of branches composed of both sexes."[8] Half a century later Lenin suggested that there should be "no special organization for women. A woman communist is a member of the party just as a man communist, with equal rights and duties." At the same time, he supported formation of special groups to carry on the work among backward peasant women, but "that is not feminism, that is practical revolutionary expediency."[9] In most cases, however, separate sections for women did emerge in the European radical parties.

Nevertheless, women's issues became secondary to the more important goal of a working-class revolution because solution of the "woman question" supposedly would accompany the revolutionary transformation of society. Acceptance of this "higher cause" of human liberation became characteristic behavior for

radical women, particularly when parties of the Left found themselves facing major international crises of war and fascism. All the
women discussed in this volume can be said to have had a feminist
consciousness, if only because they recognized the existence of a
particular "female condition" with accompanying specific needs.
However, their responses to reconciling the dilemma of this attitude
with stated party ideology and practice were quite different.

Sylvia Pankhurst, for example, moved into radical politics
through the middle-class women's rights movement in England,
and though increasingly concerned with class issues, never totally
abandoned her feminist perspective. She also succumbed to the
myth of a "higher cause" in her antiwar activities; clearly she,
Angelica Balabanoff, and Italian communist women in the interwar years preferred to dedicate themselves to "broader" social
causes rather than to what they perceived as the narrow and perhaps
selfish scope of women's rights. Other radical women, among them
Clara Zetkin, Anna Kuliscioff, and Margarita Nelken, spent the
greater part of their energies organizing women and working for
women's rights, such as the vote or improved working conditions.
They frequently confronted male colleagues on these issues, but in
the end accepted a fairly rigid class analysis of conditions and
remained within the boundaries of orthodox ideology and practice
on the "woman question."

Several other women moved further in their analysis of women's
condition and became concerned with issues such as male-female
relations, life within the family, and the oppressive nature of wom-
en's work in the home. These inquiries unfortunately put them on
shaky ground in the eyes of party leadership, and consequently
Madeleine Pelletier, Alexandra Kollontai, and Federica Montseny
suffered rather painful personal contradictions as they attempted
to adjust their perceptions of the "woman question" with established policy.

A second theme that can be traced in the lives of the women
leaders included in this volume is the distinction between their
motives and actions and those of the so-called rank and file. The
leaders, usually the product of middle-class or upper-class back-
grounds, found their inspiration in ideals and visions of the future
rather than in the pragmatic necessities of survival that weighed so

heavily on their working-class sisters. They acted more freely out of conviction and could separate their public and private lives in a way that was impossible for proletarian women, whose exploitation in the workplace seemed an extension of the oppression felt by the entire working-class family.

In examining the experiences of women radicals, care must be taken to distinguish the cultural and social norms of various periods. Whereas the idea that the "personal is political" has had considerable impact in the contemporary radical scene, individuals in the earlier movements felt no great need "for psychological insight into their own and other's behavior."[10] Personal liberation was not a conscious motive to become political.

In addition to the problems raised in the formal development of theory and party programs related to women, there is also what one might call a "private" side to the picture of women's involvement in radical politics. Regardless of principle, radical men often reflected traditional social conservatism and upheld the feminine stereotypes of their times. Women remained second-class citizens because, as Lenin noted, "the old master right of the man still lives in secret."[11] Women in the party found themselves relegated to support services, underrepresented in party deliberative groups, and victims of hostility to the very notion of their participation in the work force, while at home they were still considered nothing more than wives or mothers. Marxist theory, which placed the "women question" within the family, reinforced these attitudes, despite attempts by individuals such as Kollontai and Leon Trotsky to reevaluate the forces governing family behavior. The Left often glorified motherhood and reaffirmed the idea of "separate spheres." Such problems of attitude had particular significance to the women discussed in this collection, all of whom, by their participation in the public political arena, were inevitably breaking with traditional stereotypes. When women challenged their treatment by male colleagues, the answer frequently (and correctly) stressed that women occupied a better place in the revolutionary parties than in any other European political organization.

In the decades since the end of World War II, many of the tensions mentioned above have continued to develop in Europe; however, some new differences in the relationship of women to radical politics are visible. These changes can be explained generally by the "de-radicalization" of traditional parties, which has helped to foster pluralism in contemporary leftist politics. One large component of this more diversified radicalism is the "new feminism" whose roots began in the rush of student political activism in 1968.

A major result of the new movement has been the creation of an open confrontation between commitment to feminism and commitment to the organized Left. Radical women, pressing for more precise solutions to the problems apparent in the previous decades of left-wing political history, contend that issues of sex cannot be subsumed simply within the analysis of class struggle, pointing out the need to understand the relationship of patriarchy to modern industrial capitalism and the social control and oppression of women that follow. The socialist historian, Sheila Rowbotham, argues that "a new and non-dogmatic Marxism is in the making. . . . In exploring the dual oppression of women, feminists will provide an important remedy to the narrowness of Marxist interpretation." In other words, "feminist theory and the political practice of the women's movement can be a model for the rest of the left."[12]

In some cases the model is very practical. The women's movement has managed to push traditional parties toward a more radical stance on issues such as maternity care, divorce, and abortion. This is the discernable pattern in Italy, France, and Spain. Leaders of communist and socialist parties, concerned with the expansion of their electoral base, have been forced to recognize certain deficiencies in their approach to women's issues. In a 1974 interview, Enrico Berlinguer, leader of the Italian Communist party, agreed that the party needed to reevaluate its position on feminist issues and admitted that since the founding of the party in 1921, "the woman question subsequently has not been thoroughly examined by the worker's movement nor by the communists: there has not been any communist thinker who has ventured deeply and specifically into this material."[13]

In addition to the emphasis on feminism within the "old" parties, recent decades also have witnessed the development of an autonomous radical feminism. European radical women, involved in student political activity after 1968, became aware of their subordinate status within the groups and voiced the opinion that these movements did not meet women's needs and therefore could not reconstruct society in a truly revolutionary fashion. In West Germany, for example, "German women discovered their own experience with discrimination . . . in discussion within a political movement whose goals they had originally supported."[14] In France as well, women participating in the May, 1968, student revolt frequently arrived at similar conclusions and soon severed their connections with these radical sects.[15] The Union of Italian Women (UDI), founded in 1945 and usually composed of socialist and communist women, maintained an uneasy alliance with the radical parties until 1970, when they began searching for autonomy and a greater assertion of feminist independence. The same sort of evaluation can be made of the French Women's Union, which also dates from 1945.[16]

The experience of Ulrike Meinhof, one of the most prominent and spectacular of the new activists, though not necessarily typical of the "new feminism," must be seen as one of the variations of pluralist radicalism. She combined a fairly astute awareness of feminist issues and an eclectic dedication to what she perceived as a higher cause. She may in fact be considered in the tradition of Montseny and Nelken, both of whom condoned violence and worked closely with the terrorists of their time. For Meinhof, the connection between feminist motivations and the willingness to use violence as a means of achieving revolutionary goals never became clearly defined, but her life must be considered as one of the possible, though not necessarily desirable, forms of the relationship between women and radical politics. In the modern era a more negative assessment of women terrorists is directly prompted by popular perceptions and media coverage that link this activity with "too much emancipation," as the essay on Meinhof points out.

To understand the scope and significance of women's involvement in radical political movements, we must have some idea of the contradictions and patterns of this participation as they have appeared in the past. The struggle of other women to define ideology, translate feminist consciousness into practice, and scale major obstacles provides us with a historical base by which we can more accurately assess the current potential of feminist radicalism and understand the real portent of Herbert Marcuse's observation that the "Women's Liberation movement today is perhaps the most important and potentially the most radical political movement we have."[17]

NOTES

1. The description of these "proactive" movements is found in Charles Tilly, Louise Tilly, and Richard Tilly, *The Rebellious Century, 1830-1930* (Cambridge, Mass.: Harvard University Press, 1975). The earlier forms of activism are described in Dorothy Thompson, "Women and Nineteenth-Century Radical Politics," in Juliet Mitchell and Ann Oakley, eds., *The Rights and Wrongs of Women* (Baltimore: Penguin Books, 1976), pp. 112-38.

2. *The Woman Question: Selections from the Writings of Karl Marx, Friedrich Engels, V. I. Lenin and Joseph Stalin* (1951; reprint ed., New York: International Publishers, 1970), p. 16.

3. Ibid., p. 39.

4. Clara Zetkin, *Lenin on the Woman Question* (New York: International Publishers, 1951), p. 15.

5. Karen Sacks, "Engels Revisited: Women, the Organization of Production and Private Property," in Michelle Zimbalist Rosaldo and Louise Lamphere, eds., *Women, Culture and Society* (Stanford, Cal.: Stanford University Press, 1974), p. 209.

6. Robin Miller Jacoby, "Feminism and Class Consciousness in the British and American Women's Trade Union Leagues, 1890-1925," in Berenice Carroll, ed., *Liberating Women's History* (Urbana, Ill.: University of Illinois Press, 1976), p. 137.

7. August Bebel, *Woman Under Socialism* (1883; reprint ed., New York: Schocken Books, 1971), p. 5.

8. Hal Draper, "Marx and Engels on Women's Liberation," *International Socialism* 57 (July-August 1970): 27.

9. Zetkin, *Lenin on the Woman Question*, p. 15.

10. Ellen Key Trimberger, "Women in the Old and New Left: The Evolution of a Politics of Personal Life," *Feminist Studies* 5, no. 3 (1979): 437, 439.

11. *The Woman Question*, p. 93.

12. Jill Roe, "Modernization and Women: Recent Writings on Victorian Women," *Victorian Studies* 22, no. 2 (1977): 187; and Nancy Hartsock, "Feminist Theory and the Development of Revolutionary Strategy," in

Zillah R. Eisenstein, ed., *Capitalist Patriarchy and the Case for Socialist Feminism* (New York: Monthly Review Press, 1979), p. 56.

13. Carla Ravaioli, ed., *La questione femminile: Intervista col PCI* (Milan: Bompiani, 1976), p. 197.

14. Hilke Schlager, "The West German Women's Movement," *New German Critique*, no. 13 (1978): 63.

15. Elaine Marks and Isabelle de Courtivron, eds., *New French Feminisms: An Anthology* (Amherst, Mass.: University of Massachusetts Press, 1979), pp. 28-38.

16. For development of the UDI, see Giulietta Ascoli, "L'UDI tra emancipazione e liberazione, 1943-64," *Problemi del socialismo* 17, no. 4 (1976): 109-60; and Anna Tiso, *I comunisti e la questione femminile* (Rome: Riuniti, 1976). For a discussion of French women and the Communist party, see Joanna Durand and Sybil Fasso, "Il partito comunista francese e le donne," in Lidia Menapace, ed., *Per un movimento politico di liberazione della donna* (Verona: Bertani, 1972), pp. 303-17.

17. Herbert Marcuse, "Marxism and Feminism," *Women's Studies* 2, no. 3 (1974): 279.

1.
Anna Kuliscioff: Russian Revolutionist, Italian Feminist

BEVERLY TANNER SPRINGER

Anna Kuliscioff was one of that remarkable group of women who participated in the emergence of European socialism and feminism in the nineteenth and twentieth centuries and who were then "hidden from history" until the recent effort to reevaluate the contribution of women. In her lifetime, she associated with many of the great names of European socialism, ranging from Engels and Bakunin to Turati, and participated in major historical events in both Russia and Italy. Her activities were as diverse as membership in the Russian "going-to-the-people" movement and leadership of the Italian Socialist party (PSI) during its early phases. She also became a medical doctor, an editor, and one of the most noted Italian feminists in the struggle for universal suffrage.

Her life interacted with the major socialist tendencies of her time and gradually changed her own intellectual position from anarchism to moderate social democracy. But throughout all the changes and adjustments in her life, she remained a feminist at heart, and much that is best about her life centers on this issue.

Anna Kuliscioff was born in Russia in either 1854 or 1857.[1] In later years she refused to write an autobiography or to talk about her childhood. We do know that her family was prosperous and respected converted Jews. The family name was Rosenstein; she adopted the name Kuliscioff and was known by it throughout her adult life. Her father apparently favored Kuliscioff and encouraged her efforts for an education. He continued to give her financial support and to visit her long after she left Russia. However, her stronger ties appear to have been with her mother, who encouraged her independence. Later Kuliscioff was to support her mother when her parents separated. In many respects, the little that we know about Kuliscioff's relationship with her parents and her strong desire for education and independence is very similar to the pattern noted in biographies of her Russian contemporaries who later played leading roles as socialist feminists.[2]

After completing gymnasium (secondary school) in Russia, Anna Kuliscioff went to Switzerland, where women were allowed to attend the universities. She became part of that little group of Russian students in Zurich that J. M. Meijer has depicted so well in his *Knowledge and Revolution*.[3] But her short career in higher education came to an end when she tore up her university papers to signify her total commitment to revolutionary activity and briefly joined a Saint-Simon-inspired anarchist group. Kuliscioff was soon married to one of the group members, Peter Markelovich Makarevich, and together they returned to Russia to work clandestinely for the revolution in 1873. Even though her husband was arrested and disappeared from her life forever, she continued her work, chiefly among the "going-to-the-people" sect, narrowly escaping arrest, frequently suffering hardships, and making at least one dangerous trip abroad to obtain a printing press.[4]

The four years that she spent with other young idealists among the Russian peasants probably had a lasting influence on her feminism and populism, which were two of the most significant ideals of her adult life. She and her colleagues lived as equals, the females sharing risks and hardships with the males. From hints in the memoirs of her male colleagues we know that she was admired for her ability and her courage. She also developed a rather unique rapport with the semibarbaric people among whom they lived. Many years later she recalled her respect for them.

Kuliscioff fled Russia in 1877 to avoid arrest and never returned to her homeland. She went to Switzerland where she met Andrea Costa, a well-known Italian anarchist who later became a key figure in Italian socialist history. Kuliscioff was, by all accounts, a beautiful young woman. They became lovers in a traumatic relationship. She was a vulnerable young foreigner; he was a dedicated political activist and a somewhat traditional Italian male. They were both marked by the governments of the day as dangerous and were frequently separated by arrests, imprisonment, exile, and political missions as they moved back and forth around Switzerland, France, and Italy. For several years she tried to conform to the somewhat subservient life-style that Costa seemed to expect from her, but the hardship of her life and his lack of support drove her to desperation and even to thoughts of suicide.[5]

After the birth of a daughter in 1881, Kuliscioff determined to leave the destructive relationship with Costa and to become independent. She decided to become a doctor, probably an even more courageous decision than the one to go underground in Russia. She was alone in a foreign country where the language was still strange to her, but she kept her child with her and managed to finish her course of study. The hard work and poverty of that period seriously injured her health.

The separation from Costa was permanent. Later the bitterness of their last years together faded, and they were friends until his death. Their daughter, Andreina, remained with Kuliscioff. Kuliscioff, who had been so unconventional in her own life, became a very conventional mother, enjoying and taking pride in her daughter. She gave her a quite regular home life and sheltered the child from the turmoil of her own political life. Much later when the daughter wanted to marry into a conservative, Catholic family, Kuliscioff accepted the decision. This daughter of two fiery revolutionists led a very apolitical and traditionally Catholic family life. Later still, Kuliscioff was a very affectionate grandmother, and one of her grandsons became a Catholic priest.[6]

While Kuliscioff was studying medicine, she remained in touch with socialist developments through a network of friends and also undertook the task of fund raising to help Russian radicals who were being repressed by Czar Alexander II. In the midst of this task in 1884, she met Filippo Turati, a rising young socialist leader, who was to be her companion for the rest of her life. Her days as a "wandering Jew" were over.[7]

Turati is perhaps the best-known figure in the formative period of the Italian Socialist party. He was a refined and gentle man, not a fiery activist, a reformist socialist who directed the Socialists into parliamentary activity, becoming a prominent deputy. He disavowed violence and sought compromise. His partnership with

Kuliscioff was remarkably stable and fruitful. Together they established the Italian Socialist party and edited the most important Italian socialist journal, *Critica Sociale*.

Kuliscioff and Turati lived in Milan. Her apartment over the *Galleria* became famous as the salon where the great issues of Italian socialism were formulated and where the next generation of socialist leaders was groomed. Kuliscioff and Turati did not settle down to an unbroken, genteel existence, however. During periods of political unrest both were arrested and imprisoned. Kuliscioff's health deteriorated greatly during a harsh imprisonment from 1898 to 1899.[8] She eventually became an invalid, but continued to be involved in developments through her writing and her influence on many socialist leaders. Turati was frequently absent in Rome after he became a deputy, but he kept her informed through almost daily letters.[9] Their collaboration continued through the difficult years of World War I and the rise of fascism. It ended with her death in 1925.

Almost all socialist currents found in Europe during the nineteenth century were represented in Italy at one time or another. Leaders kept in contact with other European socialists through visits and correspondence. They regularly read each other's works and solicited essays for their own journals, and so the development of Italian socialism paralleled the general evolution of European socialism from anarchism to Marxism and finally to social democracy. In 1879 when Anna Kuliscioff entered Italy, the influence of Bakunin was beginning to wane and that of Marx to appear. Italian socialism was turning toward electoral politics and away from insurrection. Andrea Costa's career illustrates this development. As a young man he had been involved in the 1874 Bakunist insurrection in Bologna, but in 1882 he was elected the first Socialist deputy to the Italian parliament. He spent the rest of his life fighting for moderate socialism within the bounds of legality.

The PSI, organized in 1892, became a battleground for struggles among the various socialist tendencies. The party's founding marked a split between anarchism and socialism, but an uneasy balance remained between a commitment to Marx and to parliamentarianism, a dilemma that kept the party in a constant state of turmoil during the years that Turati and Kuliscioff were its active leaders. Most of the PSI members finally came to support parliamentary activity above revolutionary violence after the failures of the "Fatti di Maggio" and the repressions of the Pelloux regime. During the subsequent period, when Giolitti, who was five times prime minister, instituted a long period of relatively stable parliamentary government, the dominant faction of the PSI once again concentrated upon parliamentary activity as the focus for socialist life. The party competed successfully in electoral politics and sent an impressive band of deputies to battle for its ideals in the Chamber of Deputies. By 1911, it had become so much a part of the Italian political mainstream that Giolitti could state that "Karl Marx has been relegated to the attic."[10] This appeared to be true when seen from the floor of the parliament, but it was less true within the hall of party congresses and among the rank and file.

Anna Kuliscioff's socialism developed along lines that were close to the main PSI tendencies. Her philosophy did not totally reflect the party line, however, since at times she criticized party leaders (even Turati) and often disagreed vehemently with the party leaders over their policy of gradualness on woman suffrage. Through her long association with *Critica Sociale* she was both a participant and a critic in the evolution of Italian socialism. Her perspective was, no doubt, influenced by contacts with socialists throughout Europe and her familiarity with their writings.[11]

Although Kuliscioff left her anarchist ideas behind in Russia and was a Marxist after 1884, three themes remained constant in her thought. All related fundamentally to the fact that her basic outlook always was conditioned by humanistic values. She once stated that "certainly the hard economic doctrine of Karl Marx would not be enough to make me a socialist. What would socialism be if not the aspiration to social justice, the faith in the liberation of all humanity, not only from need, but from the brutal instincts, from spiritual meanness."[12] She and Turati also wrote: "All of life has taught us that socialism is not an end in itself, since the real end is man. . . . "[13] The three themes were populism, flexibility, and feminism. The first two will be discussed briefly, while the third will be examined more fully.

Kuliscioff's Russian populism remained an essential part of her philosophy even in the very different circumstances of Italy. She consistently rejected elitism and argued that the fate of socialism ultimately would be in the hands of the people and not in the directives of the leadership. In a famous speech she made during the Italian trial that followed her arrest in 1879, she reaffirmed this belief.

> The internationalists cannot make revolutions at their convenience because individual force can neither make revolutions nor provoke them; it is the people who make them. . . . The socialists . . . ought to take part in popular movements as in every manifestation of popular life in order to direct them to socialist principles, but they cannot create revolutions themselves. The revolution must come from the people and cannot be made against their will.[14]

Throughout her life, Anna Kuliscioff maintained her own contacts with the working class through her medical practice in industrial districts and later in various organizations she created for proletarian women. Her rapport with these women convinced her to fight elitist tendencies and to struggle to maintain the PSI as a mass popular movement. She argued that socialist policies cannot succeed if imposed from the top. They must be based on the understanding of the people. She criticized Turati and other party leaders in 1908 for becoming too distant from their own working-class constituency. Turati later joined her in criticizing the elitism of the Bolsheviks and rejected Soviet attempts to dominate European socialism.[15] At the end of her life when young party leaders came to tell her of their socialist studies, she continued to counsel them to go to the people.

Flexibility as a hallmark in Anna Kuliscioff's socialism arose from the lack of dogma in her appreciation of Marxism. She felt that Marx had been mistaken in his analysis of developments in Russia, for instance, and she always professed a belief that the roads to socialism must differ just as societies differ. She easily reconciled her acceptance of parliamentary tactics in Italy with her support of revolutionary means in Russia. In the latter, a repressive czarist regime made force a necessity. In the former, "old insurrectional methods and barricades [are] useless and anarchic." The

Italian road to socialism had to be through the defense of liberty and democracy. Turati added, "Any other way is bankruptcy for us."[16]

Kuliscioff was always more of an activist than a theoretician. Her letters are full of discussion of party strategy rather than abstract analyses of doctrine. This consuming interest kept her philosophy pragmatic and flexible. In one situation she could argue against Turati's acceptance of a cabinet post and in another argue for it. In times of serious breakdown of order in Italy she could also contemplate revolutionary activity by the socialists. She discussed such a possibility in correspondence with Engels during a crisis in 1894.[17] Later, on the eve of Mussolini's march on Rome, she wrote bitterly but perceptively, "There are only two solutions—either serious revolution with the socialists in power or a military dictatorship."[18]

The third characteristic of Kuliscioff's socialism, feminism, was perhaps the most integral part of her life. Socialism could not be complete without a feminist component. She fully accepted the ideas about the liberation of women that were common in the Russian radical movement when she participated in it, living the life of an emancipated female. However, during the early years of her relationship with Andrea Costa, Kuliscioff faced the dilemma of reconciling her feminist tendencies with her role as mistress of an Italian. A hint of the problem is found in a letter Costa wrote to her in 1880 stating, "I am certain that you could never say certain things now that you once said about the independence of the woman. . . . "[19] Costa himself professed a belief in sexual equality, but he practiced the traditional form of Latin male domination—an attitude Kuliscioff alternately accepted and resisted. Her letters recorded an increasing outrage as the end of the relationship approached. When Costa accused her at one point of having an affair, she wrote, "I see one thing, as always, that everything is permitted to men, but the woman must be his property."[20] When they parted, Anna wrote that she resented his approach to her as a sex object and not as a woman—"the desire of the species rather than a human union."[21]

Before Kuliscioff entered Italy, a small number of Italian women were involved in active organized support for women's issues. The second half of the nineteenth century was a period when feminist consciousness was growing both in Europe and in North America. Industrialization disrupted traditional life-styles, and women entered the modern work force and experienced new vulnerabilities. Among the first issues to attract an emerging feminist consciousness in Italy was educational reform. The institutionalization of education was a feature of the new industrial society, and middle-class women in increasing numbers found careers in education. The name of Maria Montessori is prominent among the women who sought to reform education and to protect the women who were making teaching a profession.[22] Other women focused on economic issues and social reforms that were relevant for life and work in an industrializing and urban society. A growing number were attracted to the universal suffrage crusade. A moderate feminism even gained respectability with token acceptance by the *Dame dei Salotti* (genteel ladies) and even by Queen Margherita.[23]

The international women's conferences that were the hallmark of feminist efforts in the decades around the turn of the century encouraged organization of women's groups throughout Italy. An organizer was assigned responsibility for Italy at the Chicago International Women's Congress of 1893. A national council of women was formed in Italy in 1898 to integrate the numerous local organizations that existed in many of the major cities,[24] but the crisis of that year diminished the significance of the event. However, organizations for women continued to grow and to create a network for female activists.

The early feminists endorsed a variety of ideologies as well as a variety of views concerning problems in Italy. Some, such as Anna Maria Mozzoni in 1881, were pessimistic about the possibility of bettering the condition of women within the existing system.[25] However, as Italy moved into the Giolitti era, most feminists began to seek specific reforms, which then seemed feasible in the more liberal political environment. Many of them focused their concern on the increasing number of women to be found in the new industrial work force, and increasingly these feminists identified with the new Socialist party.

Milan was a center for both feminism and socialism and the site for the growing interrelationship of the two movements. Kuliscioff was inevitably in contact with the participants, although her name is not among the early activists. Her concern for working-class women, whose problems she knew well through her medical practice, soon brought her into organized women's groups. Her efforts were, at first, directed toward enactment of legislation to protect working women. She gathered data, wrote legislation, and edited the first successful Italian socialist women's periodical.[26] She became a recognized authority on women and also was active as a speaker and organizer among working-class women. In keeping with her populism, she believed that lasting improvement in conditions for working-class women could be gained only through their own organized efforts.

Her feminism was moderate and compatible with both her current reformist orientation to socialism and her understanding of the needs of Italian working-class women. She advocated equal pay for women and health and safety conditions at work. She was careful not to shock accepted Italian values in regard to the family and motherhood and did not believe that the traditional legal protection of the family should be removed prematurely. In her private correspondence she could be sarcastic about the institution of marriage, but in public she defended the need of a marriage contract to protect women and children until women were able to participate equally in work and to have their children cared for. She wrote, "the economically dependent woman will always have a master."[27] She foresaw a slow evolution toward a time of freer relationships between men and women, but she knew personally the suffering that could ensue for those following such a course in the existing system. As a French feminist journalist wrote, "she has an eminently practical spirit."[28]

The long struggle that Kuliscioff carried on for votes for women combined her reformist socialism and her moderate feminism. The battle for suffrage was a major women's issue in both Europe and North American by the end of the nineteenth century. A Feminist Alliance for the Suffrage was formed by an international congress in Berlin in 1904. An Italian deputy proposed votes for women that same year, and Italian women submitted a petition in support. Kuliscioff did not become involved in the struggle until a few years later. She apparently turned to the vote in disillusion with her hopes for legislation and for the Socialist party. She endorsed universal suffrage, in part as a means to restore the populist element that she believed to be essential in socialism. She urged the Socialist party to endorse the cause in order to revitalize the party by providing an ideal around which members could rally.

Although Kuliscioff's feminism was moderate, her position on the vote showed an essential difference from moderate bourgeois feminism. She disdained the argument that the suffrage should be extended to middle-class women first and then later be given to working-class women. She noted that a similar promise had been made to working-class men during the French Revolution but had not been fulfilled, While she was not unsympathetic to the condition of middle-class women, she believed that the vote was much more essential for working-class women, who needed liberation from capitalism and not just from men.[29]

The leadership of the Socialist party did not agree with Kuliscioff on the vote. Even Turati found her total commitment to universal suffrage difficult to understand.[30] Persistently she argued her position before party meetings, submitted resolutions to party congresses, and encouraged Socialist deputies to introduce proposals for the vote into Parliament. She presented her case in *Critica Sociale* and in the feminist journal that she edited. Her battle for suffrage was the longest and most public struggle of her life, and the fact that she fought it when she was already a semiretired invalid is evidence of her commitment to the issue.

Most of Kuliscioff's feminist writings have a very modern tone, with analyses and prescriptions familiar to contemporary readers of feminist literature. Her socialist values are apparent, but she did not become entangled in the sterile debate about women as a class that is found in some Marxist feminist writings. Her major feminist work was *Il Monopolio dell'uomo*, which was first prepared for a conference organized by *Il Circolo filologico milanese* in 1890 and published as a pamphlet soon afterwards, becoming one of the first examples of socialist propaganda in Italy.[31] In it she examined the condition of women and found that they had been kept in an inferior situation throughout history. While the original cause of the subjugation of women might have been biological necessity or historical utility, the important point, she argued, was to recognize that in modern society there is no justification for the continuation of this inequality. She argued that economic subjugation is the most important aspect of the general subjugation of women because economic independence is the essential precondition for all other apsects of equality. In contemporary society, she noted that many women workers were doing the same jobs as men. Based on her study of the pay and work of women, she asserted that the work of women, even when as demanding as the work of men, always received less pay and often involved longer hours. She observed, "It would seem that almost even the work has a sex and is transformed by the sole fact that it is a woman that does it."[32] Furthermore, she noted the hypocrisy of a society that tolerated the neglect of working-class children by women in low-paying jobs but decried the demise of middle-class family life resulting from the competition of middle-class women for desirable professional positions.

Kuliscioff also wrote that the inferior status of women had harmful consequences beyond the obvious injustice to the individual woman. When women were cast in the role of "parasite" or "eternal adolescent," a virtue was made of their private martyrdom that led them to impart a reactionary political outlook to their children and neglect the needs of the larger society. She understood well the covert power and unhealthy influence that frustrated wives and mothers could assert within the traditional Italian family. She wrote, "Men make laws, but women make custom and they prevail in cases of conflict."[33] Men, children, and society would all benefit when women became responsible participants.

As for the future, Kuliscioff believed that the true character and capability of women could not be evaluated by past performance because they were so conditioned by centuries by subjugation and submission. Thus, it was incorrect to say that women could not be inventors, engineers, or whatever they wished to become, simply because they had not shown the ability to do so historically. Past performance was no measure of women's potential.

Although Kuliscioff's major work on women, written in 1890, did not mention the vote, in 1892 she wrote, "Civil and political rights are now a necessity for working women and allies them with working men. She must intervene in the great kitchen where they make laws."[34] In her subsequent writings she developed the theme that suffrage was essential for women and woman suffrage was essential for socialism. She demanded "the support of the PSI for the women's vote not as a luxury or as a pastime, but as an undeniable necessity for the life and development of the party."[35] She assumed that if working-class women had the vote, they would join proletarian men to vote an end to capitalism and exploitation.

Anna Kuliscioff's feminist writings published between 1890 and 1910 were all forceful and, at times, biting. She once stated that she did not desire women to be made over in the image of men, since she did not regard men as the ideal being of creation or the basic unit of comparison.[36] Her rationality and humanism, however, gave her writings a tone that probably made them acceptable to a wide audience. She was neither harshly antimale nor antifemale, since she recognized that men were victims as well as exploiters. She knew that feminist reforms were only a part of the total program of reform necessary to make Italy a more humane place. Perhaps surprisingly, she cherished the role of mother, which was so important in Italian culture, hoping to strengthen it, not abolish it. Finally, through her linkage of votes for women to the peaceful abolition of capitalism and exploitation, she put feminism squarely within the socialist arena in a way that no member of the PSI, male or female, could ignore.

Anna Kuliscioff did not live to see suffrage extended to Italian women. World War I, the Russian Revolution, and the turmoil that preceded Mussolini's regime intervened to pose more immediate crises for Italian socialists. When she died in 1925, the hopes of woman suffrage, Italian social democracy, and the promise of the Russian Revolution were all at their nadir.[37] Her life had spanned the great era of modern socialism as well as the seminal period of modern feminism. Few others had been able to participate in so many aspects of those significant developments.

NOTES

1. The best source on Anna Kuliscioff's life in Russia is Franco Venturi, "Anna Kuliscioff e la sua attività rivoluzionaria in Russia," *Movimento operaio* 4, no. 1 (1952): 277-86. Other sources are S. P. Afanas'eva, "Kvoprosy o revoliutsionnoi deiatel' nosti Anny Klushevoi v 1873-1892 godax," in S. D. Skaskin, ed., *Rossiia i Italia* (Moscow: "nauka," 1968),

and Alessandro Schiavi, *Anna Kuliscioff*, in the series *I Pionieri del socialismo in Italia*, 11 vols. (Rome: Opere nuove, 1955), 2. All these sources use the birth date of 1854. For the date 1857 see Ugo Guido Mondolfo and Fausto Pagliari, "Anna Kuliscioff," *Critica Sociale* 36 (1926): 1-2.

2. The writer is indebted for the ideas in this paragraph to information gained at the international conference on "Women and Power: Dimensions of Women's Historical Experience," College Park, Maryland, November 5-6, 1977. The contributions of Barbara Engels and Richard Stites are particularly valuable. See Richard Stites, *The Women's Liberation Movement in Russia* (Princeton, N.J.: Princeton University Press, 1978), and Vera Broido, *Apostles into Terrorists* (New York: Viking Press, 1977). The writer is also indebted to Dr. Kenneth Jensen who translated and analyzed Russian sources and contributed generously from his knowledge of Russian intellectual history.

3. Jan Marinus Meijer, *Knowledge and Revolution: The Russian Colony in Zurich (1870-1873)* (Assen, The Netherlands: Van Gorcum, 1955).

4. Venturi, "Anna Kuliscioff," pp. 277-86.

5. Pietro Albonetti, ed., *Lettere d'amore a Andrea Costa* (Milan: Feltrinelli, 1976), pp. 138-39 and 251-52. This recent collection of the letters of Costa and Kuliscioff is invaluable for insights into the life of Kuliscioff.

6. Andreina married a son of the Gavazzi family in 1904. Her son, Egidio, became a priest.

7. Albonetti, *Lettere d'amore a Andrea Costa*, p. 156. In November, 1880, Anna Kuliscioff wrote to Vera Zasulich that she was "immensely tired, morally tired of the life of a wandering Jew, the vagabondage of six years weighs on me more than ever." Her life with Turati had all the stability that her life with Costa had lacked.

8. Kuliscioff apparently contracted tuberculosis during an imprisonment in 1878-1879. Subsequent hardship and imprisonment resulted in serious physical disabilities.

9. The best source for an understanding of the relationship of Turati and Kuliscioff is their collected correspondence. Filippo Turati and Anna Kuliscioff, *Carteggio*, ed. Alessandro Schiavi, 6 vols. (Torino: F. de Silva, 1953-1959), vols. 1, 5, 6. An excellent dissertation is also available by Claire La Vigna, *Anna Kuliscioff: From Russian Populism to Italian Reformism, 1873-1913* (Ann Arbor, Michigan: University Microfilms, 1971).

10. A. William Salomone, *Italy in the Giolittian Era* (Philadelphia: University of Pennsylvania Press, 1945), p. 42.

11. Kuliscioff remained in contact with important Russian socialists

such as Vera Zasulich and Georgy Plekhanov. She knew personally other European socialists such as Friedrich Engels, Edward Bernstein, August Bebel, and Benôit Malon. She read the work of the British Fabians, Charles Dickens, Henry George, and a wide range of other contemporaries who dealt with topics of concern to European socialists.

12. Schiavi, *Anna Kuliscioff*, pp. 81-82.

13. "A Reggio Emiliai," *Critica Sociale* 30, no. 19 (1920): 291.

14. Mondolfo and Pagliaria, "Anna Kuliscioff," *Critica Sociale*, p. 6.

15. "A Reggio Emiliai," p. 291.

16. Turati and Kuliscioff, *Carteggio*, 1: xxix.

17. Schiavi, *Anna Kuliscioff*, pp. 109-10.

18. Nino Valeri, *Turati e La Kuliscioff* (Florence: Felice L. Monnier, 1974), pp. 139-40.

19. Albonetti, *Lettere d'amore a Andrea Costa*, p. 17.

20. Ibid., pp. 138-39.

21. Ibid., p. 302.

22. Franca Pieroni Bortolotti, *Socialismo e questione femminile in Italia 1892-1922* (Milan: Mazzotta editore, 1976), pp. 46-47.

23. Ibid., p. 48.

24. Ibid., pp. 34-35.

25. Ibid., p. 48.

26. The periodical *La difesa della lavoratrici* was first published in 1912 and continued to be produced for about ten years. Apparently Kuliscioff was actively involved in its publication for only a short period

27. Anna Kuliscioff, "Il sentimentalismo nella questione femminile," *Critica Sociale* 2, no. 9 (1892): 141.

28. Bortolotti, *Socialismo e questione femminile*, p. 74.

29. Anna Kuliscioff, "Feminismo," *Critica Sociale* 7, no. 3 (1897): 186; and idem, "Proletariato femminile e Partito socialista," *Critica Sociale* 20, no. 9 (1910): 276-78.

30. Concerning her disagreement with Turati, Kuliscioff wrote, "It is not pleasant, I confess, to dissent on a serious question, since he was a comrade in arms who [worked] for a common life for a quarter of a century." Anna Kuliscioff, "Ancora del vote alle donne," *Critica Sociale* 20, no. 4 (1910): 113.

31. Anna Kuliscioff, *Il monopolio dell'uomo* (Milan: Libreria Editrice Galle de C. Chiesa e F. Guidndani, 1890).

32. Ibid., p. 38.

33. Ibid., p. 23

34. Anne Kuliscioff, "Il sentimentalismo nella questione femminile," *Critica Sociale* 2, no. 9 (1892): 143.

35. Kuliscioff, "Proletariato femminile e Partito socialista," pp. 23-24.

36. Kuliscioff, *Il monopolio dell'uomo*, p. 43.

37. A special memorial issue of *Critica Sociale* was published in January, 1926, containing articles in praise of her by leading socialists. The title of one article, "A masculine brain, a maternal heart," expressed well the general sentiment. In that time in Italy, the salute did not have the irony it has for feminists today.

2.
Clara Zetkin:
A Socialist Approach
to the Problem
of Women's Oppression*

KAREN HONEYCUT

From the time of Plato's *Republic* to the present day, an important element in the schemes of socialist egalitarian thinkers had been the concept of equality for the female sex. Not until the development of the European socialist movement, however, and the emergence in the late nineteenth century of a socialist women's movement did the belief in a necessary connection between socialism and feminism assume organizational form. According to socialist theory, women's oppression was determined by the existing mode of production and resulting property relations. Therefore, a revolutionary transformation of society was required for women's emancipation, and this change, it was further argued, could only be realized fully under socialism.

With these views in mind, socialist women concentrated their efforts on actions and reforms calculated to further the class struggle and their liberation as a class; only those demands in favor of the female sex that could be justified in class terms were raised. Influenced by socialist ideology, as well as by the force of contemporary social and ethical norms, they shied away from challenging traditional sex roles within the family, the conventional ideals of motherhood and monogamous marriage, or the prevailing

*This article is reprinted from *Feminist Studies*, Vol. 3, no. 3/4 (Spring-Summer 1976): 131-144, by permission of the publisher, *Feminist Studies,* Inc., c/o Women's Studies Program, University of Maryland, College Park, MD 20742.

division of labor along sexual lines. This attitude on the level of theory had its practical parallel in the sacrifice by socialist women of their separate women's associations, which had been crucial in promoting sexual equality within the larger, male-dominated, socialist political organizations.

This article will illustrate these generalizations as expressed through the work and writings of the socialist-feminist leader Clara Zetkin. Although Zetkin is little known in this country, she was, after Friedrich Engels and August Bebel, the principal theoretician on the "woman question" in the European socialist camp before World War I. A leading figure in the powerful German Social Democratic party, Zetkin was widely acknowledged for her organizational work among working-class women in Germany and socialist women throughout the world. It was due in no small part to her efforts that German Social Democracy by 1914 boasted a female membership of 175,000, or 16 percent of its total membership.[1] Through her journal *Gleichheit (Equality)*, with a circulation in 1914 of 124,000,[2] and through numerous speeches which she delivered at party congresses and before the Second International, Zetkin was able to exert a powerful impact on the formation of socialist policy on the "woman question," as well as to shape the attitude of working-class women in Germany and abroad toward the socialist movement.

The principal speaker for Europe's working-class women was born Clara Eissner in a small weaver's village in Saxony in 1857. In this highly industrialized and densely populated kingdom women were already experiencing the social changes that would later take place throughout Germany. With the increase of manufactured goods and the decrease of articles produced in the home, the value of woman's traditional economic functions within the family declined. As a result, fewer women could be employed in the household economy at a cost commensurate with their upkeep. Nevertheless, the right of women to work outside the home was opposed from practically all quarters. Trade unions fought the entrance of women into factories and, failing this, seconded efforts of employers to confine women to unskilled jobs. Middle-class women were restricted in their occupational options to elementary school teaching and seamstress work. Not until 1893 were women in Germany permitted to study for the *Abitur* necessary for university entrance, and not until the following year did a German university grant women admission as matriculating students.[3]

Until 1908 women were prohibited throughout most of Germany from belonging to political organizations and barred even from attending the meetings of such organizations. As elsewhere in Europe, they were denied active and passive suffrage for national and state legislative bodies and with few exceptions for municipal legislative bodies as well. Legally subjected to paternal tutelage until marriage, a German woman stood thereafter under the legal guardianship of her husband. She was required to secure her husband's permission to work outside the home and had to turn over to him the use of all property she brought into the marriage, as well as the right of administration of all income jointly produced during the marriage. The contradiction in this situation between the forces of economic necessity compelling women to earn their livelihood outside the home and the social, political, and legal constraints limiting their capacity to do so gave rise to the German women's movement.

One of the earliest activists in this movement was Josephine Vitale Eissner, who awakened in her daughter Clara a lifelong interest in the cause of women's rights.[4] This interest was further encouraged by the young woman's contact with the two leaders of the German women's rights movement, Luise Otto Peters and Auguste Schmidt, while a student at the Steyber Institute in Leipzig.[5] Under the direction of Auguste Schmidt, the Steyber Institute provided Clara Eissner with the finest secondary schooling then available to women in Germany. Graduating at the top of her class in 1878, the young woman probably would have continued her education on the university level, had women been admitted to German universities then. University study in Switzerland, such as Clara's friend of later years, Rosa Luxemburg, enjoyed, was out of the question because of the Eissner family's limited financial resources. Since few positions in public school teaching were open to women, Clara Eissner took up work as a governess shortly after graduation.[6] The fact that she was forced to terminate her formal schooling prematurely was a loss she deeply regretted throughout her life and one that doubtless strengthened her determination to fight for justice and equality for her sex.[7]

Clara Eissner was first exposed to socialist ideas through her younger brother and a Russian schoolmate while studying at the Steyber Institute.[8] By 1878, the year of her graduation, she had become closely associated with the German Social Democratic party (SPD), although as a woman she was legally barred from becoming a member. Later that year the SPD was outlawed under Bismarck's Anti-Socialist Law, and in 1881 Clara Eissner went into exile, when the man she loved, a young revolutionary named Ossip Zetkin, was expelled from Germany as an undesirable alien.[9]

Although Clara Eissner shared a flat in Paris with her companion for most of the following decade, assumed his last name, and had two children with him, she chose to remain unmarried, so that she would not lose her German citizenship under the patriarchal marriage laws prevailing at the time.[10] Unable to secure steady employment, the couple lived on the border of poverty. The miserable living conditions took their toll on Ossip Zetkin's health, and after three years of confinement to his bed he died in 1889 of spinal tuberculosis.[11]

Under these circumstances Clara Zetkin was confronted with the task of supporting her companion, herself, and their two small children, as well as assuming most of Ossip's numerous political responsibilities.[12] Precisely because of its hardships, however, this period was crucial for Zetkin's development as a socialist and as a feminist. Although she suffered her full share of the psychological handicaps common to her sex—a lack of self-confidence, shyness before crowds, and a reluctance to make decisions on her own[13]— circumstance obliged her "to make [her] way in the world like a man."[14] This firsthand experience of poverty and disease wedded her indissoluably to the cause of the working class, and the responsibilities she had to assume as sole breadwinner for her family and substitute for her companion in his political activities developed in her capacities as a woman that otherwise might have remained dormant.

In recognition of her political activities and of the attention she had given the issue of women's emancipation in her writings for the socialist press, Zetkin was chosen to deliver the first policy statement of the European working class on the "woman question." In her address at the Founding Congress of the Second International, which convened in Paris in 1889, Zetkin argued that until the woman achieved economic independence, she would be enslaved to the man, just as the worker was to capital. At the same time, she reminded her audience, while the proletarian woman had achieved economic independence from the man, she had merely exchanged masters and "from a slave of the man she [had become] that of the employer." Only with the destruction of capitalism and the victory of socialism would the full emancipation of the female sex be possible.[15]

The refusal of the Reichstag to renew Bismarck's Anti-Socialist Law the following year permitted Zetkin and other exiled Social Democrats to return to their native land. If Zetkin's feminist consciousness had been awakened in Leipzig and her belief in her own potentialities confirmed in Paris, her attitude toward the "woman question" within the context of German Social Democracy first took form in the early 1890s under the impact of the treatment she and other socialist women received at the hands of their male comrades. Despite her writing and speaking experience during the 1880s, as well as her general political experience working within the socialist movement, not even the active support of the party's leader August Bebel and its chief theoretician Karl Kautsky could secure for Zetkin any more creative work within the party than soliciting advertisements for the party press.[16]

Although Zetkin was offered the editorship of a recently founded journal for socialist women at the end of the following year, her initial experience no doubt reinforced her impression that most German Social Democratic men, whatever their theoretical commitment to women's emancipation, had actually not freed themselves from the prejudices of the society in which they lived. Clearly, even within the socialist movement, women would have to rely on themselves to achieve their liberation.

On this issue Zetkin's view was more fundamentally feminist than that of most other leading female figures in the European socialist movement, including Anna Kuliscioff, Rosa Luxemburg, and Adelheid Popp. It was not only the product of Zetkin's personal experience as a woman within the German socialist movement, but, as will be made clear below, followed as well from her dialectical view of female social and sexual development and her conviction in the crucial role of the will, consciousness, and individual responsibility in the revolutionary process.

Basing her analysis on the work of Engels, Zetkin perceived as the root cause of women's inferior social position their economic dependence on men and the fact that they were not engaged in socially productive labor. Like Engels she saw in economic independence for the female sex the necessary precondition for its emancipation, although this could be realized fully only within a socialist society. Zetkin's attempt to demonstrate the precise and specific connection between socialism and women's emancipation was, however, not much more successful than that of her predecessors, Bebel and Engels. Like them, Zetkin proclaimed that socialism, by emancipating the whole of humanity, of necessity emancipated the female sex as well, a liberation that worked well enough in theory but not necessarily in practice. Although she failed to illustrate the exact mechanism whereby the redistribution of goods and the elimination of classes would lead to the downfall of the patriarchal social order, she did convincingly demonstrate that the destruction of private property would transform the family from a unit held together by economic interest into a "moral entity" united by understanding, love, and respect.[17] In Zetkin's view the emancipation of labor would confer a meaningful reality to woman's economic independence for the first time by mitigating the conflict between motherhood and occupational labor, while at the same time "releas[ing] feelings and powers which are today repressed."[18]

The more deeply Zetkin studied the woman question, the more fully she recognized that economic independence alone was not sufficient for women's emancipation. Nevertheless, committed to the traditional socialist view on the woman question and determined to separate proletarian women as far as possible from the bourgeois women's movement, Zetkin continued throughout the 1890s to emphasize the role of class almost to the exclusion of sex as the determinant of oppression for working-class women. In fact, she even apologized for her defense of women's rights, claiming that she supported them "only out of consideration for the value and importance of the female sex in winning over the proletariat, . . . not because I am a woman but rather because I feel myself in the first place a [party] comrade."[19] In the first major policy statement of German Social Democracy on the "woman question," delivered by Zetkin at the 1896 party congress in Gotha, she proclaimed that the place of the proletarian woman was beside the man of her class, since she was exploited chiefly as a worker of the female sex, not chiefly as a woman.[20] As on other occasions, she hastened to assure the men in the party that she was demanding rights for women not for the sake of the women themselves but "in the interest of the working class."[21]

By the late 1890s Zetkin's emphasis gradually began to shift, and she more and more frequently acknowledged the social factor of class along with the biological factor of sex as important in determining female occupation.[22] Increasingly her writings reflected an appreciation of "the woman and man" without class distinction.[23] While earlier Marxist thinkers had underplayed the fundamental problems posed by the woman's role in reproduction, Zetkin, as a woman and a mother acknowledged the profound seriousness of these problems and dealt with them at length.[24]

Adamantly rejecting the view propounded by some Anglo-American feminists at the time that women and men were in all essentials identical, Zetkin argued that they were fundamentally different, although fully equal. In her thinking on this issue she was strongly influenced by the writings of middle-class feminists, as well as by the controversies and theoretical discussions within the contemporary German bourgeois women's movement.[25] As in the case of her middle-class sisters, her conceptions were rooted to a large extent in the German idealist-romantic intellectual tradition. Precisely because women were not identical to men, Zetkin argued, society had a vital interest in the liberation of the female sex to its full creative potential, since this would result not merely in a quantitative increase in social and cultural goods from her expanded role in the world, but in a qualitative increase as well. According to Zetkin woman was neither exclusively a human being nor exclusively a sexual being, but rather a female human being whose fullest development and hence liberation required her fullest development as a female through motherhood and her fullest development as a social being through creative occupational labor. In Zetkin's dialectical view of the female condition there existed a mutually beneficial relationship between development in each of these directions. Through the experience of motherhood women matured and developed moral strengths and ethical values, which in turn contributed to their effectiveness and creativity in occupational work and other activities outside the home. Similarly, through occupational work, women widened their horizons and gained greater knowledge and experience, all of which enabled them to be better mothers and educators of their children.[26]

In approaching the woman problem from this angle, Zetkin left unquestioned the basic sexual division of labor within the family. Although she recognized that the prevailing sexual roles in the family involved many inequities, she challenged only the unequal social and economic valuation accorded the work performed by the two sexes.[27]

Zetkin's viewpoint followed logically from her conception of women's place within the larger social order and her conviction that the interests of the female sex must not be placed before those of humanity as a whole. In Zetkin's view the totality had priority over the particular, "the interest of the species" over that of the female sex, and "the welfare of humanity over the rights of the individual."[28] She dismissed as "superficial" the concept of "the woman as a 'human individual' [with] her 'natural rights' rooted in this fact," and as "cheap" the "appeal to the human rights of the woman."[29] The notion, widely accepted today, of a woman's right to control her body would have been unintelligible to Zetkin, influenced as she was by a cultural heritage and by socialist ideas that accorded priority to the good of the whole over that of the individual.

Thus Zetkin refused to consider birth control or abortion to be legitimate solutions to women's oppression and, in fact, criticized them on both political and moral grounds. Politically, she opposed party support for contraception and abortion because in her view these practices were based on erroneous Malthusian assumptions that poverty was rooted in a scarcity of goods and could be combatted by restricting individual family size. Such an approach to the social problem, Zetkin contended, ignored its actual cause, which was not a scarcity of goods, but their inequitable distribution.[30] Morally, Zetkin rejected on principle the type of liberation for women that birth control represented, dismissing it as the "easy-out of all egoists who want to have as many and as convenient enjoyments in life as possible," by "feigning bourgeois decency during adultery and sexual intercourse outside marriage and egoistically avoiding care and responsibility for a child."[31]

While most leaders in the German socialist women's movement were more sympathetic than Zetkin toward contraception, they shared her assumption that all except selfish and self-centered women "are mothers and . . . should be mothers."[32] In 1896 Zetkin proclaimed that "it cannot possibly be the task of socialist agitators to alienate the proletarian woman from her duties as wife and mother," for in these traditional female roles within the home she "achieve[d] exactly as much as the female comrades we see in our meetings."[33] In accord with this view Zetkin encouraged women to contribute to the socialist cause by using their influence as wives, sisters, daughters, and mothers upon their menfolk during strikes, elections, and demonstrations, especially in connection with such traditionally "women's" causes as the antiwar movement.[34]

At the same time Clara Zetkin hoped to develop in women capacities that would enable them to contribute to the socialist cause in more diverse ways than the traditional ones. Recognizing that both conventional female socialization and prejudice and discrimination against women limited severely the contributions they could make to the socialist cause, Zetkin proposed that special forms of agitation and enlightenment be used in the recruitment of working-class women and that the option be left open for bringing working-class women together on a regular basis for organized activities separate from those of their male colleagues. In her opinion, "If the women of the people are to be won for socialism . . . [w]e cannot make it without [utilizing] special approaches, for which the directing and driving forces are overwhelmingly women dedicated to the awakening and schooling of women."[35]

Before 1908 Zetkin's suggestions were effected to a degree even more comprehensive than she herself favored as a result of the legislation prevailing in most German states prohibiting women from joining political organizations. In this situation socialist women had of necessity to be organized outside the formal structure of the SPD and separately from the men in the party. While Zetkin often defended separate women's organizations under these circumstances on the purely pragmatic ground that they were required in order to conform with German law, she actually supported them for other reasons as well.

Outstanding among these reasons was the fact that such organizations provided a mechanism whereby socialist women, as a minority in the party, could maximize their influence and guarantee representation of their interests, since unity secured protection against disregard and discrimination far more effectively than struggle on an individual basis alone. A second important reason stemmed from Zetkin's conviction that women best understood the needs and interests of women and could most effectively appeal to women, recruit them, enlighten them, and devise methods for maintaining their involvement in the socialist cause.[36] Furthermore, separate women's groups provided Social Democratic women with the opportunity, generally withheld by society, of learning to think for themselves and to make decisions on their own. This, in turn, enabled them to contribute more fully to the socialist movement. As Zetkin pointed out, "If the female comrades can only work, but not make decisions, you take away from them the appeal to their ego, which spurs on to the greatest achievements."[37]

What feminists seventy years later recognized, so had Clara Zetkin, that women's groups help women in a number of important ways to combat the crippling effects of female socialization by providing an atmosphere unencumbered by male prejudice and discrimination or by women's conditioned and habitual deference to men. Zetkin considered women's groups especially valuable in providing a supportive milieu in which women could accustom themselves to speaking before others and could redevelop the habits of thinking for themselves and expressing their own thoughts, which had been lost through centuries of dependence upon men and exclusion from public life.

Stressing to a degree unusual among European socialists of her day the vital importance of the will in revolutionary struggle,[38] Zetkin argued that the principal factors that determined the strength of the socialist movement were "the average political maturity, intellectual energy, [and] readiness to sacrifice" of the individual organized worker.[39] Because, in Zetkin's opinion, "every single member of the Party [was] responsible for what [was] done and permitted by the leaders," she placed a high priority on the development of "strong personalities of unbroken individuality" capable of "independence of judgement and of activity."[40]

Since she believed that independence, equality, and personal responsibility could be developed and maintained only through practice, Zetkin demanded that socialist women be granted a wide scope for participation and responsible activity within the party. As she reminded the party congress in 1908, "Becoming accustomed to independence in thinking and deciding prepares [one] for conscious, vigorous action. . . . [I]t develops insight, concentration of the will, energy, and that pure idealism which drives [one] to place the entire personality in the service of the chosen cause."[41] Moreover, according to Zetkin, it released "the greatest enthusiasm, the highest ambition . . . [and] the most inexhaustible joy in work," while encouraging as well "that serious, thoughtful attitude of responsibility toward the community . . . which is the root of the most conscientious fulfillment of social duties."[42]

Thus in Zetkin's view autonomy for socialist women within the larger party structure provided a valuable means of stimulating individual and group initiative and of maximizing individual and group potential. Most important of all, it benefited the socialist movement by strengthening the moral commitment and increasing the efficiency of its female supporters.

Zetkin's stand on this issue led her to advocate the election of female delegates to party congresses and international congresses in separate women's meetings so long as legal restrictions or male prejudice prevented the election of women at sexually integrated meetings. As a consequence of her views she also called for the maintenance of separate women's groups for education and agitation and at least a limited degree of autonomy for the women in the party even after 1908, when socialist women theoretically stood on an equal footing with their male comrades. At all times she kept in mind the value of special agitational efforts for the female proletariat and the importance of permitting socialist women to hold special women's demonstrations on issues with which women particularly identified. The biweekly journal *Gleichheit*, which Zetkin edited during the quarter-century between 1892 and 1917, was published with this in mind and gave distinct preference to contributions by female socialist writers. Finally, it should be noted, Zetkin maintained a constant vigilance against discriminatory treatment of women within the socialist camp. Not only did she readily criticize male chauvinism in public, but she also defended with the full weight of her influence and prestige socialist women whose denunciations of prejudice against the female sex within the socialist movement had gotten them into difficulty with socialist men.[43]

Among Zetkin's practical achievements in this connection was the establishment of biannual women's conferences in the German party, as well as socialist women's conferences on the international level. She also played an important part as one of the chief promoters both within German Social Democracy and within the Second International of a separate women's bureau run by women and designed to act as an interim center for women's activities between conferences. Finally, Zetkin was instrumental in the establishment of International Woman's Day, which is still celebrated today with varying degrees of success throughout the communist and noncommunist world.

Zetkin's approach to the "woman question" is also reflected in her refusal to compromise on issues affecting working-class women as women. The issue of woman suffrage illustrates this well. As chief speaker on suffrage at the 1907 International Socialist Congress, Zetkin presented a resolution demanding that wherever socialist parties waged campaigns for suffrage, woman suffrage was to be "vigorously advocated in the agitation as well as in parliament."[44] In the course of the ensuing debate Zetkin criticized Austrian socialist women for refusing to propagate the cause of woman suffrage in their recent suffrage campaign out of fear that universal male suffrage might be jeopardized by association with the more controversial demand for woman suffrage.[45] Such opportunism and self-abdication, in Zetkin's opinion, made too blatant a concession to reformist thinking and to prevailing attitudes regarding the "second" sex. Although criticized for her "unsisterly" behavior toward the Austrian women, Zetkin vigorously maintained her position and ultimately won majority support for her resolution.

In the following year a new law governing political association and assembly went into effect throughout the German Reich, granting women the right to organize politically with men. The party executive of German Social Democracy responded to the new situation by advocating the dissolution within its ranks of all separate women's organizations. The Women's Bureau, although permitted to continue functioning for several more years, lost all semblance of independence. Agitational efforts among women could be carried out in the future only with the consent and agreement of the male-dominated party executive.

To reassure the socialist women that their interests were nevertheless being safeguarded under the new conditions, it was stipulated that one seat on the party executive be filled henceforth by a woman, although until 1912 she was without voting rights. Significantly enough, however, the party executive gave its support for this post not to the long-time defender of women's rights within the party and leader of Germany's socialist women, Clara Zetkin, but to a lesser known figure in the movement, Luise Zietz.[46]

While Zetkin was deeply disappointed and hurt at being thus displaced from effective leadership of the movement to which she had devoted the last twenty years of her life, she made little effort to protest the situation.[47] Apparently she failed to realize that the party executive's choice represented not merely a preference between personalities but a deliberate strategy on the part of the SPD leadership who as males, as Marxists, and as bureaucrats committed to revisionist tactics and organizational uniformity, opposed autonomy for socialist women. Blinded by conviction in the SPD's commitment to women's emancipation, Zetkin failed to see that the post-1908 situation was being consciously exploited by the party executive to eradicate that enclave of radicalism and independence which the socialist women's movement under Clara Zetkin had come to represent.

Zetkin's misunderstanding was the result of several other factors as well. In the first place, she was aware that her refusal to compromise on issues about which she felt strongly rendered her in the eyes of most party leaders unsuited for the party executive, which functioned on the basis of consensus.[48] Secondly, Zetkin labored under certain illusions regarding Luise Zietz, mistaking for commitment to principle what was in fact a tendency on Zietz's part to fall easily under the influence of others. Thus, just as Zietz before 1908 had identified herself almost wholly with the ideas of Clara

Zetkin, so after 1908 she associated herself increasingly with the interests and opinions of the party executive.[49] What the members of the party executive had no doubt already concluded concerning Zietz, Zetkin realized only too late: that she was one of those women in the party "not strong enough to escape the influence of the milieu," who out of desire "not . . . to jeopardize the position which has been achieved . . . preferr[ed] concessions to battle against the prejudices of the male comrades."[50] It was probably chiefly out of recognition that Luise Zietz was a more reliable "organization woman," more accommodating, and more willing to compromise than was Clara Zetkin, that the party executive gave preference to Zietz over Zetkin for the post in the party executive.[51]

In view of its aims the party leadership had no doubt made a wise decision, since even after 1908 Clara Zetkin continued to support the notion of separate women's groups within the Social Democratic party, each "with its own administration and its own field of activity."[52] In Zetkin's view the legal changes affecting women's political rights in Germany did not diminish the necessity, so long as sexual prejudice and discrimination existed, for women's autonomy within the Socialist party. As she summed up her viewpoint in 1913:

> If the socialist women's movement is to achieve its full outward and inward success, it must with all firm organizational connection to the movement as a whole, nevertheless possess a certain measure of independence and freedom of movement. . . . [This] is such a vital necessity for the socialist women's movement that its realization absolutely must prevail, whatever the form of the organization. If the male comrades are not judicious enough to provide this vital necessity, it must be fought for.[53]

Unfortunately for the future independence of socialist women, the men in the SPD were not judicious, and the organizational head of the women, Luise Zietz, did not want to fight. In fact, within six months of her election it was clear that Zietz would, on the whole, yield to the pressure of her male colleagues on the party executive. As Zetkin caustically summed up the situation, "One can see who pulls the strings of this marionette."[54]

In the following years Luise Zietz supported the party executive's challenge to Zetkin's independence as editor of *Gleichheit*, defended its decision to postpone the 1910 biannual Women's Conference, and in general appeared to interpret her task more as representing to the socialist women the interests of the party executive than vice versa.[55]

Although Zetkin challenged the party executive publicly over the postponement of the Women's Conference, argued for the "complete reorganization" of the Women's Bureau, and attempted to replace Zietz on the party executive with a woman more likely to resist the pressure of her male colleagues,[56] the absence of an organizational base, the restrictions on Zetkin's editorial independence, and Zietz's popularity with the rank and file as well as the party leadership limited the effectiveness of Zetkin's opposition.[57]

The one-year postponement in 1910 of the Women's Conference proved a mere prologue to its abolition, and in 1912 the Women's Bureau was also dissolved. The full ramifications of the destruction of socialist women's autonomy were not apparent, however, until after World War I. It then became clear that most women active in the party were excluded from positions of actual power and relegated to the kind of charity and welfare work conventionally considered appropriate to the female sex. The percentage of women in positions of genuine responsibility in the party seriously declined, as did this percentage figure among the delegates to party congresses.[58] Finally, the party executive closed down *Gleichheit* (from which Zetkin had already been expelled as editor in 1917 because of her antiwar activity) and provided in its place a fashion and family magazine edited by a man.[59]

Some observers have attributed the development of the socialist women's movement after 1908 to the growth of revisionism in the German Social Democratic party.[60] Others have contended that the women themselves bore the chief responsibility because they had failed to challenge the prevailing patriarchal order at its root in the existing family structure.[61] Speaking more generally, however, Zetkin's goal of realizing feminist ideals through the socialist movement was utopian for the period in which she lived. Genuine sexual equality could not be effectively instituted in the SPD, influenced and bound up as this mass party was with the institutions and ideology of the patriarchal order in which it was imbedded. Nor could a women's movement, such as Zetkin led, successfully maintain its radical feminist orientation once it had been integrated into the SPD's larger reformist, male-dominated organizational structure. In conclusion, German Social Democracy, like other male-dominated, sexually integrated political parties committed to women's emancipation, provided only limited potential as a vehicle through which women could effectively fight for their liberation.

NOTES

1. Werner Thönnessen, *Frauenemanizipation, Politik und Literatur der deutschen Sozialdemokratie zur Frauenbewegun 1863-1933* (Frankfurt/M: Europäische Verlagsanstalt, 1969), pp. 130-31.

2. Hilde Lion, *Zur Soziologie der Frauenbewegung. Die sozialistische und die katholische Frauenbewegung* (Berlin: Herbig, 1926), p. 157. Thönnessen, *Frauenemanizipation*, pp. 119, 134.

3. Margrit Twellmann, *Die deutsche Frauenbewegung im Spiegel repräsentiver Zeitschriften: Ihre Anfänge und erste Entwicklung (1843-1889)* (Meisenheim/Glan: A. Hain, 1972), pp. 127-28, 157-59; Gertrud Bäumer, "Die Geschichte der Frauenbewegung in Deutschland," Helene Lange and Gertrud Bäumer, eds., *Die Geschichte der Frauenbewegung in den Kulturländern*, in the series *Händbuch der Frauenbewegung*, 5 vols. (Berlin: S. W. Moeser, 1901-1906), 1: 96.

4. Luise Dornemann, *Clara Zetkin, Leben und Werk*, rev. ed. (Berlin: Dietz, 1973), pp. 30-31.

5. Anna Plothow, *Die Begründerinnen der deutschen Frauenbewegung* (Leipzig: F. Rothbarth, 1907), pp. 27-32; Gerd Hohendorf, *Revolutionäre Schulpolitik und Marxistische Pädagogik im Lebenswerk Clara Zetkins* (Berlin: Volk und Wissen Volkseigener Verlag, 1962), pp. 11-12, 146; interview with Konstantin Zetkin, January 3, 1973, New York City.

6. Twellmann, *Die deutsche Frauenbewegung*, p. 42.

7. Clara Zetkin, cited in Adele Gerhard and Helen Simon, *Mutterschaft und geistige Arbeit. Eine psychologische und soziologische Studie auf Grundlage einer internationalen Erhebung mit Berücksichtigung der geschichtlichen Entwicklung* (Berlin: G. Reimer, 1908), p. 304; letter of Clara Zetkin to Karl Kautsky, June 17, 1900, Kautsky Archives, Dossier XXIII (hereafter cited as KDXXIII), no. 330, Internationaal Instituut voor Sociale Geschiedenis, Amsterdam (hereafter cited as IISG).

8. G. G. L. Alexander, *Aus Clara Zetkins Leben und Werk* (Berlin: Vereinigte Internationale Verlagsanstalt, 1927), pp. 4-5. This biography is based on personal interviews with Zetkin conducted in the 1920s.

9. Ibid., pp. 5-6; Hohendorf, *revolutionäre Schulpolitik*, p. 12; August Bebel, *Aus meinem Leben*, 3 vols. (Stuttgart: J. H. Dietz, 1910-1912), 3: 152.

10. Letter of Karl Kautsky to Friedrich Engels, February 19, 1892, *Friedrich Engels Briefwechsel mit Karl Kautsky*, ed., Benedikt Kautsky (Vienna: W. Braumüller, 1955), no. XCI, p. 330; interview with Konstantin Zetkin, November 21, 1972, Long Island, New York.

11. A moving picture of this period in Zetkin's life emerges from her correspondence with Karl Kautsky, editor of German Social Democracy's theoretical organ, *Neue Zeit*, and Julius Motteler, business manager of the party's central organ, *Der Sozialdemokrat*. See letters of Clara Zetkin to Karl Kautsky, March 16, 22, and August 28, 1886; March 25 and April 9, 1888; January 30, 1889, KDXXIII, nos. 302-03, 307-310; letters of Clara Zetkin to Julius Motteler, November 15 and December 12, 1887, Motteler Archives 226, p. 7, and 1259, pp. 6-7, IISG.

12. Letters of Clara Zetkin to Julius Motteler, November 15, November 27, December 5, December 12, and December 21, 1887; February 9, 1888, Mottler Archives 226, pp. 1-15, and 1259, pp. 1-7, 31, 56-57; Alexander, *Aus Clara Zetkins Leben*, pp. 10-11, 13, 17.

13. Ibid., pp. 15-16; W. Fritz Globig, "In Leipzig hielt Clara Zetkin ihre erste Rede," *Leipziger Volkszeitung*, June 25, 1957 (based on interviews with Zetkin in 1931); letters of Clara Zetkin to Karl Kautsky, April 9, 1888; March 24, 1897; June 17, 1900; and January 16, 1903, KDXXIII, nos. 308, 315, 330, and 359; letter of Clara Zetkin to Julia von Vollmar, January 25, 1894, Vollmar Archives, IISG; letter of Clara Zetkin to Rosa Luxemburg, November 17, 1918, in "Zwischen kritischem und büro-kratischem Kommunismus. Unbekannte Briefe Clara Zetkins," ed., Hermann Weber, *Archiv für Socialgeschichte* 11 (1971): 431.

14. Letter of Clara Zetkin to Karl Kautsky, March 25, 1888, KDXXIII, no. 309, IISG.

15. *Protokoll des Internationalen Arbeiter-Kongresses zu Paris abgehalten vom 14, bis 20 Juli 1889* (Nüremberg: n.p., 1890), pp. 80-85. This speech has been reprinted in Clara Zetkin, *Ausgewählte Reden und Schriften*, 3 vols. (Berlin: Dietz, 1957), 1: 3-11.

16. Letter of Karl Kautsky to Friedrich Engels, September 8, 1890, *Engels briefwechsel mit Kautsky*, no. 72, p. 260; letter of Karl Kautsky to Victor Adler, January 26, 1891, *Victor Adlers Briefwechsel mit August Bebel und Karl Kautsky*, ed., Friedrich Adler (Vienna: Verlag der Wiener Buchhandlung, 1954), no. K19, p. 69; Dornemann, *Clara Zetkin*, p. 82.

17. "Noch einmal 'reinliche Scheidung' II," *Gleichheit* 4, no. 15 (June 25, 1894): 17; "Zur Antwort," ibid., 6, no. 25 (December 9, 1896): 200; "Notwendige Ergänzung," ibid., 11, no. 3 (January 30, 1901): 18.

18. "Mutterschaft und geistige Arbeit," *Vorwärts* 18, no. 203 (August

31, 1901): first supplement (hereafter cited as "Mutterschaft"); "Nicht Schmutzkonkurrentin, Kampfesgefährtin, Arbeitsgenossin," *Gleichheit* 7, no. 17 (August 18, 1897): 38; "Nur Etappe, Nicht Endziel," ibid., 9, no. 1 (January 4, 1899): 2-3; "Aus Krähwinkel 1," ibid., 15, no. 6 (March 22, 1905): 31.

19. *Protokoll über die Verhandlungen des Parteitages der Sozialdemokratischen Partei Deutschlands. Abegehalten zu Berlin vom 14, bis 21 November 1892*, p. 277. (Hereafter this series will be cited as *Protokoll*, followed by the place and date).

20. *Protokoll Gotha 1896*, p. 163.

21. Ibid., p. 164; *Protokoll Stuttgart 1898*, p. 112.

22. One of the earliest indications of this change appeared in "Die Frauenfrage auf dem evangelischen Sozialisten-Kongress," *Gleichheit* 7, no. 15 (July 21, 1897): 114.

23. "Nur Etappe, nicht Endziel," p. 1.

24. On this issue see Juliet Mitchell, *Woman's Estate* (New York: Pantheon, 1971), p. 106; Simone de Beauvoir, *The Second Sex*, trans. H. M. Parshley (New York: Alfred A. Knopf, 1953), pp. 50-55; Shulamith Firestone, *The Dialectic of Sex: The Case for Feminist Revolution* (New York: William Morrow, 1970), pp. 4-5, 8, 11-12.

25. See Amy Hackett, "The German Women's Movement and Suffrage, 1890-1914: A Study of National Feminism," in Robert J. Bezucha, ed., *Modern European Social History* (Lexington, Mass.: D. C. Heath, 1972), pp. 361-65, 371-73.

26. "Nicht Haussklavin, nicht Mannweib, weiblicher Vollmensch, *Gleichheit* 8, no. 2 (January 19, 1898): 9-10; "Aus Krähwinkel II," ibid. 15, no. 7 (April 5, 1905): 37; "Mutterschaft"; "Das Weib und der Intellektualismus," *Neue Zeit* 21, Part 2 (1902-1903), no. 28-29, pp. 89-90.

27. *Protokoll Mannheim 1906*, p. 353.

28. "Nicht Haussklavin, nicht Mannweib, weiblicher Vollmensch," p. 10; "Mutterschaft"; "Das Weib und der Intellektualismus," pp. 52, 89-90; "Aus Krähwinkel II," p. 37; "Wir kämpfen für unser Recht," *Gleichheit* 7, no. 14 (June 7, 1897): 106.

29. "Das Weib und der Intellektualismus," pp. 52, 88.

30. [Editorial reply following] Minna Guldner, "Zum Geburtenrückgang in Berlin," *Gleichheit* 23, no. 24 (August 20, 1913): 275; Clara Zetkin, "Gebärzwang und Gebärstreik," ibid. 24, no. 14 (April 1, 1914): 209-11; and ibid., no. 17 (May 13, 1914): 257-59.

31. Letter of Clara Zetkin to Karl Kautsky, April 5, 1902, KDXXIII, no. 353; see also letter of Clara Zetkin to Luise Kautsky, March 25, 1902, Kautsky Family Archives, folio 19, file 5.

32. *Protokoll Bremen 1904*, p. 370.

33. *Protokoll Gotha 1896*, p. 166.

34. This was a common theme in Zetkin's articles for *Gleichheit*. See, for example, "Die deutschen Genossinnen im Wahlkampf," *Gleichheit* 3, no. 15 (August 20, 1893): 118; "Jede proletarische Mutter eine Kämpferin," ibid. 6, no. 19 (September 16, 1896): 146-47. It also characterized her approach at the 1912 Extraordinary International Congress. See the letter of Clara Zetkin to Heleen Ankersmit, December 6, 1912, in "Unveröffentlichte Briefe Clara Zetkins an Heleen Ankersmit," Wilhelm Eildermann, ed., *Beiträge zur Geschichte der deutschen Arbeiterbewegung* 9, no. 4 (1967): 663; and *Ausserordentlicher Internationaler Sozialisten-Kongress zu Basel am 24, und 25, November 1912* (Berlin: n.p., 1912), p. 34.

35. Letter of Clara Zetkin to Heleen Ankersmit, September 7, 1913, in Eildermann, "Unveröffentlichte Briefe," pp. 666-67.

36. Ibid.; "Dringende Aufgabe," *Gleichheit* 14, no. 22 (October 19, 1904): 169; "Die Stellung der Frauen im Entwurf einer Organizationsstatut der sozialdemokratische Partei Deutschlands," ibid. 15, no. 16 (August 9, 1905): 91.

37. *Protokoll Mainz 1900*, p. 150; see also "Zur Frage der Frauenleseabende," *Gleichheit* 21, no. 25 (September 11, 1911): 386, 389-90.

38. See especially *Protokoll Mannheim 1906*, p. 356; and "Die Mutter als Erzieherin" [book review], *Neue Zeit* 26, Part 1 (1907-1908), no. 13, p. 422.

39. "Der Chemnitzer Parteitag," *Gleichheit* 13, no. 1 (October 2, 1912): 4.

40. *Protokoll Bremen 1904*, p. 369; *Protokoll, Nürnberg 1908*, p. 533; "Kämpfend voran," *Gleichheit* 10, no. 9 (September 12, 1900): 145.

41. *Protokoll Nürnberg 1908*, p. 533.

42. Ibid.

43. *Protokoll Frankfurt 1894*, p. 179; *Protokoll München 1902*, p. 254; "Ihr hemmt uns doch Ihr zwingt uns nicht," *Gleichheit* 5, no. 8 (April 17, 1895): 57; "Die Frauenfrage auf dem sozialdemokratischen Parteitag," ibid. 6, no. 22 (October 28, 1896): 171; "Der Stuttgarter Parteitag," ibid. 8, no. 21 (October 12, 1898): 164; "Dringende Aufgabe," ibid. 14, no. 22 (October 19, 1904): 169; "Henrik Ibsen," ibid. 16, no. 12 (June 13, 1906): 78; Letter of Clara Zetkin to "Worthy Comrade," October 11, 1900, Clara Zetkin Archives NL 5, folder 44, Institut für Marxismus—Leninismus beim ZK der SED (Zentrales Parteiarchiv), Berlin (hereafter cited as IML); letter of Clara Zetkin to Heleen Ankersmit, September 7, 1913, in Eildermann, "Unveröffentlichte Briefe," p. 667; Anna Blos, ed., *Die Frauenfrage im Lichte des Sozialismus* (Dresden: Kaden, 1930), p. 43.

44. *Internationaler Sozialisten-Kongress zu Stuttgart 18, bis 24 August 1907*, p. 40.

45. Ibid., pp. 40-47, 121-22; Julius, " 'Bravo Clara'—Clara Zetkin im Kampf mit dem Opportunismus auf dem Stuttgarter Kongress 1907," *Clara Zetkin, ein Sammelband zum Gedächtnis der grossen Kämferin* (Moscow: Verlagsgenossenschaft ausländischer Arbeiter in der UdSSR, 1934), pp. 101-03; Henriette Fürth, "Frauenbewegung," *Sozialistische Monatshefte* 11, part 2, no. 10 (October, 1907): 890.

46. *Protokoll Nürnberg 1908*, pp. 460, 547; *Protokoll Leipzig 1909*, p. 8; *Protokoll Chemnitz 1912*, pp. 516, 555.

47. Interview with Konstantin Zetkin, November 21, 1972, Long Island, New York; Dornemann, *Clara Zetkin*, p. 227.

48. Since 1895 many party leaders had harbored misgivings about Zetkin's position on the SPD's Control Commission because of her unwillingness to respect party discipline when she felt socialist principles were being jeopardized. See, for example, the letter of Clara Zetkin to Heinrich Dietz, March 4, 1909, in Ursula Ratz, "Briefe zum Erscheinen von Karl Kautskys 'Weg zur Macht'," *International Review of Social History* 12, no. 3 (1967): 473; see also Lily Braun, *Memoiren einer Sozialistin*, 2 vols. (Munich: A. Langen, 1909-1911), 2: 56, 169-71, 292, 398-99; Luise Zietz, "Zur Frauenkonferenz," *Gleichheit* 20, no. 14 (April 11, 1910): 212.

49. To cite a significant example, compare Zietz's views on the value of separate women's organizations and autonomy for the women's socialist movement before and after she became a member of the party executive. Cf. *Protokoll München 1902*, pp. 88, 252-55; *Protokoll Jena 1905*, pp. 182-83; and *Protokoll Nürnberg 1908*, pp. 244-46, 487-91, 505-06; and "Zur Frauenkonferenz," pp. 212-13; *Protokoll Jena 1911*, p. 420. Also see letter of Clara Zetkin to Fritz Westmeyer, April 26, 1912, NL 5, folder 48 IML.

50. Letter of Clara Zetkin to Heleen Ankersmit, September 7, 1913, in Eildermann, "Unveröffentlichte Briefe," p. 667.

51. The only other woman, Ottilie Baader, who had also been considered for the position by the party executive (but had declined) resembled Zietz in this regard.

52. Letter of Clara Zetkin to Heleen Ankersmit, September 7, 1913, in Eildermann, "Unveröffentlichte Briefe," p. 667.

53. Ibid., pp. 666-67; see also "Zur Frage der Frauenleseabende," p. 286.

54. Letter of Clara Zetkin to Karl Kautsky, March 14, 1909, in Ratz, "Briefe zum Erscheinen," p. 473.

55. Letters of Clara Zetkin to Karl and Luise Kautsky, August 29, 1909,

KDXXIII, no. 387, IISG, to Alexandra Kollontai, September 9, 1909, NL 5, folder 47, IML, and to Adolf Henke, Henke Nachlass, no. 35, Archiv der Sozialdemokratischen Partei Deutschlands, Bad-Godesberg; letter of Rosa Luxemburg to Clara Zetkin, September or November, 1909, NL 5, folder 47, IML; Luise Zietz, "Zur Frauenkonferenz," pp. 212-13.

56. "Notwendige Erörterung," *Gleichheit* 20, no. 8 (January 17, 1910): 113-15; "Zur Frauenkonferenz," ibid. no. 9 (January 31, 1910): 129-30; ibid. no. 11 (March 1, 1910): 164-66; ibid. no. 12 (March 14, 1910): 181-82; ibid. no. 13 (March 28, 1910): 197-98; ibid. no. 14 (April 11, 1910): 214-16; ibid. no. 16 (May 9, 1910): 251; ibid. no. 17 (May 23, 1910): 264; letters of Rosa Luxemburg to Clara Zetkin, December, 1909, and January, 1910, NL 5, folder 47, IML.

57. Marie Page Seiffert, Frieda Wulff, Luise Zietz, Linchen Baumann, and Luise Kähler, "Zur Frauenkonferenz," pp. 165, 182, 212, 263, 280; "Aus der Bewegung," *Gleichheit* 18, no. 17 (August 17, 1908); ibid. 19, no. 13 (March 29, 1909): 200-201; ibid. 22, no. 14 (April 1, 1912): 218.

58. Thönnessen, *Frauenemanzipation*, pp. 62, 97, 117, 119, 121, 134, 137-39; Gundula Bölke, *Die Wandlung der Frauenemanizationstheorie von Marx bis zur Rätebewegung* (Hamburg: Spartakus, 1971), pp. 51-52, 72, (footnote 106).

59. Lion, *Zur Sociologie der Frauenbewegung*, p. 156.

60. Thönnessen, *Frauenemanzipation*, pp. 75-79, 108, 116, 170, 173; Antje Kunstmann, *Frauenemanzipation und Erziehung* (Starnberg: Raith, 1972), pp. 84-85.

61. Bölke, *Die Wandlung*, pp. 21, 26-27, 33-34, 41-42, 58-59, 62; Sheila Rowbotham, *Woman's Consciousness, Man's World* (Baltimore: Penguin Books, 1973), pp. xiv-xv; Mechthild Merfeld, *Die Emanzipation der Frau in der Sozialistischen Theorie und Praxis* (Reinbek bei Hamburg: Rowalt, 1972), pp. 22-23, 25-28, 42, 45, 50-51, 61-62, 76-78, 105-107.

3.

When Radical and Socialist Feminism Were Joined: The Extraordinary Failure of Madeleine Pelletier

MARILYN J. BOXER

France was the land of revolution and of great ladies, of the Declaration of the Rights of Man and of Madame de Staël. During the "Great Revolution" of 1789, Paris witnessed the birth of the first groups of women organized for political rights, and the term "feminism" came into common usage a generation later in another period of social upheaval in France. The synthesis of feminism and socialism, with its assumption that women could achieve equality in alliance with oppressed workingmen, emerged during Flora Tristan's *tour de France* in 1843-44. Whether in militant behavior—the *Pétroleuses* of the Paris Commune of 1871—or avant-garde literature —the *Lelia* of George Sand—Europe could look to France for clues to the future of women in society.[1]

Yet Frenchwomen waited longer than their sisters in England, Germany, Russia, Scandinavia, the U.S., and most other industrialized countries for access to political and civil rights. The vote came one war later than elsewhere, in 1945, and legal access to birth control waited until 1972. The French feminist heritage failed because republican leaders feared that women in public life might facilitate, on the one hand, a resurgence of clerical influence, and, on the other, a diminution of the nation's already low birthrate. Maintenance of a sharp separation between family and society satisfied both political and personal goals of the majority of Frenchmen.[2]

Nevertheless, if social progress for Frenchwomen, as measured by acquisition of political and civil rights, was delayed, France continued to provide feminist exemplars. It is common today to distinguish between a nineteenth-century feminist movement composed largely of leisured ladies and a mid-twentieth-century force more diverse in its constituencies and more global in its critique. Where the earlier feminism concentrated on education, employment, and equality in law, the contemporary movement extends its scope to sexuality, reproduction, and social relationships. Instead of equality with men in a male-defined world, today's feminists envision a social order reconstructed to include female and male presence in equal measure, or androgyny. A significant fraction of the new feminists aim also for economic equality, blending feminist insights about women's oppression under patriarchal sexual structures with Marxist class analysis. Most of this contemporary feminist critique was contained in the work of Dr. Madeleine Pelletier, a French socialist-feminist who belonged to that remarkable generation of women born about 1870 and coming of age in the stormy decade of the 1890s.[3]

Unlike her contemporaries Angelica Balabanoff, Emma Goldman, Alexandra Kollontai, Krupskaya, Rosa Luxemburg, and Adelheid Popp, Pelletier remains virtually unknown, perhaps because of a paradox of French history. While advancing for all Europe an ideal of revolutionary political change, French cultural leaders maintained allegiance to traditional relationships in primary social institutions. "Underneath the dramatic conflicts which characterized the [nineteenth] century, and which have drawn most of the attention of historians in the past," Theodore Zeldin noted, "there were assumptions which people did not question and which are perhaps more difficult to write about." Traditional French histories, including studies of socialism, are silent on personal and private matters. Pelletier, notorious in her day because she challenged ever hoary assumption and venerated institution, has been ignored. Yet, while devoted to feminist advocacy, she also played, for a brief time, a notable role in French socialism. This essay will attempt to restore her to a place in the sisterhood of women outstanding in radical politics of the early twentieth century.[4]

Unlike most women who played leading roles in the radical movements of the late nineteenth and early twentieth centuries, Madeleine Pelletier did not emerge from the comfortable classes. Born in May, 1864, in a poor greengrocer's shop in Paris, she was one of very few among her generation of radical women who could speak with the authority of experience about working-class life. Raised by a disabled father and a fanatically religious, slightly crazy mother responsible for the family's survival, Pelletier described her childhood as impoverished, dirty, and bleak. The shop fared badly because her mother's antirepublican, even royalist, sentiments alienated the neighbors. Pelletier recalled that "customers who came to buy a kilo of potatoes didn't want to hear a sermon," preferring the shop across the street whose proprietor held less extreme opinions. Her father, perhaps a former cab driver, interjected a measure of skepticism and taught her to read. But clearly Pelletier's mother, who allowed her to go to school unwashed, uncombed, with lice that "swarmed on my head and fell on the table," dominated her childhood. She told her child tales of torture and damnation for sin, took her to church to "see God," and forbade her to celebrate the Republic (which she called the "ruine publique") on July 14. Thus introduced early to religious and political conflict, Pelletier developed a precocious class consciousness, noting that despite her brilliance in school, prizes went to "little girls with combed hair who rode to school in carriages." Living amid people who struggled to make a barely adequate living and observing a woman who earned with hard work neither respect, comfort, nor independence, Pelletier resolved not to repeat the pattern of her mother's life.[5]

In common with many radical women of her era. Pelletier aspired to a career in the healing professions. Unlike most others however, she did not limit her goal to nursing or midwifery. Encouraged by the nuns who were her early instructors, despite their alleged preference for her clean, lace-trimmed schoolmates, Pelletier persisted. Steeling herself to ignore the insults of both classmates and professors, she won a degree in medicine. In 1902 she applied for an internship in a mental hospital. Despite her superior qualifications, she was denied access to the required competitive civil service exam, on the grounds that she had not fulfilled a term of military service, for which, of course, she was disqualified by sex. Pelletier carried her story to Marguerite Durand's all-woman daily *La Fronde*, won attention in the feminist press, and later got her position.[6]

While little information is available about Pelletier's medical career, she apparently spent the early years in medical research, publishing a number of studies dealing with psychological manifestations of physiological functions.[7] But medical practice and scientific research failed to satisfy her catholic interests; above all, they offered too little opportunity for social action.

The chief purpose of Pelletier's life was to work for social reconstruction. Schooled in class and sexual oppression and extremely well read, she began writing for the socialist, anarchist, and feminist press. She published dozens of articles and brochures, several books, and, between 1908 and 1914 (and briefly after the war), her own review of the women's movement, *La Suffragiste*.[8] At the same time she aggressively entered the socialist movement and moved rapidly toward the top, attaining by 1910 membership on the central executive committee of the S.F.I.O. (French Section of the Workers' International). Pelletier attended the 1906 congress at Limoges, becoming the first woman to speak at a national assembly of the newly unified party. Between 1906 and the war, she served as a delegate to the S.F.I.O. national congress seven times, and also represented France at the Stuttgart meeting of the Second International in 1907. In 1910 and again in 1912 she ran for legislative office, under S.F.I.O. auspices.

While Pelletier wrote and spoke on numerous political, economic, and social issues, she clearly committed herself above all to amelioration of the condition of women—without which she considered socialist reconstruction unattainable. Believing that the political naiveté and religiosity of women presented a formidable obstacle to elevation of the working classes, and that without the symbolic equality represented by the vote, women would remain undereducated, she placed woman suffrage alongside the right to work as her two leading feminist demands. During the months of preparation for the national congress in 1906, she waged a virtual one-woman campaign to persuade the party to charge its deputies with immediate presentation of a universal, "not unisexual," suffrage proposal in the Chamber of Deputies. Interest in the political emancipation of women had increased since the foundation of the National Council of French Feminists in 1901, though a proposal for limited suffrage introduced that year had disappeared in committee. Another was attempted in 1906. Now Pelletier called for urgent action.

Addressing the national congress at Limoges, she refuted, one by one, all the common charges of the opposition. Not only were women not intellectually inferior to men, but the argument based on intelligence was specious, since no test of intellectual capacity was required of male voters. No "law of nature" disqualified the female sex, for there were none, merely natural phenomena transformed by custom. "Nature gives women the burden of reproduction, but is it nature which decrees that she makes the soup and washes the socks, that she has no horizon beyond the kitchen and the bedroom?" The famous "clerical peril" supposed to ensue from woman suffrage was an echo of the old ideas of Michelet. If the enfranchisement of women were, as alleged, a "leap in the dark," how could socialists, as partisans of revolution, be moved by such a feat? Actually, along with justice, party interest in converting wives from adversaries to colleagues demanded that women vote.

A brief debate ensued, after which the congress, "unanimously less six votes," affirmed a resolution declaring the extension of the franchise to women "legitimate and urgent." Socialist deputies were charged with sponsoring the measure "as soon as possible this year." Yet the party remained divided, many believing, in the words of a proposed substitute motion, that "the question of the vote for women will and can be resolved only with the question of labor by the collective appropriation of all the instruments of production." The socialist deputies who greeted feminist delegations that Pelletier led to the Chamber promised, but indefinitely delayed, legislative action. Ultimately Pelletier expressed her dissatisfaction by throwing stones into windows at the polls on election day.[9]

By the time of Pelletier's arrival on the socialist political scene, the separate parties that characterized French socialism in the 1880s and 1890s had heeded the advice of the Second International and united. However, factions grouped around early leaders such as Jean Jaurès, Jules Guesde, and Jean Allemane, or newer contenders like Gustave Hervé, persisted. At first Pelletier associated herself with the Guesdistes, whose Marxist program and refusal to countenance socialist participation in coalition ministries marked them, she felt, as "men of doctrine" committed to the class struggle. But she quickly became disillusioned with the parliamentary games that elected officials of red as well as other stripes played and accused Guesde and his men of using the proletariat for their own advancement. Explaining that "only Don Quixote is capable of serious social transformation," she moved toward Hervé, whose group disdained parliamentarianism altogether and called for direct action, even military insurrection. Recognizing earlier than most observers that bureaucratization compromised revolutionary fervor, she criticized the party for its tendency to follow elected officials who had won, with their seats, a vested interest in the status quo. She also agreed with the Bernsteinian revisionists that the bourgeoisie, far from diminishing as capitalism advanced, reconstituted itself in new ways that undermined orthodox Marxism. "Far from destroying the middle classes," she wrote, "industrial concentration reconstitutes them on a new basis. The engineer earning 10,000 francs has no interest in a social upheaval." An even greater problem with Marxism, she thought, lay in effects of historical determinism; not only did it rob people of a sense of control over their own fate, but it also falsely assured them of victory, if only they waited long enough. "Thus," she pointed out, "German Social Democracy could regiment a million workers under Marx's banner without having taken a step toward revolution." A "voluntarist" by personality as well as persuasion, perhaps also politically ambitious, in 1909 and early 1910 Pelletier joined Hervé, several others in his camp, and a few anarchists in a short-lived attempt to form a self-proclaimed antiparliamentary, revolutionary elite party.[10]

Thanks to this new connection and an attempt at proportional representation within the party, Pelletier earned a place representing Hervéism on the S.F.I.O.'s central committee, a singular honor for women (reduced, however, in significance by the fact that party rules proscribed committee seats for elected officials and thus sharply limited the group's actual power). Only a few months later, she obtained nominal support from the party for presenting herself as a candidate in legislative elections, still an unusual if not unprecedented form of political participation for Frenchwomen. She conducted a brief campaign in which she minimized her feminism and carefully elucidated the socialist program for the electors of the hopelessly reactionary district to which the party assigned her. Advised to "put reformist water in her revolutionary wine," she conformed and won more votes than the previous socialist candidate.[11]

Pelletier was a principled opportunist, attracted by all parties that might offer a platform, anarchism as well as Guesdism and Hervéism. While her disillusionment with electoral politics might appear to be the source of her movement toward the insurrectionist and libertarian groups, the pattern of her work demonstrates no consistently leftward evolution. It appears instead that she covered the left side of the political spectrum, always seeking acceptance for her feminist ideas and an outlet for her political ambition. At the beginning of her career as well as at the end, she wrote for anarchist journals, publishing in them some of her most radical views, such as the benefits of military conscription for women and the rights of women to freedom of contraception and abortion. She left the Guesdists soon after the failure of her suffrage campaign and rejected the insurrectionists with the explanation that "the Hervéists are not feminists." Hervé himself had criticized her unmodish, masculine attire. But she engaged in party politics when offered S.F.I.O. support for her 1910 and 1912 campaigns. The political parties had resources no feminist group in France could command.

French feminism in the early Third Republic counted a number of small factions, grouped around a singular individual, idea, or journal. Major political questions of the day, such as the separation of church and state, economic conflict, resurgent militarism, and nationalism, formed a backdrop against which women's groups discussed access to higher education and the liberal professions, the right of married women to control their own earnings and to participate in legal action, prostitution and the "white slave" traffic, the right of unmarried mothers to sue for support of their children, and occasionally, women's right to work. After the turn of the century, the demand for the vote was heard more often.[12] In 1904 centennial celebrations for the Napoleonic Code focused feminist attention on the double standard in law and morality. When Caroline Kauffman, president of the most radical feminist group, *La Solidarité des femmes (Solidarity of Women)*, interrupted ceremonies at the Sorbonne by releasing balloons inscribed "The Code Crushes Women!" she attracted Pelletier, who had addressed to the Ministry of Justice a letter asking to be named to the all-male commision charged with revision of the Code.

Enlisted by the aging Kauffman, Pelletier succeeded to the presidency and attempted to engage the *Solidarité* in a campaign of feminist militance modeled on the British "suffragettes." Advocating "virilization" and even violence, she sought allies "who do not fear illegality."[13]

But these were comfortably bourgeois women who disdained Pelletier's style. In her autobiographical novel, *La Femme vierge (The Virgin Woman)*, she describes them as a "lamentable group of old women, [of whom] few were liberated, judging from their appearance." Their costumes, adorned with flowers, feathers, and lace, contrast sharply with the severe dress worn by Marie Pierrot, Pelletier's thinly disguised alter ego. Criticizing the *Solidarité* as "feminists by feeling" rather than by reason, Pelletier finds even more unacceptable their devotion to fashion: while wearing ordinary clothes to *Solidarité* meetings, they dress up to attend those convened by Marguerite Durand. Kauffman even urges her to wear décolletage to feminist evenings, while she considers such exposure "a symbol of serfdom." Her own appearance dramatized her uncompromising stand on women's equality: she wore a man-tailored suit jacket, white blouse or shirt, sometimes with a man's false collar, and straight skirt. With her mannish haircut, all she had to do to pass unnoticed in public places forbidden to women was switch to trousers. Apparently she adopted this mode of dress early in life as a defense against criticism of her "unfeminine" determination to walk alone and freely through the streets of Paris.[14]

While Pelletier succeeding in mobilizing the *Solidarité* to demonstrate for the vote, leading one hundred fifty "suffragettes of Paris" to the Chamber on a stormy day in December, 1906, she failed to instigate a campaign in the British mold. She enlisted a number of well-known feminists as contributors to her journal. However, she represented within French feminism such an extreme position that, according to some historians, she lent little positive momentum to the movement. Embodying the worst fears of feminist revolution, that it would turn women into men, she might have made moderate feminism seem respectable—or, she may, it has been suggested, have turned the public away altogether from women's rights issues. However, in the development of feminist ideology, she moved ahead of all other women of her generation.[15]

In common with many radical women, Pelletier owed her feminism to the need to escape from the stifling world of her childhood. Like the Russian generation of the 1860s, whose commitment to women's rights originated in defiance of arranged marriages, Pelletier discovered early that unless she asserted her right to an existence independent of her family, she would find herself a wife and mother, her individuality consumed like her mother's by repeated pregnancies. (Her mother had eleven.) Given her social situation, she could hope at best for marriage to a small shopkeeper, which also promised a constant struggle against poverty. In the novel that follows Pelletier's life so closely, Marie rejects proposals, engineered by her mother, for marriage to a tailor and a café-keeper. She determines to resist her instincts and to develop her intelligence.[16]

Most women of Pelletier's class and era lacked the means to an independent life. While no quantitative study has yet been made of the socioeconomic origins of French feminists, literary evidence as well as lists of delegates to feminist congresses strongly suggest that a large majority were secure, bourgeois women. Even among those who belonged to socialist parties, most were petty bourgeois, often lay teachers or wives of members, most of whom were artisans.[17] Struggling to support herself, Pelletier belonged to the minority.[18] She recognized that dependency on marriage for economic subsistence destroyed women's chances for equality. Therefore, she made economic independence, the "right to work," the cornerstone of her feminist philosophy. In defense of Emma Couriau, the typographer rejected by her husband's union in a celebrated struggle against antifeminist syndicalists, Pelletier declared: "Only by Work will Woman have the means to live free of dependence on man and will she be able with him and like him to enjoy all that brings happiness in life, materially, morally, intellectually and emotionally."[19] She also observed that most radical men, whatever their class, envisioned nothing but traditional roles for women, even in postrevolutionary society. "In the society envisioned by Kropotkin," she protested, "women do not work. They have only

to be mothers of families." They foresaw for women not reconstruction but restoration. Parodying the socialist message to wom-
en, she wrote,

> Citoyenne, the bourgeoisie has torn you from your casseroles to
> drag you into the workshops. Let your husband vote for us. When
> we are your masters, we will restore you to your kitchen and your
> kids. Your dresses are of cotton; they will be of silk.[20]

French workers and the working-class movement were divided
over the question of women's work outside the home. Many responded negatively to the employment of female labor in workshops and factories, charging the "industrialization of women"
with destruction of both the workers' home and ultimately, through
decreased fertility, the French nation. Although the percentage of
women employed in industry grew quite slowly after mid-century,
opponents of change in traditional sex roles predicted disastrous
effects on the health and morality of women and the wages of men.
Heavily influenced by the antifeminism of Proudhon, French
workers debated women's right to work, and the broader "woman
question," at many labor congresses. Not until 1935 did the major
federation of French labor, the C.G.T. (General Congress of
Workers) fully acknowledge women as legitimate workers. In the
period of Pelletier's prominence in socialist circles, before World
War I, it was common to attribute defense of women's economic
rights to bourgeois feminism. Feminist demands such as control of
one's own property were challenged as irrelevant to working-class
women, who owned virtually nothing of value, and feminist pro-
tests against "protective" legislation that limited women's working
hours and conditions were criticized as inconsiderate of poor women
whose labor in laundries and factories returned only a meager
paycheck. Women working for less than subsistence wages in unskilled jobs would prefer, it was asserted, to be supported by well-
paid husbands.

If there was no agreement between working-class and women's
parties on the right of women to work, there was not even a ground
for discussion of the second point in Pelletier's bill of women's
rights: sexual emancipation. By this she meant absolute destruction

of the double standard. She believed that women should be as free as men to express their sexuality, with no more fear of the consequences. How else could women develop into full human beings? As a girl, she had been punished for her desire to enjoy walking about the city; as a woman, she was criticized for traveling alone. A girl was limited in her access to the world for one reason: to preserve her virginity "so that her husband won't be deceived on the quality of his merchandise." Indeed, she asserted, "all the servitude of the young girl and the married woman has at bottom a sexual goal."[21]

In the new world that Pelletier envisioned, both sexes enjoyed total freedom of sexual expression. She wrote a utopian novel, *Une Vie nouvelle (A New Life)*, in which "love ceased to be a combat; one said yes or no, and that was all." Provided early sex education and ready access to contraception and abortion, women of the future would prevent unwanted consequences.[22] Pelletier also demanded these rights in her own society, in such works as "The Right to Abortion" and *The Sexual Emancipation of Woman*.

Although French literature of the period includes several notable portraits of women who effectively liberated themselves from maternity through homosexuality, Pelletier seems never to have suggested lesbianism as an alternative life-style. Since she anticipated virtually every aspect of current radical feminism, defending a woman's right to control of her own body and adopting for herself a masculine appearance, profession, and life-style, she might be expected to have at least broached the subject of homosexuality. Such a discussion is noticeably missing from her work. On the contrary, her analysis of female sexuality seems limited to heterosexual relationships. Her longest study on the subject, *L'Emancipation sexuelle de la Femme* (1911), includes a condemnation of the double standard, an attack on the traditional family, advocacy of the right to abortion, and an unpatriotic suggestion that a bit more "depopulation," through contraception, might improve the quality of French life. While she often called for women to "virilize" themselves, she meant only that they should emulate such "masculine" virtues as self-assertiveness, ambition, and independence. She termed nonsense the charge of some feminists (and antifeminists) who accused her of "wanting women to renounce their sex."

Obviously, she said, "no one would think of changing women into men or men into women, for to succeed one would have to be a God." She aspired to transform only the material and moral circumstances of women's lives.[23]

Nor did Pelletier preach abstinence. She favored celibacy, a "superior state," but not chastity. As an animal function, sexual desire demanded expression. Society called it love and used affection to exploit women.[24] Aware that the public questioned her own sexual identity, Pelletier suggested that she was essentially a woman like any other, extraordinary only in refusing to be exploited. Her fictional self, Marie, looking back over a celibate life, reflects that "certainly she wasn't without sexuality; she also felt these desires, but she had to repress them in order to remain free. She didn't regret it." While this is the voice of Marie, not Madeleine, the resemblance is extremely close: She attributes Marie's fears of sexuality to a sense of horror awakened during lessons in sex education given by her father, an experience that parallels her autobiography. During her youth, Marie explains further, she had hoped to be loved by a "superior" man, with whose help she might have overcome her sexual aversion. Perhaps Pelletier speaks here also of herself.[25]

Trained in psychotherapy and familiar with Freud, Pelletier cannot have ignored the implications of such revelations for her own biography. To furnish information that permitted an inference that she was motivated even slightly by any factor other than free and rational choice was to open herself to further scorn, as well as to denigration of her work. Therefore, barring the discovery of new biographical materials, it seems best to accept Pelletier as she presented herself: a heterosexual woman with extraordinary talent and modest means, for whom the price of sexual expression in her society was too high.

In rejecting the maternal mystique embraced by most of her contemporaries, including the feminists and socialists, Pelletier attacked the most sacred institution in French society: the family. Against a tidal wave of praise for traditional agrarian, familial values provoked by fears of decreasing population, increasing nationalism, and the declining power of the Church, she termed the "molecular" family the enemy of women, children, and all "superior" men.[26] She reversed a common belief in private virtue and public vice, to locate the worst of human behavior in the individual family in its inviolable home. The Napoleonic Code, awarding virtually unlimited legal power to husbands over wives and parents over children, had only aggravated an essentially destructive institution. Although marriage and the home were "the official symbols of the good life," the family, as Freud had shown, actually fostered hate. "Freudism," she declared,

> has revealed to us the real situation of the child within the family. Far from thriving, he suffers beneath the nagging authority of his parents; often far from loving them, he detests them and represses the morbid desire to kill them. His greatest aspiration is to grow up so that he can become free and no longer subject to humiliation.[27]

Pelletier painted a bleak picture. Drawing on her own emotionally and financially impoverished childhood and her medical practice among working-class wives subject to repeated pregnancies, overwork, and too often, alcoholic husbands, she identified the family as a source of oppression. In the family, men also lost their liberty, for "the master is in some measure a slave of the slave." But women, subject to the Code, lost liberty, property, and not infrequently, their lives—if not actually in childbirth, then morally.

> Unless she finds her equal, which is rare, the marriage of an intelligent woman is a moral suicide. Many wives lose in marriage all the benefits of a brilliant education. Piano, song, culture, all lost beneath the dull preoccupations of daily life.

Foreshadowing the work of feminist sociologists in the mid-twentieth century, she pointed out that spinsters, or "old girls" in the French phrase, looked younger, lived longer, and enjoyed life more than married women. Single men died earlier.[28]

Like other French socialist feminists before her, Pelletier proposed a radical solution to the problems of family. Following Engels, she believed that wage labor for women, by eliminating their economic dependence on individual men, was of primary importance. Revision of the Code to equalize civil and political rights must follow. Elimination of the double standard in sexual behavior and social customs was equally essential. Finally, maintenance and education of children at state expense would be required. Going beyond her predecessors, she envisioned a society in which reproduction of the species was a mere animal function performed by women for moral satisfaction, and with the tangible reward of a year's paid vacation—decidedly not, however, to be spent in child care! Pelletier's novel, *Une Vie nouvelle*, opens with Claire, its female lead, casually walking to the hospital to give birth for the fourth time to a child whom she will never see but will donate at once to the state. With the science of puériculture (child raising) far advanced, the expectant mother is confident that her child will grow up healthy, happy, and free. She can fulfill her duty as a citizen and retain her freedom.[29]

In the last decade of her life, Pelletier gave free rein to her imagination in utopian novels. Earlier she published countless shorter works clearly grounded in reality, and she often called for limited reforms that seemed feasible in contemporary society. Uncompromising in principle, she was open in tactics to every opportunity. Because she acknowledged a core of truth in fears of a "clerical peril" should women get the vote, she suggested that socialist leaders might first propose an enfranchisement limited to municipal elections. She modified her demand that Masonic lodges open membership to women by proposing an entrance exam. She looked to reform even of the family if husbands would accept their fair share of child care and housework. Within the present social, economic, and political structure, feminists might increase their influence in civic life and improve women's condition by creating a "women's society." Thus she anticipated the alternative institutions crucial to the contemporary women's movement.[30]

Pelletier was not oblivious to the faults of women. Like Mary Wollstonecraft and Charlotte Perkins Gilman, she bemoaned the triviality of many "feminine" concerns, attributing them to faulty education and social subordination. Accustomed to wearing chains, women had difficulty even imagining themselves free. Criticizing female acceptance of inhibiting fashions, she noted that French socialist women had scorned their German sisters at an international meeting where some of the latter appeared without corsets.[31] She was dismayed at women who, during the war, supported militarism and attacked her because, suppressing her fears, she rode her bicycle into the battle-torn outskirts of Paris to help the wounded of any nation. Before the war she had advocated military service for women because it would, like her masculine costume, symbolize the equality of the sexes and moreover open some civil service positions to women veterans. The war had in fact served feminism by creating opportunities for women to perform "men's work" and to earn independent incomes. In many countries, it also brought in its wake access to political equality with men.[32]

But most women, like most working-class men, continued to bow down in an age-old "posture of inferiority." Only in violence, through war or revolution, might they overcome the fear of change which, according to Pelletier, affected all human beings, even feminists, socialists, and anarchists. "Almost all social progress," she wrote, "has been the result of revolution."[33] As a woman who had herself overcome obstacles of class and sex, achieving economic independence and, since she was willing to pay the price, considerable social freedom, she might have retired to enjoy a comfortable life. But she aspired to change the world. Like her continental European counterparts—Krupskaya and Kollontai in Russia, Luxemburg and Zetkin in Germany, Popp and Schlesinger in Austria, Kuliscioff and Balabanoff in Italy—but in contrast to Anthony and Stanton in the U.S. and Emmeline and Christabel Pankhurst in England—Pelletier believed that radical social reconstruction was essential to human liberation. Since most feminist groups, she felt, lacked a comprehensive understanding of social problems and none had mobilized a party with any potential for winning power, she could reach the masses and play a significant role in politics only in a larger movement. Therefore she joined the socialist movement, attempting to move men of the Left to fight for feminist goals, while leading feminists, she hoped, toward sympathy and support for the working classes. She failed on all counts. Revolutionary socialists considered her support for feminism as deviation, mere bourgeois reform. Feminists complained of socialist antifeminism: attacks on women's right to work, ambivalence about woman suffrage, continuing adherence to the double standard in behavior. Caught in a reform-revolution dichotomy, Pelletier escaped by placing her faith in education, which many socialists considered another bourgeois solution. Pelletier, however, distinguished between reforms that might defer the revolution, by improving the material conditions of the workers, and others that, by encouraging workers to control their own lives, might turn them into rebels. In this second category she placed education, contraception, and temperance.[34]

Unfortunately for the feminist cause, French socialists in this period interpreted their Marxism narrowly. Economic determinists, they focused on the workplace, and they viewed women as well as men primarily as workers. Calling for the emancipation of the working classes "without distinction by sex," the French Workers' party adopted at its inception a program calling for the equality of the sexes in all phases of life. But having decided to mobilize for economic power by parliamentary means, they could offer little more to the disfranchised sex than an opportunity to speak from the public platform—which they did, and support for woman suffrage —on which they wavered and delayed.[35] Seeking to win votes in a nation shaken by periodic political crises and continuing "conflict over moralities," socialist leaders sought to charge the bourgeoisie with responsibility for economic instability and social immorality. Vulnerable themselves to accusations that socialism sought to destroy the family, to tear women from their homes, and to promote "free love," they saw little profit in causes that seemed to promote the "industrialization of women" and threaten the declining birthrate. Instead, while opposing the forces of clericalism, nationalism, and militarism on political and economic issues, they might deflect criticism on social issues by allying with the right to "protect" women, children, and the traditional family. Thus, after a long debate against proponents of free enterprise, the socialists joined with the Catholic party of Count Albert de Mun to enact the first labor legislation that imposed restrictions on the hours and conditions that women might work in industry. This combination of Left and Right continued to develop in the interests of defending tradition in private life. The political capital thus gained surely outweighed the loss of support from a few hundred feminist women, most of whom, in any case, belonged to enemy classes.[36]

But neither was Pelletier free from inconsistency. While disdaining bourgeois morality, she adopted the bourgeois faith in education and herself pursued a typically bourgeois path of upward mobility. Her strong resentment of the leisured classes was matched by considerable disdain for the working classes with their "souls of slaves." In fact she placed her faith not in "the people," but in meritocracy. In the new world of her utopian novel, revolution results in chaos until a benevolent dictator imposes his will and an ideal society on the undisciplined masses. But how else might women be liberated if, as she charged, men of the working classes were the most antifeminist of all?[37]

Pelletier found herself caught in a double, double bind: between reform and revolution, between feminism and socialism. Reforms advocated by feminist allies, which promised some measure of amelioration for women in the near future, were ignored or opposed by socialists bent on revolution, which aimed to empower men with limited visions of women's roles. Unable to reconcile the conflict, unwilling to forsake feminism in socialism or socialism in feminism, Pelletier finally withdrew from party politics. In the last decades of her life she turned, on the one hand, to fictional worlds where total resolution was possible and, on the other, to the reality of women's lives, where the radical act of abortion could solve immediate problems. In the end she was arrested as an abortionist, declared "legally incompetent," and incarcerated in a mental institution where, six months later, in December, 1939, she died.[38]

Along with her more famous sisters, the radical women born in the decade of the Paris Commune, Pelletier belonged to the first generation of women for whom higher education was available and participation in mass political parties open. They shared not only the heritage of the Russian nihilists—Chernyshevsky's fictional Vera, Breshkovskaia, Perovskaia—they also grew up with stories of the Paris Commune and Louise Michel, whose funeral Pelletier and Kollontai attended. Despite their sex, all joined socialist parties formed in the 1890s; because of their sex, none totally escaped the conflict between sex and class loyalties. Feminism necessarily made demands on their conscience. Their ultimate political choice perhaps depended on the relative strength of feminism and socialism in their respective milieus. The German women found a large established socialist party open to them, while feminist groups struggled to organize. Italian socialism offered less, but feminism hardly existed. Russia offered a long heroic tradition of female social revolutionaries. Feminism boasted greater success only in America. In France perhaps the options were nearly equal and the paths of development rought parallel. For Pelletier the choice was difficult.

Caught in the middle, Madeleine Pelletier, the infamous *doctoresse* of her day, withdrew from politics. Ignored by historians of socialism, who have been concerned primarily with struggles for power and party structure, unknown to historians of feminism, who have written mostly of the Anglo-American movements, Pelletier's memory and work lay hidden until discovered by a new generation seeking in women's history a usable past. Madeleine Pelletier anticipated contemporary radical and socialist feminism. She envisioned a socialist feminism containing almost every goal of the present women's movement. She died incarcerated for practicing what she preached, in the struggle to improve women's lives. She belongs in the international feminist pantheon.

NOTES

1. On the history of feminism and the socialist-feminist relationship in France, see Jane Abray, "Feminism in the French Revolution," *American Historical Review* 80, no. 1 (1975): 43-62; Marilyn J. Boxer, "Socialism Faces Feminism in France, 1879-1913," (Ph.D. diss., University of California, Riverside, 1975); idem, "Socialism Faces Feminism: The Failure of Synthesis in France," in Marilyn J. Boxer and Jean H. Quataert, eds., *Socialist Women: European Socialist Feminism in the Nineteenth and Twentieth Centuries* (New York: Elsevier, 1978), pp. 75-110; S. Joan Moon, "Feminism and Socialism: The Utopian Synthesis of Flora Tristan," ibid., pp. 19-50; Karen M. Offen, "Aspects of the Woman Question during the Third Republic," and "The 'Woman Question' as a Social Issue in Nineteenth Century France: A Bibliographic Essay," in *Third Republic/Troisième République* [hereafter cited as *TR/TR*], nos. 3-4 (1977): 1-19, 238-99; Charles Sowerwine, "Women and the Origins of the French Socialist Party: A Neglected Contribution," and "Women, Socialism and Feminism, 1872-1833: A Bibliography," ibid., pp. 104-27, 300-366; and idem, *Les Femmes et le socialisme* (Paris: Presses de la Fondation national de science politique, 1978). For the *Pétroleuses* see Edith Thomas, *The Women Incendiaries*, trans. and ed., J. and S. Atkinson (New York: George Braziller, 1966).

2. On the retardation of the woman suffrage movement in France, see Steven C. Hause, "Hubertine Auclert's Second Suffragist Career, 1893-1914: To an Unchanging Goal with Constantly Changing Tactics" (Paper read at the Fourth Berkshire Conference on the History of Women, Mt. Holyoke College, South Hadley, Mass., August 24, 1978); idem, "The Rejection of Women's Suffrage by the French Senate in November 1922: A Statistical Analysis," in *TR/TR*, nos. 3-4 (1977): 205-37; and idem, "Women Who Rallied to the Tricolor: The Effects of World War I on the French Women's Suffrage Movement" (Paper read to the Western Society for French History, San Diego, November 9, 1978); and Steven C. Hause and Anne R. Kenney, "The Development of the Catholic Women's Suffrage Movement in France, 1896-1922," (forthcoming) *Catholic Historical Review*; and idem, "Legalism and Violence in the French Women's Suffrage Movement, 1901-1914" (Paper read to History Department Colloquium, University of Missouri, St. Louis, Missouri, March, 1978). On attitudes toward the family, see Marilyn J. Boxer, "French Socialism, Feminism and the Family," in *TR/TR*, nos. 3-4 (1977): 128-67.

3. While some earlier feminists offered a radical critique of marriage, even they accepted traditional attitudes about maternity. See, for example, Mary Wollstonecraft, *A Vindication of the Rights of Women* (New York: Pelican, 1975), pp. 142, 146-47; Eleanor Flexner, *Mary Wollstonecraft: A Biography* (New York: McCann & Geoghegan, 1972), p. 158; and Charlotte Perkins Gilman, *Women and Economics* (New York: Source Book Press, 1970), pp. 177-97.

4. The birth date of Balabanoff was 1878; Goldman, 1869; Kollontai, 1872; Krupskaya, 1869; Luxemburg, 1871; Pelletier, 1874; Popp, 1869. See Theodore Zeldin, ed., *Conflicts in French Society: Anticlericalism, Education and Morals in the Nineteenth Century* (London: Allen & Unwin, 1970), p. 10.

5. Pelletier's deathbed autobiography, "Anne dite Madeleine Pelletier," wartime diary, and other biographical sources are available at the Bibliotheque Marguerite Durand (BMD), Dossier PEL, Paris. See also Madeleine Pelletier's novel, *La Femme vierge* (Paris: V. Bresle, 1933).

6. "Anne dite Mad. Pelletier;" *La Fronde*, December 2, 4, 7, and 21, 1902; and January 1, 1904; and "Anne dite Mad. Pelletier," *La Petite République*, December 3 and 19, 1902. In 1906 there were only 573 female physicians in France.

7. Earliest publications of Pelletier include *L' Association des idées dans la manie aiguë et dans la débilité mentale* (Paris: J. Rousset, 1903); idem, *Les Lois morbides de l'association des idées* (Paris: J. Rousset, 1904); idem, *Les Membres fantômes chez les amputés délirants* (Paris:

J. Rousset, 1905); and idem, with Marie Vaschide, *Recherches expériment-ales sur les signes physiques* (Paris: Impr. librairie de Montligeon, 1904).

8. For bibliography, including location and call numbers, see Sower-wine, "Women, Socialism and Feminism," pp. 300-366. Madeleine Pel-letier's major works included *L'emancipation sexuelle de la femme* (Paris: M. Giard and E. Brière, 1911); idem, *Philosophie social. Les opinions—les partis—les classes* (Paris: M. Giard and E. Brière, 1912); idem, *L'in-dividualisme* (Paris: M. Giard and E. Brière, 1919); and idem, *Mon voyage aventureux en Russie communiste* (Paris: M. Giard, 1922).

9. See *4e Congrès national tenu à Nancy, 11-14 Août 1907* (Paris: Le Libertaire, 1907); and Boxer, "Socialism Faces Feminism," pp. 232-340.

10. "Marxisme néfaste," *Le Libertaire*, November 22, 1913. On the Hervéist period, see *La Guerre sociale*, August 14, September 4, September 25, December 4, 1907, May 20, July 1, 1908, and February 9, 1910; *L' Humanité*, April 13, 15, November 29, 1909, February 10, 1910; *La Suffragiste*, July, 1919; *Le Socialiste*, February 27, 1910; Archives Nation-ales F7, 13071, reports dated February 19, 1910 and May, 1911; F7, 13072, folder on Congrès de St. Etienne (1909); Boxer, "Socialism Faces Femi-nism," pp. 251-52; and Charles Sowerwine, "Women and Socialism in France" (Ph.D. diss., University of Wisconsin, 1973), pp. 247-54.

11. Madeleine Pelletier, "Ma Candidature à la députation," *Documents du progrès*, July, 1910.

12. See, for example, the proceedings of the *Congrès international de la condition et des droits des femmes* in 1901.

13. On origins and composition of *Solidarité*, see Sowerwine, "Women and Socialism in France," pp. 236-38; on uses of illegality, see ibid., pp. 249-50. For Pelletier's impressions of *Solidarité*, see *La Femme vierge*, pp. 94-95, 128, 134-36.

14. A photograph of this costume is reproduced in Boxer and Quataert, *Socialist Women*, p. 99. Pelletier's dress, adopted to avoid unwanted attention from men in the streets (*La Femme vierge*, p. 53), was criticized by Hervé (*La Suffragiste*, July, 1919) and Paul Lafargue (quoted in *La Femme vierge*, p. 186); such criticism struck her as "moral rape." A pre-decessor who found that in men's clothes she could "fly from one end of Paris to the other" without risk was George Sand. See Joseph Barry, trans. and ed., *George Sand: In Her Own Words* (Garden City, N.Y.: Anchor Books, 1979), p. 321.

15. Anne R. Kenney, "A Militant Feminist in France: Dr. Madeleine Pelletier" (Paper read at the Fourth Berkshire Conference on the History of Women, Mt. Holyoke College, South Hadley, Mass., August 24, 1978). Kenney argued that Pelletier's extremism made moderate feminism more acceptable. Antifeminists such as Theodore Joran used her views on sexual-

ity and marriage to identify feminism with criminality. See Theodore Joran, *Au Coeur du féminisme* (Paris, n.p., n.d.), p. 13. A reviewer for *Le Mouvement socialiste*, July, 1910, considered Madeliene Pelletier, *La Femme en lutte pour ses droits* (Paris: V. Giard and E. Brière, 1908) "odious."

16. Pelletier, *La Femme vierge*, chaps. 5 and 11. In it, Marie becomes a teacher, but unlike her creator, is not a serious scholar. Pelletier's works abound with references to her wide readings, including Bachofen, Balzac, Barbusse, Dostoevsky, Flaubert, Fontenelle, Frazer, Freud, Galileo, d'Holbach, Ibsen, William James, Kant, La Boétie, Lamarck, La Rochefoucault, Jack London, Malthus, John Stuart Mill, Molière, Nietzsche, Pascal, Plato, Proudhon, Ricardo, Rostand, Rousseau, de Sade, Spencer, Spinoza, Tolstoy, and Voltaire. Pelletier also received feminist or socialist journals from numerous countries in Europe, as well as North and South America and Australia.

17. A quantitative study of socialist women in Germany in the early twentieth century indicates that more than half were housewives. See Jean H. Quataert, "The Making of an Ideology: The Social Bases of Socialist Feminism in Imperial Germany" (Paper read at the Fourth Berkshire Conference on the History of Women, Mt. Holyoke College, South Hadley, Mass., August 25, 1978). Also see Karen Honeycut, "Socialism and Feminism in Imperial Germany," *Signs* 5, no. 1 (1979): 31.

18. Another exception, Louise Saumoneau, daughter of a carpenter and one of the few working-class socialist women, was strongly antifeminist. See Charles Sowerwine, "Le Groupe féministe socialiste," *Le Mouvement social* 90 (1975): 87-120; and Boxer, "Socialism Faces Feminism," in Boxer and Quataert, *Socialist Women*, pp. 92-97.

19. Madeleine Pelletier, *L'Equité*, December 15, 1913. On the Couriau case, see Boxer, "Socialism Faces Feminism," pp. 292-306; Madeleine Guilbert, *Les Femmes et l'organisation syndicale avant 1914* (Paris: Centre national de la recherche scientifique, 1966), pp. 63-65, 409-12; Charles Sowerwine, "The Organization of French Socialist Women, 1880-1914; A European Perspective for Women's Movements," *Historical Reflections* 3, no. 2 (1976): 18-20.

20. Madeleine Pelletier, "Admission des femmes dans la franc-maçonnerie," *L'Acacia* (n.p., 1905).

21. "Le Droit à la vie sexuelle," clipping from unidentified journal in Dossier PEL, BMD.

22. Madleine Pelletier, *Une Vie nouvelle* (Paris: E. Figuièrre, 1932), p. 134.

23. Madeleine Pelletier, "Les Femmes et le féminisme," *La Revue*

socialiste, January, 1906), p. 44. A woman attacking Pelletier's suffragism in an anarchist periodical pointed out, "I am a *women*, yes Madam, a woman who does not deny her sex, a woman who is wife and mother." Madeleine Vernet, "Une question à Madam Madeleine Pelletier," *La Libertaire*, July 26, 1908.

24. Madeleine Pelletier, *Le Célibat, état supérieur* (Paris: Impr. caennaise, n.d.), p. 7.

25. Pelletier, *La Femme vierge*, pp. 231, 241; idem, "Anne dite Madeleine Pelletier," p. 8.

26. Pelletier, *Le Célibat*, p. 7. See also Madeleine Pelletier, *La Désagrégation de la famille* (Paris: Sauvard, n.d.); idem, "Famille," in Sébastien Faure, ed., *L'encyclopédie anarchiste*, 4 vols. (Paris: Le Libertaire, 1911), 2: 779-83; and idem, *Le Féminisme et la famille* (Paris: G. Coquette, 1919), p. 6.

27. Pelletier, *Le Célibat*, p. 7.

28. Pelletier, *Le Féminisme et la famille*, p. 6.

29. For a more extensive analysis of Pelletier's views on the family see Marilyn Boxer, "French Socialism, Feminism and the Family," *TR/TR*, nos. 3-4: 128-67. See also Pelletier, *La Femme en lutte*, p. 77.

30. Pelletier anticipated current feminist emphasis on the sharing of domestic responsibilities and on development of alternative institutions. But she had more faith in transforming the individual household than in overcoming male resistance to housework. See Pelletier, *Le Féminisme et la famille*, n. 13; idem, "La Femme seule," *La Suffragiste*, February, 1914; idem, "Le Droit un travail pour la femme," *Brochure Mensuelle* 107 (1931): 22; and idem, "La Classe ouvrière et la féminisme," *La Suffragiste*, July, 1912.

31. Cf. the reactions to braless women today.

32. Madeleine Pelletier, "Le Féminisme et la guerre," *La Suffragiste*, June, 1919.

33. For her views on revolution, see Pelletier, *Philosophie social*, pp. 83-84.

34. See her debate with Bracke on whether the worker's belly or brain should receive attention first: *Le Socialiste*, December 30, 1906, January 6, 1907. The opinion that the working class needed education, especially regarding class structure and women, pervades her work; see especially Madeleine Pelletier, *L'Etat éducateur* (Paris: by the author, 1931); idem, "Le Socialisme et la culture intellectuelle," *La Revue socialiste* 45, pt. 1 (1907): 107-17; and idem, *Le Libertaire*, April 18, 1914.

35. See Boxer, "Socialism Faces Feminism," or Sowerwine, "Women and Socialism." In an article, Sowerwine suggests that failure to organize

separate women's sections, following the German model, doomed the French socialist women's movement. Charles Sowerwine, "The Organization of French Socialist Women," *Historical Reflections*, pp. 18-20. He also notes that Pelletier was ambivalent on separatism. Sowerwine, "Women and Socialism," p. 252.

36. Theodore Zeldin points out that this same combination influenced Charles de Gaulle's decision to introduce woman suffrage by decree in 1944; Theodore Zeldin, *France, 1848-1945: I, Ambition, Love and* (Oxford: Clarenden Press, 1973), p. 360.

37. On attitudes toward peasants and the working classes, see *La Suffragiste*, June, 1919; and Pelletier, *La Désagrégation de la famille*, p. 8.

38. For accounts of arrest and death notice, see Dossier PEL, BMD.

4.
Sylvia Pankhurst: Suffragist, Feminist, or Socialist?

LINDA EDMONDSON

"Life is nothing without enthusiasms."
Richard Marsden Pankhurst
to his children

The name Pankhurst is associated in the public mind almost exclusively with the militant suffragettes whose campaign, launched on the British political scene in 1905, contributed conspicuously to the turbulence of the succeeding decade. For Emmeline Pankhurst and her eldest daughter Christabel, these were the years of greatest influence and fame, never regained thereafter. But for Mrs. Pankhurst's second daughter Sylvia the suffragette years were just the beginning of a highly eventful career dedicated to the promotion of radical causes and the quest for a higher civilization. Her life defies categorization, as it was distinguished by a fierce individualism and refusal to conform to the dictates of orthodoxy or compromise. Beginning her political life as a suffragette and concluding it, half a century later, as a passionate supporter of Ethiopian nationhood, she embraced in the intervening years a variety of enthusiasms, from communism and antifascism to Esperanto and world government. To each she brought a sense of purpose and disregard for petty considerations of expediency that were remarkable for any public figure at any time.

Since doing justice to such a varied career in a single chapter would be difficult, this essay will be confined mainly to the period from 1906 to 1924, the years of Pankhurst's most radical activity.

Estelle Sylvia Pankhurst was born in 1882, the second of five children. Her father, whom she idolized, was a barrister with radical views and considerable learning. He was a prominent figure in the provincial world of his native Manchester (though not perhaps as eminent as his daughter later suggested) and ranged himself on the side of all the progressive causes of the time, including woman suffrage. His wife, whom he married when he was forty-four and she twenty, was a good-looking young woman with a Parisian education and wardrobe but also an active mind, which readily responded to her husband's political enthusiasms. She immediately involved herself in his political career and, after the birth of her fifth child, began to take a more energetic role in public life on her own account.

In 1865 the family moved to London, where it was hoped that Dr. Pankhurst's political career would prosper. The eight years the family spent in the capital did not yield the anticipated prize of a seat in Parliament, nor did the Pankhursts' finances flourish, despite Mrs. Pankhurst's attempt to supplement her husband's income by running a "fancy goods" shop. But if their stay in London brought little material gain (and one tragedy in the death of their four-year-old son), it did help to broaden their political horizons, introducing them to the stimulating company of socialists and anarchists, nationalists and republicans. As a small girl Sylvia met an enchanting assortment of left-wing celebrities at her parents' house: the Russian populists Stepniak and Chaikovskii, Louise Michel, the *Pétroleuse* of the Paris Commune, the Italian anarchist Malatesta, English socialists such as William Morris, as well as numerous campaigners for women's rights.

Their influence was long-lasting. When the family returned to Manchester, Dr. and Mrs. Pankhurst shed their old associations with the Liberal party and soon joined the infant Independent Labour party, founded in 1893 to increase working-class representation in Parliament on a platform of nondoctrinaire socialism.[1]

The Pankhurst children received a somewhat haphazard education, largely because of their mother's prejudice against formal schooling. Sylvia was already eleven when she and her sister Christabel were first sent to school, an institution she came to detest for its cold discipline and uninspired teaching. Neither sister seems to have suffered from the lack of a steady school career, for which the informal education received at home more than compensated. Their father had a passion for books and learning, which Sylvia, in particular, inherited. Like her younger siblings she spent much time alone, often in a world of dreams and fantasies. This childhood tendency might have been unremarkable had it not been carried into her adult life, shaping her political ideas. The "childish fancy" of a world of beauty from which poverty and unhappiness would be banished was the inspiration of all her undertakings in later life.[2]

Despite the failure of Dr. Pankhurst's political ambitions and the accumulating financial anxieties with which he and his wife had to contend, Sylvia's childhood was generally happy, and she lovingly preserved memories of it. But when she was sixteen, her security was rudely shattered by the sudden death of her beloved father. His death seemed to hit her with particular severity, leaving a scar that never entirely healed. She felt that the bond between them had been especially close (compensating perhaps for her mother's obvious preference for Christabel), and in her political career years later she consciously sought to uphold his ideals with the same tenacity that he had shown. But for the other members of the family, too, Dr. Pankhurst's death was a terrible loss, both emotionally and materially. Mrs. Pankhurst was distraught and retired from active political involvement for several years. She was also obliged to provide the family's income, as her husband had left no money and none of the children was fully grown.

Although plagued by recurrent illness in the year following her father's death, Sylvia had one resource that she was able to put to good use: her artistic ability, the one sphere in which as a child she excelled over her elder sister. At seventeen she won a free place at the Manchester School of Art, where she studied for three years. After several months in Italy, she went on to the Royal College of Art in London, the city that thereafter was her home. At this stage she had every intention of making art her life's work.

In the meantime, however, the movement for woman suffrage in Britain had begun to take on new life, after forty years of eloquent campaigning but little achievement. The new campaign began in northern England. Unlike the earlier suffrage movement, whose members were overwhelmingly from the professional classes, the new phase owed much of its vigor to the working women of the textile towns around Manchester, who formed a large part of a skilled and relatively well-paid work force and had an unusual amount of time to spare for union work and politics. In 1901 Christabel Pankhurst became involved in a suffrage organization, the North of England Society for Women's Suffrage, which aimed to appeal directly to such working-class women. Mrs. Pankhurst had meanwhile revived her contacts with the Independent Labour party (which Sylvia also joined) but was disconcerted to discover that many of her male comrades gave woman suffrage very low priority in the party program. By 1903 Mrs. Pankhurst had decided that working women needed a new organization combining the functions of suffrage society and political pressure group, and in October she established the Women's Social and Political Union (WSPU).

Until 1905 the union remained a small, provincial society, largely unknown outside Lancashire and maintaining strong ties to the Independent Labour party. By 1905 Mrs. Pankhurst and Christabel, who had begun to work for the WSPU too, had grown weary of the old tactics of persuasion by petitions and speeches and had begun to consider more eye-catching methods, such as lobbying Parliament and disrupting public meetings.[3] By this time Sylvia Pankhurst was studying in London. Although she worked when she could for her mother's organization, she had not been intimately involved for its development and was not entirely happy with its new tactics. But when the focus of the WSPU's campaigning was transported to London early in 1906, she found herself devoting all her spare time to the cause.

With London as its base the nature of the WSPU began to change. It grew narrower in social composition, more autocratic in structure (after a schism in 1907), and more extreme in its tactics. From heckling at meetings the union soon adopted the policy of harassing government ministers on all possible occasions, each time inviting arrest and rough treatment. Suffragette demonstrations were the scene of progressively more violent clashes with the police, but little lasting damage was inflicted until 1909 when suffragettes first threw stones at the windows of government buildings. In prison they began a policy of hunger strikes to gain their release, but the government retaliated by forcibly feeding them, using methods that were both degrading and dangerous, and were much criticized at the time. A truce in 1910, while a "Conciliation Bill" was under discussion in Parliament, was followed by renewed stone throwing and arrests. In 1912 Christabel Pankhurst, who had increasingly dominated the organization since 1907, escaped to Paris to direct in safety a campaign that now included arson and vandalism.

Until 1912 Sylvia Pankhurst immersed herself in the work of the WSPU, writing and campaigning. She toured the United States for the union, designed exhibits for it, and went to prison twice. But her doubts grew, not only about the level and nature of violence, but also about the WSPU's divorce from its working-class supporters. At the end of 1912 she decided to seek her own independent base among working-class women, and set up shop in the East End of London. At first she managed to get financial support from the WSPU, but aid was soon withdrawn and the East London Federation of the WSPU (as it was christened) had to depend on its own resources.

For the first time Pankhurst was in charge of her own campaign and threw herself into it with total commitment of body and soul. She supervised the creation of six district branches of the federation, spoke at innumerable public meetings, played cat and mouse with the police countless times, and submitted to the agonies of the hunger and thirst strike (about which she wrote in almost masochistic detail). Her greatest coup was to force the prime minister into receiving a delegation of working women, by threatening to fast to her death. In March, 1914, she set up a weekly paper, *The Woman's Dreadnought*, which catalogued the activities of the East London Federation and exhorted its readers to support the cause.[4]

It is difficult to say what would have been the fate of the suffragette movement if World War I had not intervened. The WSPU had reached an impasse, having failed by arson, vandalism, and hunger strikes to force the government into conceding votes for women. Whether Sylvia Pankhurst's organization would have achieved more by mobilizing working-class women is doubtful, unless it had successfully broken out of its East End confines and recaptured the women in the industrial towns of the north.[5]

In any event, the war brought the suffrage movement to an abrupt halt. The two leading organizations, the WSPU and the moderate National Union of Women's Suffrage Societies (NUWSS), suspended their campaigning and committed their members to support of the war. However, not all suffragists were prepared to rush to the aid of the government. The NUWSS lost most of its leadership (though little of its rank and file) to the international women's peace movement, and some members of the WSPU were unable to stomach their leaders' sudden conversion to bellicose chauvinism.

Meanwhile the East London Federation of Suffragettes characteristically swam against the tide. While her sister and mother became unofficial recruiting officers for the same government that only months before had been their sworn enemy, Sylvia Pankhurst immediately pledged her federation to oppose the war and to continue the battle for the vote.[6] Living as she now did in the most depressed area of London where a high level of unemployment was endemic, she appreciated at once the economic consequences of the war for working-class families. Although conscription would not be introduced for another two years, enlistment was quickly forced upon men as much by the impossibility of finding work as by the social pressure on them not to "shirk" their duty. Women, too, suffered from the immediate rise in unemployment as peacetime industries closed down. Many were later absorbed into war work, especially in munitions factories, but the work was often unpleasant and even dangerous.[7]

Pankhurst seized upon the widespread distress of women in the East End, as in working-class areas all over Britain, and kept up a constant barrage of complaints to the authorities for their failure to administer relief efficiently or guarantee an adequate minimum wage and prevent food hoarding and speculation. The federation became an unofficial welfare center, which by early 1915 had set up three "Cost Price Restaurants," a maternity clinic and day nursery (in an abandoned pub), and a small toy factory, paying reasonable wages to its women workers.[8]

The war brought economic hardship and personal loss to the British population and also a substantial curtailment of civil liberties. Successive Defence of the Realm Acts introduced censorship and surveillance over individuals and organizations, while the creation of a war economy was accompanied by restrictions on trade union activity and the suspension of much protective legislation. As the months wore on, Pankhurst began to devote less of her energy to the hardships endured by women alone and more to the campaign to prevent military conscription (finally introduced in January, 1916) and industrial compulsion.

By the end of 1915 her articles in the *Dreadnought* had begun to show signs of a new if still tentative interest in the international socialist movement. Woman suffrage was supplanted by the slogan of "human suffrage," and a hitherto somewhat vague pacifism became a "determination to strive for the time when the People's International shall put an end to war for all time."[9]

But not until after the February Revolution in Russia did she depart from the standard rhetoric of nonrevolutionary socialism and pacifism. From the first she was deeply skeptical of the provisional government in Russia, believing that the new leaders intended to prosecute the war as before, with the same imperialist ambitions. Initially impressed by Kerensky, she very soon dismissed him, pinning her hopes instead on the socialists in the Soviet to take Russia out of the war. Her journal (renamed *The Workers' Dreadnought*) began to demand the establishment of soviets in Britain (an idea of revolutionary councils much canvassed by the Left at this time) and the refusal of war credits to the government. By early autumn the *Dreadnought* was openly supporting the Bolsheviks and greeted the October Revolution with enthusiasm:

> Our eager hopes are for the speedy success of the Bolsheviks of Russia: may they open the door which leads to freedom for the people of all lands![10]

Much of Pankhurst's efforts in the coming months were channeled into the campaign to support the Bolsheviks at the Brest-Litovsk negotiations, by which the Russians eventually signed a humiliating truce with the Germans. She was particularly disgusted by the hostile attitude of the trade unions and the Labour party toward the Bolsheviks and in 1918 joined the predominantly Marxist British Socialist party for a short time.

The focus of Pankhurst's work had shifted remarkably in the previous two and a half years. From being a purely women's association, ELFS (renamed the Workers' Suffrage Federation and then, in 1918, the Workers' Socialist Federation, or WSF) had become a radical political organization, pledged to a People's Peace, the abolition of Parliament, and Soviet power in Britain. As part of its propaganda the WSF established a Russian People's Information Bureau, and some issues of the *Dreadnought* carried little but news of Russia. Pankhurst also played a prominent role in the "Hands Off Russia" campaigning, which aimed to rouse working-class opinion against Allied intervention after the November armistice.

Until 1919 socialists in Britian made few efforts to form a native communist party. Political agitation was conducted mainly through the existing parties and through the shop stewards' movement (a form of industrial syndicalism) which was particularly strong on Clydeside in Scotland. But the turbulent state of European politics after the war and the founding congress of the Third International in March, 1919, inspired thoughts of a British communist party to weld those left-wing groups that were disillusioned with the existing political system into a coherent revolutionary force.

Among those groups was the Workers' Socialist Federation, which in June, 1919, took the name "Communist party" with Pankhurst as honorary secretary.[11] It made overtures to other organizations to form a united party and seek affiliation with the Third International, but the negotiations proved acrimonious. Pankhurst found herself on the extreme left wing of the movement and became the target of a strong rebuke from Lenin. To argue her case more forcefully, she set off at the last minute for the Second Comintern Congress, which opened in Moscow at the end of July, 1920. Her presence at the congress made no difference to the outcome, but she had the opportunity to meet Bolshevik leaders (including Lenin, who impressed her greatly at the time) and see something of the country that she had been so vigorously defending since 1917.

During the summer and autumn of 1920 the handful of communist organizations in Britain that accepted Lenin's policy agreed to sink their differences and form the Communist party of Great

Britain (CPGB). Pankhurst's faction joined as a dissident minority. She, meanwhile, was arrested in October on a charge of sedition, based on four articles that had appeared in the *Dreadnought*, and served a six-month prison sentence.[12] Her imprisonment removed her from the scene at a critical point in the history of the Communist party, and by the time she was released, she had lost whatever chance as she had possessed of influencing its future development. Relations between the party and the *Dreadnought* deteriorated as Pankhurst exercised to the full her right to criticize. The CPGB repeatedly demanded that she hand the journal over to its executive; she naturally refused and was expelled from the party.

Despite its perennial financial difficulties, Pankhurst kept the *Dreadnought* afloat for three more years. She made it a forum for all dissident communist opinion in Europe and deplored what she saw as a steady drift to the Right in Russia itself.[13] She was equally alarmed by the growth of right-wing nationalism on the continent, denouncing "the murderous Mussolini" and the antics of Hitler in Munich.

But falling circulation and her own failing interest led to the *Dreadnought*'s demise in the middle of 1924, and with it the end of Pankhurst's communist phase. By that time she had moved out of the poverty-striken East End to a semirural suburb, where she opened a café called the Red Cottage and withdrew from organized politics.

She had first demonstrated her ability to write in 1911, when she had produced a history of the militant suffrage movement, to promote the WSPU's campaign.[14] Since then she had written numerous pamphlets, besides editing the weekly *Dreadnought*. Now, with that burden removed, she turned to new intellectual interests, which included village communism in India and the prospects for an international language.[15] Both confirmed her continuing search for the ideal which, despite her disillusion with organized politics, she still believed people could attain.

In 1931 she brought out *The Suffragette Movement*, a work that was partly a definitive history of the militant suffrage movement as she saw it and partly an autobiography. Besides being a detailed account of WSPU activities, the book was noteworthy for its idealization of her father, its suggestion of Mrs. Pankhurst's failings as a mother, and its pointed criticisms of her sister Christabel's direction of WSPU tactics. The following year she produced *The Home Front*, a memoir of her war work in the East End of London.

Her creative instincts did not find fulfillment in writing alone. In December, 1927, at the age of forty-five, she gave birth to a son, whom she named Richard after her father. The child's father, Silvio Corio, was an Italian political émigré, also of middle age, with whom she was living and with whom she had worked for the past decade. Despite the scandalized comments of the press, Pankhurst refused to marry and continued to live in a "free union" with Corio until his death in 1954.

Living with an émigré from Italy, Pankhurst was naturally involved in the opposition to Mussolini, a cause that she had already taken up in the *Dreadnought*. Until 1934, however, her commitment remained general. But when Mussolini provoked war with Ethiopia to justify an invasion, Pankhurst was among the first to come to the victims' defense. With Corio she produced leaflets to be smuggled into Ethiopia, lobbied politicians, and spoke at innumerable meetings. In 1936 she and Corio brought out a news sheet, *New Times and Ethiopia News*, which, despite its improbable title, reached a circulation of 40,000 at its peak and came out regularly for the next twenty years. She first met Haile Selassie during his exile in England. A republican since her youth, she was nonetheless overwhelmed by the imperial presence and became his devoted and lifelong disciple. Unlike the majority of liberals and radicals whose interest in Ethiopia was ephemeral, Pankhurst's enthusiasm for the country developed with the years. Even when Haile Selassie had been restored to his throne and fascism was finally defeated, Pankhurst's war on Ethiopia's behalf continued. She was totally convinced that Ethiopia's territorial claim to Eritrea was right and published two books on the subject.[16] During the last two decades of her life, in addition to her fund raising and propaganda activities, which continued unabated, she produced a number of works on Ethiopia, notably a 700-page cultural history. In 1956, at the age of seventy-four, she packed up her belongings and emigrated there with her son and daughter-in-law. In Addis Ababa she inaugurated a new journal, *The Ethiopia Observer*, and worked for her new homeland with the same vigor she had given to all her enthusiasms. She died in September, 1960. An agnostic all her life, she was given a state funeral in Holy Trinity Cathedral in Addis Ababa with Emperor Haile Selassie first among the mourners.

Throughout her extremely varied career Pankhurst's political philosophy remained fundamentally the same. She was in essence an individualist who believed passionately in collectivism and the responsibility of the community for the welfare of its members. From her parents, particularly her father, she inherited a compelling need to be of service to others. "If you do not grow up to help other people," she quoted her father as saying, "you will not have been worth the upbringing."[17] He passed on his own unyielding principles and refusal to compromise for the sake of personal gain to his daughter who cherished them all her life. Possessing an unshakable sense of right and wrong, she found it difficult to comprehend how others, particularly those blessed with health, education, and material comfort, might be less firm in their convictions. She assailed corrupting influences in society, whether they be alcohol, the capitalist mode of production, or in later years American commercial cinema, for destroying the creative potential that she believed lay in each human being.

Coupled with a strong moral sensibility was an aesthetic revulsion against ugliness and poverty. Her writings are full of powerful visual images that evoke the decay of a slum landscape or the pathos of a human tragedy.

> Those endless rows of smoke-begrimed little houses, with never a tree or a flower in sight, how bitterly their ugliness smote me! . . . The misery of the poor, as I heard my father plead for it, and saw it revealed in the pinched faces of his audiences, awoke in me a maddening sense of impotence; and there were moments when I had an impulse to dash my head against the dreary walls of those squalid streets.[18]

In common with many English socialists, such as William Morris a generation earlier, Pankhurst envisaged a society of the future in which not only would material want be satisfied but also a striving for beauty, a society whose very structure lent itself to the arts.

It would be hard to describe Pankhurst at any point in her career as a true Marxist. Even during her years as a committed revolutionary the ideas of Marx never sat comfortably on her shoulders, and she was as likely to quote Morris or Kropotkin as the author of *Das Kapital*. At her most bloodthirsty she was not quite at home with the concept of class warfare. "Deep down beyond all race and class distinctions we are human beings, with the same needs and instincts," she wrote in 1915, and her outlook never really changed.[19] Although she talked of "smashing capitalism," she was happier contemplating the time when communism would be achieved. For this reason she was in her element during the "early heroic days" of the revolution in Russia when a new civilization seemed to call to a world exhausted by an endless war:

> Out of the welter rises the Russian Revolution. Oh, human race with the wonderful brain creative, crushed to the lowest ebb of endurance, pressed beyond bearing, comes to you then divine revolt, forging out new conditions, changing the old world's face to a higher civilisation.[20]

She seized upon the soviet as the answer to the problem of the world's government, substituting for the old system "under which the people suffer" an alternative "built upon an occupational basis, of which the members shall be but the delegates of those who are carrying on the world's work."[21] For Pankhurst the soviet was a living entity embodying and fulfilling the dreams of men and women, not the rigid structure it soon became in Russia. Indeed her faith in it did not long survive her loss of faith in Lenin's revolution, and by the end of 1921 she had begun to suggest that although the soviet structure "presents the best form of organisation yet evolved, ... there is always the possibility of something higher, as yet undiscovered."[22]

After her break with the Communist party her ideas drifted still farther from Marx, to a collectivism that had more in common with the Russian populists of the 1870s and 1880s. Like them she came to believe that the village commune of prerevolutionary Russia, or India, provided the basis for the realization of an "earthly paradise" founded on a "great fraternity of mutual aid." The Soviet government's endeavors to break up the peasant communal system during the New Economic Policy (NEP) was one more indication to her that the Russian regime had been made morally and ideologically bankrupt.[23]

Inspired as she was by a conception of human motivation that was idealistic in the extreme, it is not hard to see why her involvement in the communist movement should have been so short-lived. Hers was no orthodox communism trimming its sails to the wind from Moscow, but rather a vision of spiritual regeneration that permitted little compromise on tactical issues. Yet it was with tactical issues above all that the communist movement had to grapple in these years. The problem was to determine the degree to which the party could participate in the bourgeois system in order to undermine it without thereby becoming compromised by it. Specifically in Britain the controversy revolved around the questions of affiliation to the Labour party (whose constitution permitted a diversity of opinion), involvement in trade unionism, and participation in Parliament.

Pankhurst was intransigent throughout in her opposition to any such collaboration. By 1910 she had become convinced that Parliament was grossly unrepresentative and "a waste of time."[24] Carried away by the Russian example, she advocated the use of industrial action to bring capitalism to its knees (exactly how she never specified) and the immediate establishment of a system of soviets. She had no patience with those who urged caution:

> The deeds of pioneers are calling to us to do something. . . . mass action alone can succeed, but those who are ready for action must act and thereby cause the mass to move.[25]

She condemned the Labour party and the trade unions which were the Labour party's principal constituency as "social patriotic" organizations which "the revolutionary opposition" must "make ready to attack."

> We must not dissipate our energy in adding to the strength of the Labour party; its rise to power is inevitable. We must concentrate on making a communist movement that will vanquish it.[26]

Her refusal to consider any sort of tactical compromise was not well received by many of her comrades or by Lenin. In the summer of 1919 he suggested, not too forcefully, that an excessive commitment to ideological purity would be misplaced under existing conditions, and he proposed that if factions in Britain were unable to agree, then two separate communist parties should be formed. Eight months later he had become more impatient with leftist dogmatism and devoted several pages of his pamphlet *"Left-wing" Communism, and Infantile Disorder* to demolishing the arguments that Pankhurst and those who thought like her had put forward. He insisted that unless British communists learned to compromise with the parliamentary system, they would stand no chance of capturing the masses. The history of Bolshevism "is *full* of cases of maneuvering, of conciliation, of compromises with other parties, including bourgeois parties," he wrote. By collaborating with the Labour party, in and out of Parliament, communists would be doing no more than support the Labour leaders "as the rope supports the man being hanged." The worst that the Communist party could do would be to rush into revolutionary action before the masses were ready to follow.[27]

Lenin's strategy prevailed, but Pankhurst would not accept his arguments nor submit to his authority. The more she was threatened with disciplinary action, the more her libertarian instincts were roused. Whereas in 1920 she had reproved a colleague for questioning the right of the Third International to direct the activities of member parties, a year later she was raising the same question herself and soon prepared to welcome the dissident Fourth International, which had been recently inaugurated in Berlin.[28] The *Dreadnought* carried critical accounts from returning visitors of conditions in Russia under the NEP and reported the imprisonment there of anarchist and communist opponents of the Soviet government.

However, Pankhurst was never tempted into supporting Trotsky. He had been too closely associated with Lenin's leadership at the time of her own battle with the Third International for her to be able to do more than register his conflict with Stalin. "Trotsky is, of course, right in all this," she wrote of his denunciation of bureaucratic tyranny in the Soviet regime, "but he has been somewhat late in discovering it, and even now he does not see the full extent of the evil and its causes."[29]

At home, too, she championed the cause of inner-party democracy. "To stifle discussion . . . is to dig the grave of the Communist Party," she pronounced during her battle with the party executive.[30] On its attempt to silence the *Dreadnought* she wrote:

> Those who may differ from the Executive on any point of principle, policy or tactics, or even those whose method of dealing with agreed theory is not approved or appreciated by the Executive, are therefore to be gagged.[31]

Yet there are hints that her castigation of censorship, at least in the party, was limited to the censorship of the Left. Moreover, she appeared to be suggesting that this censorship was inexpedient rather than morally wrong. She conceded that strong discipline might be necessary during war and revolution, but argued that freedom for the left wing of the party was essential to prevent the growth of "Right opportunism and laxity!"[32] This attitude contrasts strangely with her wholesale condemnation of government censorship during World War I, but is in keeping with her later support for the autocratic rule of Haile Selassie in Ethiopia. Although sincere in her support of free speech, she was prepared to put it in abeyance when circumstances seemed to dictate.

Pankhurst's influence on the communist movement in Britain was negligible, although she achieved a certain notoriety in the press at the time. The fact that she was middle-class in a largely working-class party and had no personal experience of industry may not have been in her favor. But her temperament was more telling than her social origins. She was not one to submit easily to orders, especially when she believed those orders to be incorrect. Her assessment of the political situation in Britain was at odds with the policy of the Third International and with the views of her comrades, and she would not alter her assessment to suit party bureaucracy. Equally, her conception of the communist future was not in accord with orthodox communist ideology.

Indeed, her unorthodoxy was the most notable feature of her political personality. Neither as a member of the Communist party nor later would she fit into a convenient pigeonhole. This undeniably cost her something in influence. Neither a communist nor a "fellow traveler" in the 1930s and having cut herself off from the

Labour party years before, she played only a small role in shaping left-wing attitudes in Britain. General interest in Ethiopia evaporated once the Spanish Civil War broke out, and there were few in Britain whose enthusiasm for Haile Selassie survived his restoration to the throne.

But her isolation was of her own choosing and wholly characteristic of her career. Throughout, she preferred to remain in charge of her own minority campaign and keep faith with her ideals rather than be a functionary in the organization of others, however worthy the cause.

Submerged in a world of revolutionary politics, which paid scant regard to the women's movement in Britain, Pankhurst had allowed herself to be diverted from those feminist issues that had been her principal concern until World War I. By 1917 she had all but left the movement; as a socialist she repudiated her suffragette past, belittling the act of Parliament that finally gave women the vote. But although she was never again part of a purely women's organization, she remained instinctively a feminist, with a passionate concern for the rights of women and their welfare. In particular she retained a deep compassion for those women who, she felt, had neither the education nor the economic advantages to fight for their independence.

To analyze the nature of Pankhurst's feminism, one has to return to her years in the suffragette movement, her break with the Women's Social and Political Union, and the establishment of her own East London Federation. Feminism was, of course, part of her family inheritance. But for her the campaign for the vote at any price was not the exclusive obsession that it became for her mother and Christabel. Indeed, it was a sign of her individuality that none of the established suffrage societies, the WSPU included, was able to fulfill her aspirations. Despite considerable working-class support (especially in the north of England), they were all predominantly middle-class in leadership and, perhaps more significantly, in immediate goals. None of them advocated universal female suffrage; all of them, from moderate to extremist, supported legislation which, being based on a property qualification, would have enfranchised no more than 2 million women. While in the early stage of WSPU militancy Sylvia Pankhurst accepted the necessity of a limited bill to establish the principle of woman suffrage, her doubts about its widsom developed simultaneously with her doubts about suffragette violence.

The extent of her disagreement with WSPU policy before 1912 is difficult to gauge. Undoubtedly there was a strong element of family rivalry influencing both her behavior at the time and her subsequent interpretation of it. The rift with her mother and Christabel in 1914 was total and may well have colored her recollections. Nonetheless, she had good reason to criticize WSPU policy, which was alienating many supporters of woman suffrage, and one may readily accept the explanation she gave almost twenty years later:

> I believed, then and always, that the movement required, not more serious militancy by the few, but a stronger appeal to the great masses to join the struggle.

But she went on to explain why she failed to make a stand earlier:

> Yet it was not in me to criticize or expostulate. I would rather have died at the stake than say one word against the actions of those who were in the throes of the fight.[33]

Distressed by the WSPU's neglect of its original working-class support, as by its resort to arson, she also intensely disliked its autocratic structure and sought to create in the East London Federation that "equalitarian society of mutual service" which in later years became an integral part of her political creed.[34] Working in the East End, she found herself for the first time in her suffrage career completely at one with her coworkers:

> They were to me, in Gladstone's phrase *vox populi, vox dei*, the touchstone of eternal vertities; my mothers, my sisters, my daughters. I had need of no other kin than they.[35]

Yet even in ELFS a hierarchy emerged. For all her aspirations to collective organization, Pankhurst was too much the leader, too strong-willed and inclined to dogmatism. ELFS was dominated as much by Sylvia as the WSPU was dominated by Christabel and

Mrs. Pankhurst; it fulfilled her need for total commitment, but was less successful in cultivating working-class initiative in the long term. Despite her democratic principles, there was more than a hint of condescension in her attitude to East End women (as there always was toward the working class in general). Notwithstanding her admiration for the resourcefulness and initiative of individual ELFS members, she tended to think of them as "my brood" whom she had aroused "from the voiceless millions of the submerged poor."[36] There were times when their reactions distressed her, as in their initial refusal to accept her pacifism at the outbreak of World War I:

> As children unable to comprehend the long words in the story-book, they stared at me, nonplussed; their minds all dazed and glamoured by the torrents of Press rhetoric, and the atmosphere of excitement and rumour growing apace in every street. I saw in those two questioners the type of millions. How should one rend from their eyes the veil of illusion, how unravel for them the tangled and knotted skein?[37]

It was, therefore, in keeping with her sentiments at the time that her chief contribution to the East London Federation after the outbreak of war should have been in the nature of a rescue operation, a type of unofficial social work. The low-price meals, the baby clinic, and the toy factory were all a response to the immediate crisis rather than the implementation of theory and as such were highly successful. Pankhurst clearly possessed the ability to inspire great loyalty in those among whom she worked as on those occasions when she led them up to Whitehall demanding redress for grievance.

But ELFS was not able to grapple with the fundamental social and economic problems which first caused women to come to it. When Pankhurst began to appreciate the strict limits of the federation's usefulness, the Russian Revolution was already beckoning, and she turned to new solutions for the social crisis.

Her work with ELFS does, however, tell us a good deal about her views on certain feminist issues, such as equal pay and protective legislation. On these questions, as on the question of adult suffrage, her opinions had become notably more outspoken since her move to the East End. The mainstream of the women's movement in Britain had never given prominence to the demand for equal pay, even in middle-class occupations, choosing to concentrate instead on establishing the basic principle of a woman's right to work at all in those professions. There were few occupations, manual or white-collar, where the female labor force earned more than two-thirds the male income, and frequently the differential was much greater. In many areas of employment, and notably in the East End, the problem was compounded by a sexual division of labor in which women took low-paid jobs, often dependent on seasonal demand.[38] In the garment industry women were employed in small workshops or took in work at home and remained to a considerable extent outside the industrial economy.

The war had brought instant unemployment in many "female" occupations, depressing women's wages still further. But women soon found themselves taking jobs in essential industries hitherto reserved for men, and the question of equal pay began to assume a more obvious relevance. Pankhurst was among the first to demand the raising of women's wage rates, not only in jobs where direct comparison with men's rates was possible but also in specifically female occupations. She used the *Dreadnought* to publish regular assaults on employers who continued to exploit women's low bargaining power, agitated for a minimum female wage, organized demonstrations to demand equal pay and woman suffrage, and refused to fill in her National Register form (which she saw as a prelude to industrial conscription), because women in war work were being paid at lower rates than the men they replaced.[39]

She was equally vigorous in her defence of protective legislation in the workplace. She had little sympathy with the opinion, common among feminists, that legislation to regulate hours and conditions of employment merely served to protect men from the competition of female labor. She had seen enough of the conditions in which women worked in the East End to appreciate that existing legislation, especially relating to small workshops, was still inadequate and poorly enforced. The problem was exacerbated by the war, during which much of the statutory legislation was suspended. Pankhurst's was only one of many voices urging greater government controls in munitions factories, in particular to prevent women from working excessively long shifts and to protect them from overexposure to toxic chemicals. But despite considerable publicity of the worst abuses, the view prevailed that nothing should be allowed to impede the nation's effort in time of war. Pankhurst's own pacifism was undoubtedly strengthened by what she felt to be the government's disregard for the health and safety of those women who were providing the country with vital military equipment.

At the heart of Pankhurst's feminism, evident in her work with ELFS, was a concern for women as mothers and housewives. Although her feminist involvement took second place to revolutionary politics toward the end of the war, her socialist utopia did not neglect the housewife. In one of her rare direct appeals to working women during this period, she called on them to emulate their Russian sisters and set up street committees to further the revolution.

> These are the workshop committees of the mothers, for the streets and the houses they live and work in are *their* work-shops. The women must organise to protect themselves and their families and to help in the general struggle of the working class to conquer the power of government.[40]

There is no suggestion in her writings at this time that she envisaged serious antagonism between workingmen and women, but she did believe that women had their own particular interests. For this reason she advocated a system of household soviets "in order that mothers and those who are organisers of the family life of the community may be adequately represented, and may take their due part in the management of society."[41] Clearly even as a revolutionary, she saw no need for a radical restructuring of sexual roles. While making allowance in her scheme for "individual men and women who have no housekeeper to care for them," she unquestionably intended the household soviet primarily for women in their position as housewives. Women whose main occupation was outside the home would, she felt, be adequately represented in workshop soviets; while the possibility of men and women sharing housework and the upbringing of children equally was never seriously considered.[42]

As for the day-to-day management of the household, she dreamed of a total liberation from drudgery, through the provision of communal laundries, kitchens, crèches, and so on. These would be run on the most up-to-date lines by the women of the neighborhood, eliminating back-breaking toil and social isolation and leaving housewives with time to develop their minds. Like many socialist utopias, Pankhurst's was in some respects the epitome of the suburban dream, clean and somewhat antiseptic.

Nor did she aspire to abolish the family; if anything, she sought to strengthen it by elevating the role of housewife in society. In her utopia, marriage would be transformed by the removal of legal bonds into a free union of equals. Parenthood would be "based on mutual love and mutual intention . . . an ardent zest for producing and cherishing splendid offspring."[43]

Of all the aspects of women's lives, their role as mothers most aroused her sympathy. The subject of motherhood (and particularly its relation to national efficiency) had been under close scrutiny since the end of the nineteenth century. With a falling birthrate and an infant mortality rate that was actually rising, the earlier Malthusian nightmare of an uncontained population explosion had been superseded by a fear that only the physically and mentally "unfit" would continue to breed, resulting in the degeneration of the race.[44]

Pankhurst' concern did not take this form. Hers was for the health and happiness of mothers themselves. She was horrified by the conditions under which most working-class women endured pregnancy and childbirth and, like other practical feminists, conceived the solution in simple terms: The community must intervene to provide facilities for motherhood. When she herself became a mother, her feelings grew more personal. "Motherhood is a great mystery," she wrote in 1930. "Those who fail to know it have missed an element of the essential fabric of life."[45] But she also became more explicit in her prescription for maternity care. She denounced the existing provisions (which had improved considerably since 1918) for their failure to lower the persistently high level of maternal mortality in Britain and advocated a comprehensive national maternity service, including not only care by an obstetrician and good medical facilities but also trained home help and generous maternity insurance.[46]

Her enthusiasm for motherhood made her critical of attempts to control population. She spoke of abortion as a "terrible and dangerous expedient" and, although she supported proposals for free access to contraceptive advice, clearly did not regard contraception as a prerequisite for women's liberation.[47] Rather, she believed that no woman would fear pregnancy once the community appreciated "her great service and her great need":

> The true mission of Society is to provide the conditions, legal, moral, economic and obstetric, which will assure happy and successful motherhood.[48]

Once society had been reconstituted on equitable lines and poverty abolished, she felt, women would be free to fulfill their biological role and breed a healthy race of contented human beings, the hope of the future.

None of Pankhurst's ideas were startling in its originality. Her feminism belonged securely to the radical wing of the women's movement, which looked beyond the campaign for the vote to social reform for the solution to sexual inequality. Her socialism was derived largely from William Morris and Kropotkin, idealistic in essence and only temporarily influenced by Bolshevism. Far from being an innovator, she was part of a school of English socialism that drew as much on memories and myths of an age gone by as on theoretical models of the future. One can discern in her philosophy a romantic yearning for the rural idyll, peaceful and unchanging.

But a tendency to idealize the past was more than matched by a desire to change the present. To this end she committed her whole adult life. As a young woman she sacrificed a promising career as an artist to work for the suffragette movement and later gave up material comfort for the sake of her East London work. She committed seven years of hard labor to the *Workers' Dreadnought* and another twenty to Ethiopia. She was sustained throughout by a faith in the ability of the human race to transform its environment. In this lay her strength. She never doubted for one moment that "a new type of human being will gradually be evolved: one that will be nobler and more balanced in sentiment . . . than any amongst us today."[49]

NOTES

1. The party's leader, Keir Hardie, became a good friend of the family. Years later, during the suffragette campaign, he and Sylvia developed a very close relationship, which lasted until Hardie's death in 1915. In her obituary she called him "the greatest human being of our time" and honored his memory for the rest of her life. See *The Woman's Dreadnought* [hereafter cited as *Dreadnought*], October 2, 1915, pp. 329-31. See also Kenneth O. Morgan, *Keir Hardie: Radical and Socialist* (London: Weidenfeld and Nicholson, 1975), pp. 164-66, 270-71.

2. E. Sylvia Pankhurst, *The Suffragette Movement: An Intimate Account of Persons and Ideals* (London: Longmans & Green, 1931), p. 104. Biographical information relating to Pankhurst's childhood and youth comes mainly from this source.

3. For an account of the WSPU's history see Andrew Rosen, *Rise Up Women! The Militant Campaign of the Women's Social and Political Union 1903-1914* (London: Routledge and Kegan Paul, 1974).

4. The East London Federation of the WSPU was renamed the East London Federation of Suffragettes (ELFS) after WSPU support was withdrawn. The title of *The Woman's Dreadnought*, with its warlike connotation, was apparently not Pankhurst's choice; see Pankhurst, *Suffragette Movement*, p. 525.

5. It did establish nine branches outside London by 1915 but failed to expand into a truly national organization.

6. Initially her pacifism was out of tune with sentiment in the East End, which responded with a burst of patriotism to the call to arms. "Ruthless economic pressure," however, soon dissipated the euphoria. E. Sylvia Pankhurst, *The Home Front: A Mirror to Life in England during the World War* (London: Hutchinson, 1932), pp. 16-18. Her attitude toward the war completed the rift between herself and her mother and sister. Ibid., p. 67.

7. The number of women in industry rose from 2,178,600 in July, 1913, to 2,970,600 in July, 1918. By July, 1924, it had dropped to 1,987,990; see Pankhurst, *Home Front*, p. 160.

8. The toy factory later closed due to mismanagement.

9. *Dreadnought*, December 18, 1915, pp. 384, 388.

10. Ibid., November 17, 1917, p. 886.

11. The following year it formally established itself as the Communist Party (British Section of the Third International). Ibid., June 26, 1920, p. 1.

12. While in prison, she composed a short account of her visit to Russia, full of admiration for what she had seen there. E. Sylvia Pankhurst, *Soviet Russia As I Saw It in 1920* (London: Dreadnought Publishers, 1921).

13. Among other translations from European communist dissidents, the *Dreadnought* published Alexandra Kollontai's *The Workers' Opposition* in the only translation to appear in England even to the present day.

14. E. Sylvia Pankhurst, *The Suffragette: The History of the Women's Militant Suffrage Movement 1905-1910* (London: Gay and Hancock, 1911).

15. E. Sylvia Pankhurst, *India and the Earthly Paradise* (Bombay: Sunshine Publishing House, 1926); idem, *Delphos or the Future of International Language* (London: Kegan Paul and Co., 1927). A regular feature in the *Dreadnought* from 1921 had been the weekly Esperanto lessons, with the Communist Manifesto as the primary text. By 1927, when *Delphos* was published, she had rejected Esperanto in favor of the rival Interlingua.

16. One of these was written in collaboration with Pankhurst's son, who had become an authority on the area. E. Sylvia Pankhurst and Richard Kier Pankhurst, *Ethiopia and Eritrea: The Last Phase of the Reunion Struggle 1941-1952* (Woodford Green, England: Lalibela House, 1955).

17. Pankhurst, *Suffragette Movement*, p. 67.

18. Ibid., pp. 125-26.

19. *Dreadnought*, August 14, 1915, p. 298.

20. Ibid., June 15, 1918, p. 1020.

21. Ibid., February 16, 1918, p. 948.

22. Ibid., November 26, 1921, p. 1.

23. Pankhurst, *India and the Earthly Paradise*, "Preface"; *Dreadnought*, January 6, 1923, p. 5.

24. *Dreadnought*, December 7, 1918, p. 1143.

25. Ibid., May 10, 1919, p. 1321.

26. Ibid., February 21, 1920, pp. 4-6.

27. Vladimir Ilyich Lenin, *Polnoe Sobranie Sochinenii* [Complete collected works], 55 vols. (Moscow, 1958-1970), 41: 1-104. A condensed version is to be found in *Lenin on Britain* (London: Martin Lawrence, 1934), chap. 7.

28. *Dreadnought*, October 16, 1920, p. 3; October 8, 1921, p. 4.

29. Ibid., January 5, 1924, p. 5.

30. Ibid., July 30, 1921, p. 5.

31. Ibid., September 17, 1921, p. 1.

32. Ibid.

33. Pankhurst, *Suffragette Movement*, p. 316.

34. Pankhurst, *Home Front*, p. 126.

35. Ibid., p. 51.

36. Ibid. Members of ELFS seem to have accepted her position as leader. The federation's minutes record Pankhurst's vain attempts to force her members into becoming more independent of her. See Sheila Rowbotham, *Women, Resistance and Revolution* (London: Penguin Books, 1972), pp. 130-31.

37. Pankhurst, *Home Front*, p. 16.

38. For an interesting discussion of women's employment in the East End in an earlier period, see Sally Alexander, "Women's Work in Nineteenth-Century London: A Study of the Years 1820-1850," in Juliet Mitchell and Ann Oakley, eds., *The Rights and Wrongs of Women* (London: Penguin Books, 1976), pp. 59-111. Compare the low status of women there with the greater equality in the textile mills of Lancashire; see Jill Liddington and Jill Norris, *One Hand Tied Behind Us: The Rise of the Women's Suffrage Movement* (London: Virago, 1978), pp. 47-63.

39. *Dreadnought*, September 12, 1914, p. 102; May 29, 1915; August 14, 1915, p. 299, and elsewhere. In her denunciation of women's war work, Pankhurst glossed over the real increase in wages that such work brought. Although rates rarely equalled men's, union resistance to the invasion of their preserve by women and unskilled men tended to keep wages higher than they might otherwise have been. For a more balanced interpretation of war work, see Arthur Marwick, *Women at War 1914-1918* (London: Fontana, 1977).

40. *Dreadnought*, March 27, 1920, p. 3.

41. Ibid., June 19, 1920, p. 1. A similar idea was proposed in 1919 by two of Pankhurst's male colleagues in the communist movement; see Sheila Rowbotham, *Hidden from History* (London: Pluto Press, 1973), p. 114 fn.

42. Her own household some years later seems to have been more progressive. Corio did most of the cooking, leaving Pankhurst free to write and campaign; see David Mitchell, *The Fighting Pankhursts: A Study in Tenacity* (London: Jonathan Cape, 1967), pp. 246-47.

43. Pankhurst, *India and the Earthly Paradise*, pp. 163-64.

44. For a stimulating essay on the questions of eugenics and its relation to society's view of mothers and maternity, see Anna Davin, "Imperialism and Motherhood," *History Workshop Journal* 5 (1978): 9-65.

45. E. Sylvia Pankhurst, *Save the Mothers: A Plea for Measures to Prevent the Annual Loss of about 3,000 Child-bearing Mothers and 20,000 Infant Lives in England and Wales and a similar Grievous Waste in other Countries* (London: Alfred A. Knopf, 1930), p. 33.

46. Ibid., passim. Before World War I, the Women's Cooperative Guild, an association composed largely of working-class women, had campaigned for maternity benefits and other measures, with some success. In 1915 the guild published *Maternity: Letters from Working Women*, which drew a picture as harrowing as anything Pankhurst wrote of working-class women's experiences of pregnancy and childbirth. Margaret Llewellyn Davies, ed., *Maternity: Letters from Working Women*, rev. ed. (London: Virago, 1978). By the time Pankhurst wrote *Save the Mothers*, maternity services had improved immeasurably in many parts of the country, as a result of postwar legislation.

47. Pankhurst, *Save the Mothers*, p. 107.

48. Ibid., pp. 110, 132.

49. Pankhurst, *India and the Earthly Paradise*, p. 618.

5.

Alexandra Kollontai and the Russian Revolution

RICHARD STITES

A few years ago, during one of my trips to Leningrad, I found myself by chance in front of the house where the child who would become Alexandra Kollontai was born. It is situated in Srednaya Podyacheskaya Street amid a web of crooked lanes and bending canals in the old section of St. Petersburg. I tried to gain entry into the apartments that had housed Kollontai's family, the Domontoviches, but to no avail. A half-dozen families now share those spacious premises. Kollontai's father, Mikhail Domontovich, was a general of Ukrainian origin; her mother was half Finnish. A childhood sojourn in Bulgaria, lately rid of the Turks, and regular summer visits to the Finnish countryside encouraged Alexandra's natural linguistic gift and stimulated the growth of the cosmopolitan outlook that would mark her revolutionary life and subsequent diplomatic career. (It should be noted that polygot tendencies and a love of travel were common characteristics of upper-class Russian women, radical or otherwise.) From her father, little Shura, as she was called, seems to have absorbed the critical sense of justice that marked (and almost ruined) his career; from her mother she acquired the personal rebelliousness that led both mother and daughter to flaunt the conventions of their milieu for the sake of romantic and sexual fulfillment.[1]

During the family's stay in Bulgaria after 1878 young Shura, a child of six, first perceived the outlines of her personality. "There, [in Sofia]," she later wrote, "I began to observe and think; there my character began to take shape."[2] Her father had been assigned to the administration of Bulgaria after its liberation from the Ottoman Empire in the recent war. She once chanced to see a band of Bulgarian "partisans" (perhaps bandits or *haiduks*) being led before a firing squad. Her reaction as she recalled, was to think: "When I and all the other children grow up to be partisans, we will eliminate the cruelties and stupidities of grownups."[3] It was a fitting premonition of her later offensives against "the cruelties and stupidities" of "realists" who did things in the name of maturity and practicality. When her father suffered minor political persecution for siding with a liberal faction in the new Bulgarian parliament, Shura was furiously indignant. She once embarrassed her parents by refusing to pass a cigarette box to a house guest of known conservative views. It would be wrong to exaggerate the significance of such childhood episodes; many upper-class women of Russia who experienced similar feelings failed to develop into revolutionaries. But Shura was certainly a nonconformist and recognized this at a precocious age. "From childhood I brought my mother a good deal of trouble and woe by my determination 'not to live like others'."[4] She fantasized about returning her poodle to human shape, sided with the servants (a very common impulse among gentry children), and dreamed of being a "heroine" who would rescue children, dethrone tyrants, and liberate the common folk from oppression.

In later years, Kollontai would claim that her entire political career was molded by her preoccupation with the "woman question." There is little about it in her recollections of her early years. But the dramatic assassination of the czar in 1881 by a band of terrorists led by a woman, Sofya Perovskaya, seems to have left an imprint of which she was only dimly aware. The nine-year-old girl, whose family had been put in temporary disrepute because of her father, was mystified but unexplainably elated by the exploit. Kollontai's mother was shocked and angered and felt pity only for the mother of the regicide. But Shura, even at that tender age, must have heard of the veritable legion of radical women who, in the 1870s, had worked and fought strenuously alongside their male comrades to pull down the autocracy.[5] Much later, the mature Kollontai would pay an eloquent tribute to the terrorist Perovskaya for her "daring 'man's mind' and ability to subordinate her woman's 'ego' and her loving, passionate heart to the cause of the revolution.''⁶ It was an ability that Kollontai would envy and seek to emulate throughout her career.

The Domontovich household was filled with books, both foreign and Russian, and Shura, who was tutored at home, became an avid reader at an early age. Eventually, her youthful moral yearnings were refitted and defined by her reactions to the works of Buckle, George Sand, Turgenev, Victor Hugo, and the Russian radical publicists and fashioned into a vague feeling of populism *(narod-nichestvo)* by her friends and tutors. As a political doctrine and a program for action, populism—one current of which had led to the terror campaign against the autocracy—was clearly in eclipse in the 1880s, but it served for a long time as a moral magnet for sensitive and "repentant" persons of the privileged classes who looked to "the people"—the peasantry—as the social and spiritual base of Russia's regeneration.⁷

In 1888 the girl Shura became the young lady Alexandra, passing her examination to become a teacher after receiving a fine domestic education at the hands of a progressive-minded teacher, Mariya Strakhova. Romance and education now began to compete for Alexandra's attention. Her first (apparently tender and innocent) crush ended with the suicide of her admirer, for reasons that are still obscure. She wished to study at the Bestuzhev Courses in St. Petersburg, a university-level program for women created in 1878 by the government under pressure from feminists. Her mother, fearing the alleged radical atmosphere there, did not permit it, and she attended private courses. While there, she fell in love with a distant relative, Vladimir Kollontai, the son of a Polish political exile. Her parents quickly shipped her off to Europe where her interest in Russian populism was replaced by a growing attraction to Marxism. Upon her return Alexandra's will to marry prevailed, and she and Vladimir wed in 1893. The marriage lasted five years and produced a child, Mikhail Vladimirovich (Misha). Alexandra's commitment to public activity on behalf of workers and her increasing attachment to Marxist socialism conflicted with her engineer husband's interests and occupation. At Narva, where Vladimir served in a large armament works, she witnessed the appalling scenes of factory life that were a part of Russia's cruel industrial revolution. When her husband came home one evening with two tickets to an operetta, she realized how far they had drifted apart. In 1898 she left him.

Two of Kollontai's biographers, both of whom knew her in a Scandinavian setting, have suggested a link betweeen her desertion and the influence of the Norwegian writers Ibsen *(Doll's House)* and Bjornson *(The Glove)*, whose works were well known to her.[8] Chiefly through the critic Georg Brandes, who was enormously popular in Russia in the 1880s and 1890s, the Russian reading public was indeed taken up by Scandinavian treatment of the "woman question." But this is misleading: Russian women themselves had pioneered in sexual freedom during the 1860s, in a movement—loosely called "nihilism" at the time—whose inner nature was largely unknown in the West.[9] There was no lack of real-life precedent for what Alexandra Kollontai had done; indeed, her mother had left another man for Domontovich a generation earlier. Furthermore, Ibsen's Nora was made to leave home and husband with no clear alternative in mind, whereas Kollontai wanted to be free to pursue education and political interests. Her marriage was interfering with her ego and her desire for development and activity, a problem that was to pursue her throughout the coming years.

She spent the ensuing seven years, up to the dramatic turning point of 1905, partly in Europe and partly in Russia. Kollontai defined her place in the socialist movement by her negative reaction to her professor at Zurich University who was sliding to the right, to the Webbs in England, and to Peter Struve who had just abandoned Marxism; and by her attraction to such pillars of Marxian orthodoxy as Kautsky, Plekhanov, and Rosa Luxemburg. She parted ideological company with her old liberal friends and began spreading illegal socialist propaganda among the workers of the Nevsky District in St. Petersburg, By 1904 Kollontai was drifting rapidly into a life of radicalism, but there was little in her life as yet to indicate that the liberation of women was to be a major preoccupation in the coming years.

Kollontai was never a brilliant Marxist scholar or an innovative theoretician as was her friend Rosa Luxemburg, for example. She "discovered" Marx in a copy of Communist Manifesto which she picked up in a bookstore in Germany during the cooling off period forced on her by her parents. It quickly replaced her populism, which had been shallow and emotional, and seemed to pull her previous ideas together in an intellectually satisfying form—a common experience for many Marxist converts. Before her activity on behalf of women began, she wrote several Marxist tracts; one of them was a solid study of the emergence of capitalism in Finland and its social consequences and another was a brief pamphlet on the politics of class struggle in Russia.[10] Neither these works nor her later "straight" Marxist writings on war, imperialism, and revolution were distinguished by originality or depth. Kollontai was far more at home writing about the personal, the social, the humane dimension of politics; her best works are those that deal with the moral regeneration of women and workers. But her human radicalism and her political militancy were slow in unfolding. At the time of the 1905 revolution, Kollontai, though she later claimed that she "sympathized with the spirit of Bolshevism," was a Menshevik. Her admiration for Plekhanov, her own inclinations, and the slowness of the Bolsheviks to respond to the "woman question" helped to keep her in that camp for the next ten years.

Kollontai's baptism by fire as a revolutionist was Bloody Sunday (January 9, 1905), the day on which the czarist government allowed its troops to shoot down hundreds of peaceful workers who were intent upon serving a petition to Czar Nicholas II. Against the advice of the local Social Democratic Committee, she decided to participate in the march toward the Winter Palace and was therefore a direct witness to the chilling events. This experience converted her into a full-time revolutionary agent: she distributed propaganda, provided liaison with the Finnish Social Democrats whose leaders she had met, composed brochures, raised money in "good" society, and acted as treasurer for the committee. At illegal factory meetings in St. Petersburg, Kollontai made her real debut as a tribune of the people, her musical and impassioned voice and her immaculate grooming enhancing rather than weakening the impression she made upon the raw proletariat of the industrial slums. Kollontai was hardly a pioneer among her sex in this role: Sofya Bardina, Betti Kaminskaya, and Sofya Perovskaya had moved among the factory barracks and plants back in the 1870s with their message of social revolution. But witnesses recall the stunning impression that she made then and again, on a larger scale, in 1917. The spectacle of a cultivated daughter of the landed-military aristocracy preaching violent insurrection to the gray masses would in later years lead critics to call her a traitor to her own class.[11] In fact, had she not turned her energies to the women's struggle, Kollontai might have remained just another female radical agitator, one of hundreds in the ranks and in the leadership of the socialist parties before the revolution.

It is also worth considering whether Kollontai would have taken up the cause of women so early or in such a big way had not the "bourgeois" feminists presented her with a challenge in 1906. Previously Russian feminism, which had emerged about fifty years earlier, had concerned itself mostly with charity, self-help for educated women, antiprostitution work, and the struggle for education. There had even been a woman's movement of sorts, loosely held together by vigorous but moderate public leaders like Naezhda Stasova (whose niece became a well-known Bolshevik), Anna Filosofova, and other members of the upper class. The first organization with national pretentions was founded in 1895 as the Russian Women's Mutual Philanthropic Society, headed by Filosofova and Dr. Anna Shabanova. Though hoping to unify all Russian feminists, the society was emphatically nonpolitical. The events of 1905 electrified educated society as much as they alienated large sectors of the working population. Two new feminist groups emerged almost overnight with a program of woman suffrage in the new Duma and a series of other reforms. These were the Union of Women's Equality (1905-1908) and the Women's Progressive Party (1905-1917). Though differing greatly in spirit and outlook, the society, the union, and the party all hoped to win votes for women in the new Duma recently established by the czar. The union, the most militant of the three, also looked with sympathy on the plight of working women and hoped to enlist them in an "all-women's" struggle in support of both general reform and specific rights for women.[12]

Kollontai responded in an almost visceral way to this effort to "win away" proletarian women from the proletarian cause. But there was little enough in Marxism that could guide her steps.

Marx and Engels, though generally endorsing—as had many pre-Marxist socialists—the complete emancipation of women through work and proletarian revolution, had had very little to say about it. August Bebel, in *Women under Socialism* (1883), helped fill this void by outlining the process by which women were inevitably being drawn into production and thus toward economic independence and by describing the bright lot of women in a socialist future. But his remarks about feminist movements and the proper socialist response to them were limited and ambivalent. Clara Zetkin removed the ambiguity in 1889 by a formula that called for sharp hostility to "bourgeois" (that is, nonsocialist, all-woman) feminism, the recruitment of working females into a "proletarian women's movement"—meaning an army of female workers marching side by side with men toward the overthrow of capitalism—and the establishment of campaigns for such recruitment and for dealing with the problems of working women as women (such as maternity protection).[13] Echoes of these formulations in Russia, including a small brochure, *The Woman Worker* by Lenin's wife, Nadezhda Krupskaya, were few in number and not widely known.[14] There was, moreover, little in the Russian experience to prepare socialist women for a struggle with the newly organized feminists. Kollontai herself seems to have known little of the theoretical literature on the subject until 1906. Therefore, her initial steps were tentative and spontaneous.

Kollontai's first brush with organized feminism (which she and other Marxists insisted on calling bourgeois feminism) was probably the opening conference of the Union for Women's Equality in St. Petersburg in April, 1905. Kollontai was appalled at the determination of these women to capture the hearts of factory women for their struggle, at the spectacle of some socialist women joining the union, and at the indifference of the party to all of this. She spoke out sharply against "classless" feminism, urging working women to join the Social Democratic party and merge their struggle with that of the proletariat. She began her work by making direct contact with a small number of female servants, artisans, and textile workers and reading them original lectures on the "woman question" from the Marxist point of view. In 1906 and in 1907, she attended international conferences of socialist women in Germany.

There her hostility to the feminist movement and her determination
to launch a "proletarian women's movement" were encouraged
and fortified by Zetkin, who was also in the process of posing an
Arbeiterinnen-Bewegung to the *Frauenbewegung** in Germany.
Back home in Russia, Kollontai encountered imposing obstacles to
her ambitions. First, the Russian feminists, though divided and
weakened by reaction, still displayed remarkable vigor and a willingness to return Kollontai's venom in good measure. Second, it
was very difficult to reach and organize working women because of
a shortage of people interested in such work, continuous harass-
ment by the police, and a persistent tension between factory women
and women of the intelligentsia who endeavored to guide their
development. The final—and in the long run most serious—obstacle
was the indifference and even hostility with which most party leaders
(including women) greeted these efforts to carve out a special
women's movement within the socialist struggle.

The peak of Kollontai's activities, and of the movement she
fostered, came in 1908 with the writing of *The Social Bases of the
Woman Question* and her appearance at the All-Russian Women's
Congress. *Social Bases* offered a Marxist interpretation of women's
history in Russia and in the West, a critique of modern family and
sexual culture, and a withering assault upon European feminists
and their Russian counterparts. The last theme clearly dominates
the book, the longest ever written by a Russian socialist on the
subject. At the basis of Kollontai's attack upon organized feminism
is the conviction that upper-class women (or *burzhuiki*, meaning
bourgeois "types," as she consistently and inaccurately calls them)
cannot possibly represent the interests of working women, but she
does not explain how individual exceptions, such as herself, can
sometimes manage to do so. She is also unfair to the feminists by
inappropriately lumping them together with their less socially
minded European counterparts and by singling out episodes and
certain groups to illustrate a general pattern of Russian feminism,
without ever conceding that many of these women were in fact
"social" feminists and not mere conservatives. On the other hand,
her book did illuminate the narrow scope of the movement and did

*Working class Women's Movement vs. Women's Movement.

so at a rather early phase of the suffrage movement. Unfortunately, it did not appear in time to "unmask" feminism at its 1908 Women's Congress.[15] Kolontai herself did appear, however, and she unburdened her views on an all-women's movement upon an angry congress. But the effect was marred by her own party's initial reluctance to send women to the congress, by clashes of opinion within the working women's delegation, and by the fact that Kollontai had to quit the proceedings prematurely because the police were about to arrest her for assorted illegal activities. Both the feminist and the socialist women's movement entered into a decline thereafter. Kollontai fled abroad and remained in Europe for the next ten years.[16]

Love, as most grownup people know, can be as much a debilitating distraction as a fulfilling and ennobling experience. Kollontai first felt the full meaning of being "emptied out" by romance during the bleak decade of exile in Europe (1908-1917). Caught in a mood of despair by the renewal of reaction in Russia, by loneliness for her friends, and by the malaise she felt among her European socialist comrades, Kollontai was perhaps at this moment exceptionally vulernable. The object of her affair was P. P. Maslov, a scholarly, middle-aged (and married) economic theoretician of the Menshevik movement. As she later acknowledged, it was a mismatch. Maslov, weak, selfish, and traditional like many antiheroes in Kollontai's later fiction, wanted mostly sex and extramarital adventure. Kollontai wanted respect for, and attention to, her intellectual and political activities. After a series of passionate rendezvous in European hotels and bitter partings at railroad stations, Kollontai ended the affair and returned to full-time political propaganda for the party. Maslov returned to his wife and children. Her perception of Maslov's weakness may have helped frame her eventual image of Menshevism as indecisive. In any case, the affair of 1910-1911 further darkened the unhappy years of exile and led her to take a fresh theoretical look at the all-consuming "great love" that could—as she saw it—so malevolently deflect the energies of a person (especially a woman) from the main concerns of life: work, study, or revolution.[17]

The fruit of these and earlier ruminations about sexual relations was a series of articles that Kollontai wrote shortly before World War I and that were published in the émigré press. The immediate occasion was her reading of *Die sexuelle Krise* by Grete Meisel-Hess, a Marxist with an interest in psychoanalysis. Indissoluble marriage, according to Meisel-Hess and Kollontai, failed to allow for incompatibility and poor mating and often ended with the rapid erosion of tenderness and concern. Prostitution was even worse, for, in Kollontai's words it "suffocates love in human hearts; from it Eros flies in fear of soiling its golden wings." But the third alternative, the so-called free union, was also inadequate because it usually took the form of "great love"—a painful, all-consuming, and tragic mistress-lover relationship that drained the energy of both partners and flattened the ego of the woman. The modern woman who eschewed these three modes of erotic life, said Kollontai (borrowing her terminology from Meisel-Hess), could realize her "love potential" by means of "love play," an erotic friendship requiring attentiveness, awareness, and sensitivity to one's partner without incarcerating or annihilating his or her inner soul. Addressing herself to "the new woman," the single independent female whose numbers were being swiftly augmented by industrialization, Kollontai admonished her to display "self-discipline instead of emotionalism, recognition of the value of freedom and independence instead of submission and a faceless personality, assertion of individuality instead of the naive attempt to absorb and reflect the alien nature of the 'beloved'." She must become, in short, not "the shadow of a man" but "a Woman Human Being."[18]

Kollontai believed and reiterated many times that the ultimate liberation of the personality—male and female—would have to await the dawn of a socialist order. But unlike most Marxists, she felt compelled to fill in the scenario for that indeterminable period during which living people would have to wait for the new day to break. Her Marxism, her firm belief that capitalism by its very workings negated the possibility of women becoming genuinely free and fulfilled, always lay at the base of her comments on the "woman question." But—and here she was unwittingly allied to the feminist enemy—she also believed that problems of man-woman relations had to be faced (if not solved) here and now; the battle for personality had to be fought simultaneously with the larger campaign to drag down the fortresses of capital. Dissatisfied with the flat and often arid proclamations of absolute equality of the sexes issued both by the Marxists and by the indigenous Russian radicals who drew their inspiration from the 1860s, Kollontai felt compelled to raise questions about sexual intimacy, about the relationship between love and work and between love and eroticism that were of little concern to most other Marxists, particularly male ones. She was not wholly alone in this search for clarity and definition. At about the same time that Kollontai finished her articles on sex, Inessa Armand, her future colleague and uneasy comrade under the Bolshevik regime, was posing similar questions to Lenin in a well-known spurt of letters. Lenin's replies (we do not have Armand's actual questions) left no doubt that she was concerned about the deeper levels of sexual culture both in the capitalist present and in the socialist future and no doubt also that Lenin considered—as he would affirm emphatically a few years later to Clara Zetkin—such questions to be unessential, unanswerable, and posed in the wrong spirit.[19]

When the world war erupted in 1914, Kollontai, like her female comrades in the international socialist movement—Krupskaya, Zetkin, Armand, and Balabanoff—was sickened by its horror and by the nationalistic behavior of her former colleagues, about whom she had just published a very critical book, *Around Workers' Europe*.[20] Although she did not attend a Bolshevik-sponsored International Women's Socialist Conference at Bern in 1915 (the first step in the Zimmerwald Movement), Kollontai nonetheless threw herself vigorously into the antiwar movement. Caught in Berlin at the outbreak of the war, she made her way to Sweden, where she was arrested for socialist antiwar agitation and banished "eternally" from the land to which she would return fifteen years later as Soviet diplomatic representative. Facing hostility in Denmark as well, she found refuge in Norway. In contrast to Russian feminists at home, Kollontai lashed out at the war, and her radicalism deepened. This and the disillusionment with Menshevism and European Social Democracy led her into Lenin's camp. In 1915 she became a Bolshevik, acting as one of Lenin's chief contact people in neutral Scandinavia—a crucial base for Zimmerwaldist and Bolshevik agitation. She also fell in love with another energetic agent of Lenin, Alexander Shlyapnikov. This love affair with a man of working-class background does not appear to have diminished her capacity for work. Twice she visited the United States and toured more than eighty cities from coast to coast, delivering her antiwar message in Russian, German, French, and English to hundreds of American workers and socialist politicians. She also wrote one of the most effective antiwar pamphlets of the period, *Who Needs War* (1916).[21] Early in 1917, she heard about the overthrow of the czar in Petrograd and hastened to end her exile and return to witness the unfolding revolution.

The year 1917 found socialist women again locked in a struggle against organized Russian feminism. The first day of the revolution, February 23 (March 8 by the Western calendar), was also International Women's Day, a socialist holiday established by Zetkin back in 1910 and observed periodically and semilegally in Russia since 1913. Armand, Krupskaya, and other Bolshevik women had been among its organizers in the prewar years and had also started a journal for working women, *Rabotnitsa*. After the fall of the monarchy, Bolshevik women began to rebuild a proletarian women's movement by enlisting the energies of factory women and other poorer elements of Petrograd and by opposing the feminists' programs. The feminists, divided more by labels than by issues, were in the full flush of unity and determined to extract suffrage from the provisional government in return for their resolute support of that government's war effort. This continuation of feminist wartime tactics eventually led them to endorse the so-called Women's Battalions, a female military movement of 1917 that attracted thousands of volunteer recruits for the war. Kollontai, now a Bolshevik, returned via Finland in March and threw herself at once into the antifeminist campaigns. She appeared at a big women's rights demonstration at the Tauride Palace where she bitterly attacked the suffragists' militarist position, and she wrote heated articles pouring scorn on the female battalions. More important, she lent her rhetorical skills to winning over lower-class women such as soldiers' wives and laundresses by supporting their economic grievances in return for their endorsement of Bolshevik political slogans. In spite of lapses and serious disagreements among themselves, Bolshevik women enjoyed visible political success. Many also participated or acted as auxiliaries in the fighting that attended the October Revolution.

Although Kollontai was not the only leader of the Bolshevik women's effort of 1917, she certainly was the best-known Bolshevik woman in the revolution. In the midst of her agitation on women's issues, she carried out important party missions to Finland and Sweden and among the volatile and militant sailors of the Baltic and adorned the rostrum of the Ciniselli Circus and other popular tribunals of the time. She was one of the few to endorse Lenin's first utterances when he returned to Russia in April; she sided with him again at the famous rump meeting of the Central Committee on October 10, 1917, when Lenin urged the seizure of power. She saw the inside of a prison when she was apprehended by the provisional government after the July Days. For John Reed, the Amercan radical and author of *Ten Days that Shook the World*, she seemed to symbolize the euphoric joy among the Bolshevisks at the Second All-Russian Congress of Soviets, which greeted the establishment of Soviet power. And she seemed also to symbolize the new role that women would have in the socialist society when, soon after the October Revolution, she was appointed commissar of public welfare, the first cabinet post occupied by a woman in modern history. Given the conditions of the time and compared with other commissariats, Kollontai's tenure was far from unsuccessful. Though hesitant at first to use force to occupy the premises of her ministry, she was convinced by Lenin's words that revolutions are not made with white gloves, and she ordered some arrests. In facing the Church, however, she moved too quickly, attempting to convert the opulent Alexander Nevsky Monastery into a veteran's hospital overnight. The clergy and pious laity marched against her, called her the Whore of Babylon, and apparently burned down the children's shelter hastily rigged up by the Bolshevik welfare agency. It was the Brest-Litovsk negotiations, which resulted in a humiliating truce with the Germans, and Kollontai's affair with a revolutionary sailor, Paul Dybenko, that brought an end to her brief career as a government minister.

Kollontai's taste for cultivated upper-class men may have been

soured by the officer Vladimir Kollontai and the intelligent Paul
Maslov. Her major work, *Social Bases*, exhibits a profound belief
in the spontaneous political virility and moral nobility of the proletariat, a belief that eventually blossomed into the Workers'
Opposition Movement. Perhaps this was a part of her attraction to
the proletarian figure Shlyapnikow during World War I. There
seems to be no doubt that Dybenko's attraction was precisely his
raw physical presence and his revolutionary energy. They had met
during one of her propaganda sorties to the Baltic. They were
lovers, seeing each other when time permitted, and both became
commissars in the new Soviet state. Kollontai was reluctant to
sanctify the affair by marriage. Perhaps she was embarrassed by
the fact that she was forty-five and he only twenty-eight, but
eventually she was persuaded to marry him. Bolshevik leaders were
not overly happy with this union of commissars: Lenin once remarked that he distrusted "women whose love affair was inter-
twined with politics." Stalin made very crude jokes about the
couple to Trotsky. When Dybenko, an impetuous figure to begin
with, made some lapses of judgment and discipline, he fell afoul
of the authorities and was reprimanded, jailed, and later pardoned
by a party tribunal. Kollontai protested vigorously; she resigned
her post after the signing of the Brest-Litovsk Peace Treaty with
Germany, which Bolsheviks of the Left opposed vehemently. By
March, 1919, the couple was again serving together in the Ukraine.
During the Civil War, their marriage flourished briefly, then became
dessicated and perished. Kollontai had discovered again how difficult it was to combine revolutionary politics with revolutionary
love.

Alexandra Kollontai reached the peak of her political activity,
if not her power, during the Civil War. She served for a while as
commissar for propaganda in the still disputed Ukraine and covered
huge distances on an Agitation Train, bringing, as she saw it,
Bolshevik enlightenment to the benighted peasants and other backward elements of the front-line zones. She also found time to grind
out brochures describing the virtues of the Red side and the reactionary evils of the Whites. But her interest in capturing the allegiance of Russian women never flagged. She attended and arranged working women's conferences in Petrograd and organized

the first major Soviet congress of women in Moscow in 1918. There she, Inessa Armand, and others laid the foundations of the Zhenotdel, the women's section of the Communist party, headed intially by Armand (1919-1920). When Armand died, Kollontai was chosen to succeed her. During her two-year tenure as the administrator of Zhenotdel, Kollontai fed all her abundant energy and optimism into the work of organizing and recruiting masses of women into an active role in the state and economy. Centered in Moscow, Zhenotdel was a network of female Communists and nonparty volunteers which set up training centers, reading cabins, literacy classes, and family counseling centers all over Soviet Russia. Poorly staffed, underfunded (like most early Soviet agencies), and often criticized and hampered by Communist officials, the Zhenotdel nevertheless made startling progress, particularly during Kollontai's tenure, in drawing women into Soviet life, drafting laws to protect women, and acting as an affirmative action group to open opportunities for women in the new society. Kollontai's best-remembered gesture was to bring Muslim and other "eastern" women to Moscow to tear off their veils, symbolically demonstrating their liberation.[22]

Kollontai's political demise, at least on the domestic scene, came in 1922 as a result of her participation in the Workers' Opposition Movement, led by Shlyapnikov and other dissident Communists who resented the party's, the government's and the manager's heavy-handed treatment of the proletariat—the element that had, after all, stormed and razed the bastions of czarism and private property in the revolution. Kollontai, whose physical love affair with Shlyapnikov and platonic love affair with the proletariat predated the revolution, naturally gravitated into its ranks. In a famous pamphlet, *The Workers' Opposition*, she advocated "the collective, creative effort of the workers themselves" as against the bureaucratic, centralistic, and authoritarian style that was becoming the norm in the new regime. Kollontai's sense of spontaneity, syndicalism, and faith in the moral energies of the working class—paralleled in Bogdanov, Machajski, and other leftist thinkers —led her into a passionate and fatal struggle against the party leadership in 1921 and 1922. Her fundamental belief (now widely held by proponents of workers' self-administration) was that collective and interpersonal relations among producers generated greater productivity than did those of hierarchical authority and control.[23] When she said as much at a number of party meetings, she was removed from her Zhenotdel post, stripped of whatever political influence she had left, induced to recant and break with her friends in the opposition, and sent off to Norway on a minor diplomatic mission. In the meantime, she had broken with Dybenko, who was attracted to younger women. The year 1922 was the very nadir of her career and the low point in her emotional life as well.

Throughout these turbulent and painful years, the feminist voice in Kollontai could not be stifled, in spite of her unhappy personal life. Her writings on sex in the postrevolutionary years (1918-1923) were generally more schematic and simpler than the lengthy ruminations of her émigré period. She was writing for uneducated women and men and for many half-educated party comrades. The message and content were essentially the same as before, but the readership was wider and the misunderstanding more profound. Old marriage forms, she announced in 1918, were to be obliterated and replaced by a "comradely union" of two equals whose offspring, if any, were to be raised with the help of the state. This was hardly novel; one can find it among the writings of the intelligentsia as far back as the 1860s. But Kollontai insisted that *de facto* (unregistered) unions should have as much legal and moral force as registered ones. Her 1921 book on prostitution, while assaulting any sort of commercially inspired liaison, allowed for "fleeting physical attraction," implying that the state would be ultimately responsible for all children, born in or out of wedlock. Kollontai was emphatically opposed to any official concept of illegitimacy, to alimony, to interference in sex life, and to any restraints on premarital sex. In her celebrated essays on "The Winged Eros" (1923), however, she muted the militant tone of these pronouncements, vigorously opposed vulgar, physiological and "materialistic" theories of sex, and advanced her own rarefied concept of "winged Eros," a later version of "love game" requiring refined passion and consideration toward the erotic partner, who was defined as a friend and comrade. She also reaffirmed the need for independence in the love relationship and looked forward to a collectivist environment under communism, which would allow all sorts of tender and erotic relations to flourish in a "love collective" of workers.

Motherhood was never a dominant motif in Kollontai's life as she freely admitted. On the other hand, she neither rejected nor ignored it as some writers have maintained. Nor did she ever sponsor a law requiring girls to become mothers automatically on reaching the age of twelve, a charge leveled at her at the time of the revolution. Kollontai, herself a typical Russian revolutionary mother, believed that maternity was not only a natural function for women but also a moral duty for Communist women; they were to care for themselves during pregnancy, nurse and love their own children, and help provide the care and loving attention for all other children in their particular collective—whether of work or residence. She also devoted her largest book and her skills at legislative lobbying to a program of comprehensive maternity protection for working women, one of her major contributions to the Soviet approach to the "woman question." Like other Communist women, she accepted the 1920 law legalizing abortion as a necessary evil that would soon be made obsolete when material conditions had improved. She also insisted that whereas the state had the obligation to care for *all* children, whatever the legal status of their parents, the parents had *no obligation* to avail themselves of this aid if they did not choose to do so. Her final themes was the recurrent plea to abolish individual kitchens and housekeeping and replace them with communal facilities (collective kitchens and the like).

All these motifs are illustrated in two of her major fictional characters of the time: Zhenya of *Love in Three Generations*, who scandalized good, older communists by her flippant irresponsibility and her casual attitude to sex (which Kollontai frowned upon but tried to understand); and Vasilisa of *Vasilisa Malygina*, who asserted her independence, broke with a weak and corrupt husband, decided to have her own child without a husband, and established a commune for women based upon mutual self-help.[24]

Kollontai hoped for the dawn of a "new morality" under communism. She had no illusions that the dawn was imminent; yct she reacted with pained surprise to the coarseness and vulgarity that so quickly enveloped the new revolutionary sexual culture in everyday life. Toughened soldiers, workers fresh from the village, and still-green Komsomols exhibited little comprehension of or interest in

Kollontai's exalted notions of the sex relation. Abuses were inevitable in the atmosphere of disorder and rebuilding. What disturbed so many older revolutionaries, whose morality was drawn from Chernyshevsky and Bebel, was the counterfeit ideology that sprang up to defend the "new" sexual ethos: the notion that "communist" sex meant total freedom of contact plus total lack of liability for its results. Lenin as early as 1920 was appalled at the "glass of water" theory of sex, which allegedly taught that sex was simply a biological function like drinking.[25] Although it is easy to prove that Kollontai was in no way responsible for, and indeed was repelled by, this hedonistic impulse masquerading as a new culture, she was nonetheless blamed by many in the party for ventilating sexual themes too openly, too enthusiastically, and too apocalyptically. A minor press campaign was launched against her "winged Eros" (rarely understood by those who attacked it), and she was cited again and again as the villain who had inaugurated an era of "life without control." Her teachings were flatly discredited without ever being sufficiently examined or analyzed. By the end of the 1920s, long after she had physically left the scene, those in power were beginning to squirm at the results of the family revolution: abandoned wives, myriads of abortions, and armies of homeless children. In the mid 1930s, Stalin, supported in the main by the party, proceeded to reestablish some of the traditional legal, moral, and sexual constraints upon Russian men and to revive some of the traditional values surrounding women, particularly as mothers.[26]

The years 1922 and 1923 mark the end of Kollontai's career as a political and moral force in the Russian Revolution. Her major statements on women had been made, the Workers' Opposition was in ruins, and she herself as a kind of polite punishment was sent off to Norway to assist in trade negotiations. Ironically, this was the beginning of a brilliant new career. Lenin was dead, she made her peace with Stalin, and she managed to survive the murderous purges that swept away all her own comrades of the early years, including two of her former loves, Shlyapnikov and Dybenko, who were both shot by the new dictator during the terror. After her mission to Norway was completed, she served a while in Mexico City in the mid-1920s. Later she was assigned to represent the Soviet Union at the Royal Court of Sweden. Her services there, especially during the Finnish War and World War II, have been recounted elsewhere.[27] She ended her diplomatic career by being named the first female ambassador (to Sweden) in modern times. Covered with honor, she returned home, went into retirement, wrote some memoirs, and died in Moscow in 1952. Her grave is still to be seen among those of other prominent (but second-rank) Communists in the Novodevichi Monastery in the capital.

The central theme in the life of Alexandra Kollontai is the struggle between socialism and feminism, a theme much treated in recent literature. This struggle, it ought to be noted, is not necessarily, as some would insist, between two mutually alien opposites. In Kollontai, it was also a struggle of radical feminism against conventional feminism and a struggle of an anthropological socialism, which aspired to remake human relations as well as resorting political, social, and economic forces, against the political socialism, embodied in revolutionary Bolshevism. Kollontai is perhaps the best example in our century of the dual commitment to feminism and socialism and of dual defeat at the hands of the revolution she helped to make. At the very dawn of socialism in Europe, Flora Tristan neatly illustrated the problem of dedicating oneself to the liberation of both *ouvrier* and *femme*, but she died before the deeper levels of the problem fully manifested themselves.[28] At the beginning of the twentieth century, women like Lili Braun, a German Social Democrat, painfully broke with socialism because they perceived it to be inimical to their view of female liberation. And Russian radical women of the nineteenth century often left behind a feminist-minded youth in order to bury themselves in the deadly revolutionary struggle with the czarist regime.

Kollontai eschewed what she took to be the narrow goals of feminists who sought merely to put women higher up within the system via educational, economic, and political rights, while ignoring both the socioeconomic inequalities of their milieu and the deeper problems of sexual life. By the same token, Kollontai found that even her own chosen brand of socialism—Bolshevism— focused far more on the achievement and preservation of power, the reshaping of class and property relations, and economic development than on the refashioning of the social psyche and the human condition. Kollontai found herself in the vanguard of both movements. As a feminist she fought for all the established feminist goals but added to them the search for a new woman and an erotic culture that would liberate women, humanize men, and envelop both in a novel and noble collective of life and labor; as a socialist she advanced from a vaguely populist moral impulse to Marxism, from Menshevism to Bolshevism, from propagandist to fighter, and finally, on the eve of her fall from prominence, from bureaucrat to iconoclastic syndicalist in the Workers' Opposition Movement. The tragedy of her life was that she stood almost alone in her dual struggle.[29]

NOTES

1. This article is based upon research growing out of my book, *The Women's Liberation Movement in Russia: Feminism, Nihilism, and Bolshevism, 1860-1930* (Princeton, N.J.: Princeton University Press, 1978). The best study of Kollontai in any language is Barbara Clements, *Bolshevik Feminist: The Life of Aleksandra Kollontai* (Bloomington, Ind.: Indiana University Press, 1979). Another fine work is Beatrice Farnsworth, *Alexandra Kollontai: Socialism, Feminism, and the Russian Revolution* (Stanford: Stanford University Press, 1980). Thanks are in order to both these authors for their comments, for allowing me to read their works in manuscript, and to Priscilla Roosevelt for reading this piece. It would be impossible to cite all the biographical literature on Kollontai in this brief sketch; therefore only references to quotations are given along with other useful works. The chief sources for the subject's life are *Den första etappen,* tr. T. Nordstrom-Bonnier (Stockholm: n.p., 1945); "Avtobiografiya," *Entsiklopedicheskii slovar* [Encyclopedic dictionary] (Granat) 41, no. 1: 194-201; "Avtobiograficheskii ocherk," *Proletarskaya revolyutsiya* 3 (1921): 261-302; *Iz moei zhizni i raboty* (Moscow: n.p., 1974); and *The Autobiography of a Sexually Emancipated Communist Woman*, ed. I. Fetscher, trans. S. Attanasio (New York: Herder and Herder, 1971)—all autobiographical.

2. A. M. Itkina, *Revolyutsioner, tribun, diplomat*, 2d ed. (Moscow, 1970). It should be noted that standard Russian bibliographies do not usually list publishers since all publishing is done by the state.

3. C. Halvorsen [G. Johansson], *Revolutionens Ambassadør* (Copenhagen: Gyldendal, 1946), p. 23; Itking, *Revolyutsioner*, p. 11.

4. Kollontai, "Avto. ocherk," p. 261.

5. For the role of women in the terrorist movement, see Stites, *Women's*

Liberation, chap. 5; Vera Broido, *Apostles into Terrorists* (New York: Viking Press, 1977); Barbara Engel and Clifford Rosenthal, eds., *Five Sisters* (New York: Alfred A. Knopf, 1975); and Robert H. McNeal, "Women in the Russian Radical Movement," *Journal of Social History* 2 (Winter 1971-1972): 143-63.

6. Alexandra Kollontai, *Polozhenie zhenshchiny v evolyutsii khozyaistva* (Moscow, 1922), p. 126.

7. For some fascinating insights on family relations among the Russian gentry and intelligentsia, see the essays by Jessica Tovrov and Barbara Engel in David L. Ransel, ed., *The Family in Imperial Russia* (Urbana, Ill.: University of Illinois Press, 1978).

8. Halvorsen, *Ambassadør*, p. 75; Isabella de Palencia, *Alexandra Kollontay* (New York: Longman's, 1947), p. 31.

9. On this phenomenon, see Stites, *Women's Liberation*, chap. 4.

10. *Zhizn finlyandskikh rabochikh* (St. Petersburg, 1903); *K voprosu o Klassovoi borbe* (St. Petersburg, 1905). The fullest bibliography of and on Kollontai is in Clements, *Bolshevik Feminist*, pp. 315-44. Among recent editions of Kollontai's works, the most useful are *Izbranny stati i rechi* (Moscow, 1972); Alix Holt, ed., *Alexandra Kollontai: Selected Writings* (Westport, Conn.: Greenwood Press, 1977). See note 24 for Kollontai's fiction.

11. This theme is treated wittily in an otherwise romanticized Soviet film on Kollontai entitled *Posol Sovetskogo Soyuza* (Ambassador of the Soviet Union).

12. The best work on these groups is Rochelle Ruthchild, "The Russian Feminist Movement, 1859-1917," (Ph.D. diss., University of Rochester, Rochester, N.Y., 1976). For a shorter published treatment, see Stites, *Women's Liberation*, chaps. 3 and 7.

13. For an up-to-date critical discussion, see Alfred G. Meyer, "Marxism and the Women's Movement," in Dorothy Atkinson et al., eds., *Women in Russia* (Stanford, Cal.: Stanford University Press, 1977), pp. 85-112; and Jean Quataert, "Unequal Partners in an Uneasy Alliance: Women and the Working Class in Imperial Germany," in Marilyn Boxer and Jean Quataert, eds., *Socialist Women: European Socialist Feminists in the Nineteenth and Twentieth Centuries* (New York: Elsevier, 1978), pp. 112-45.

14. N. K. Krupskaya, *Zhenshchina-rabotnitsa* (n.p., 1901). It was originally written in 1899.

15. Alexandra Kollontai, *Sotsialnye osnovy zhenskago voprosa* [The social bases of the woman question] (St. Petersburg, 1909). For an introduction and commentary, see Stites, "Note on Kollontai's Social Bases of

the Woman Question (1909)," in idem, *Women's Liberation*, pp. 423-26; for a brief excerpt in English and an intelligent and informed comment by Alix Holt, see her edited work on Kollontai, *Selected Writings*, pp. 29-38, 58-74.

16. A good recent account and analysis of this congress is Linda Edmondson, "Russian Feminists and the Women's Congress of 1908," *Russian History* 3, no. 2 (1976): 123-50.

17. Her novel describing this affair is *Bolshaya lyubov* (Moscow, 1926). For its background, see Stites, "Kollontai, Inessa, and Krupskaya: A Review of Recent Literature," *Candadian-American Slavic Studies* 9, no. 1 (1975): 84-92.

18. These prewar writings are collected in *Novaya moral* (Moscow, 1919). See excerpts in Holt, *Selected Writings*, pp. 237-49.

19. *Bolshevik* 13 (1939): 58-62. Clara Zetkin, *Lenin on the Woman Question* (New York: International Publishers, 1934), one of many editions.

20. Alexandra Kollontai, *Po rabochei Evrope* (St. Petersburg, 1912). See excerpts in Holt, *Selected Writings*, pp. 88-98.

21. *Komu nuzhna voina?* (St. Petersburg, 1917).

22. For two accounts of Zhenotdel, see Carole Eubanks Hayden, "The Zhenotdel and the Bolshevik Party," and Richard Stites, "Zhenotdel: Bolshevism and Russian Women, 1917-1930," both in *Russian History* 3, no. 2 (1976): 150-74, 174-93.

23. Aleksandra Kollontai, *Rabochaya oppozitsiya* (Moscow, 1921); Barbara Evans Clements, "Kollontai's Contribution to the Workers' Opposition," *Russian History* 2, no. 2 (1975): 191-206.

24. For recent interpretations of Kollontai's sexual program, see Cathy Porter, "Introduction," and the stories in Alexandra Kollontai, *Love of Worker Bees* (London: Virago, 1977); Alix Holt, "Morality and the New Society," and the excerpts in that section in Holt, *Selected Writings*; Clements, *Bolshevik Feminist*, pp. 225-41; and Stites, *Women's Liberation*, pp. 346-58. Soviet writers have, unfortunately, offered almost nothing by way of commentary on Kollontai's ideas on love and sex. On her fiction, however, see Ragnfrid Stokke, "Aleksandra Kollontaj—kommunist, kvinnefork-jemper og forfatter," in M. B. Nielsen and G. Kjetsaa, eds., *Kvinnen i russisk litteratur* (Oslo, 1979), pp. 103-18.

25. Zetkin, *Lenin*.

26. Beatrice Farnsworth, "Bolshevism, the Woman Question, and Alexandra Kollontai," *American Historical Review* 81, no. 2 (1976): 292-316. See also Rudolf Schlesinger, ed., *The Family*, vol. 1, in *Changing Attitudes in Soviet Russia: Documents and Readings*, 2 vols. (London:

Routledge & Paul, 1949); and H. Kent Geiger, *The Family in Soviet Russia* (Cambridge, Mass.: Harvard University Press, 1968).

27. Clements, *Bolshevik Feminism*, pp. 242-72.

28. See S. Joan Moon, "Feminism and Socialism: The Utopian Synthesis of Flora Tristan," in Boxer and Quataert, *Socialist Women*, pp. 19-50.

29. My reading of Kollontai's life and its meaning is closer to that given in the Clements and Farnsworth books than that given by Simon Karlinsky in his review article, "The Menshevik, Bolshevik, Stalinist Feminist," *New York Times Book Review* (January 4, 1981): 3.

6.
Feminism:
The Essential Ingredient
in Federica Montseny's
Anarchist Theory

SHIRLEY FREDRICKS

The most interesting women in modern European history appear in the ranks of radical political movements. It is difficult to find conservative or traditional counterparts equal to Louise Michel, Emma Goldman, and Rosa Luxemburg. Even Isadora Duncan, creator of modern dance, flirted with communism. More thoughtful and articulate and certainly as politically active as any of these women is the lesser known Spanish anarchist, Federica Montseny. On asking what attracted these women to radical politics, one discovers in each a commitment to feminism. No person, not even Emma Goldman, explored this necessary relationship between feminist and socialist principles more provocatively than did Federica Montseny. Therefore, an understanding of Montseny's thought and actions provides a persuasive explanation of this connection.

Born to anarchist parents in 1905, Federica Montseny was nurtured according to their anarchist principles. Her own career, begun at age eighteen, deeply affected the life of the Spanish working class; she became a highly vocal, widely read anarchist theoretician during the 1920s and 1930s. She showed an acute awareness of events outside of Spain. Often she wrote of the Bolshevik betrayal of the Russian Revolution, the unjust treatment of Sacco and Venzetti, and the rise of reactionary governments throughout the world. Furthermore, she knew the ideas and work of leading artistic figures such as Herman Hesse, Isadora Duncan, Eleanor Duse, and Romain Rolland. She criticized major Spanish institutions and customs, including those of government, religion, education, marriage, and most adamantly, the status of women.

Montseny presented these ideas to the working class in a variety of ways. Her family published the journal *La Revista Blanca* and the newspaper *El Luchador*; Montseny regularly contributed to both. Her theories provided the foundation for speeches of unrelenting social criticism delivered at workers' rallies, speeches that called attention to the extreme injustice permeating society. Montseny influenced the National Confederation of Labor (*Confederación Nacional de Trabajo*, or CNT) through her leadership in the Iberian Anarchist Federation (*Federación Anarquista Ibérica*, or FAI). Throughout the 1920s, she traveled extensively in Spain with other leading anarchists. They discussed with the people the social ills of the country, insisting that only through organizations such as the FAI could the people improve their socioeconomic status.

In addition to her political activity, Montseny wrote many novels that describe the relationship between the sexes, positing the ideal against the real. These popular polemics attempted to educate the nation's women. Montseny believed that once women became aware of their plight, they would demand change. In her own life, she lived as did the heroines in her novels, trying to set an example for her sex.

In the summer of 1936, the Spanish Civil War convinced Montseny that the long-awaited, long-sought, often planned social revolution had arrived. She actively aided the Republican cause, serving as minister of health and public assistance in the Largo Caballero government. By assuming this position, Montseny became the first and only woman ever to hold portfolio in the Spanish national government. From this office, she did much to promote the education, technical training, and employment of women by working closely with such organizations as *Las Mujeres Libres*.

Because of complex political machinations, both at home and abroad, the social revolution in Spain was lost. In the freezing cold of mid-winter 1939, Federica Montseny fled with her parents and children into France just ahead of General Francisco Franco's troops. She remained there in exile for thirty-eight years, returning to her homeland in April, 1977. Her whole life has been committed to securing an anarchist revolution for the Spanish people.

For many years Montseny argued that before the anarchists could establish a truly libertarian society, there had to be a revolution in the relationship between the sexes.[1] For this reason, her commitment to female emancipation continuously outweighed all other aspects of her anarchist concern. She knew from experience that socialism, of whatever variety, had not produced equality for women. She knew, too, that most women, consciously or unconsciously wishing self-identity, liberty, freedom, self-expression, and respect equal to their talents, had joined socialist movements because in their minds the principles these movements embodied seemed to hold out the best opportunity for the equality that they so desperately wanted. They all soon discovered that the male leadership was as ingrained in traditional attitudes about women as were more conservative thinkers.

Montseny began with this awareness, so she argued in the reverse. If women would demand an emancipation that was in keeping with their human potentials, they would cause a social revolution, not far out of line with the tenets of anarchist philosophy. Male anarchists, not being able to shake their traditional attitudes about women, could not, in truth, produce the social revolution they wanted because they could not first secure equality for women.[2] Montseny accepted the fact that this elusive emancipation would develop slowly and that it would have to begin first "in the souls of women."[3] For her, the equality was not only desirable, but was absolutely essential for the revolution that the anarchists sought.

In an attempt to promote this revolution in thinking about the nature of women, Montseny analyzed every facet of the topic. She examined the deplorable status of women in contemporary society. She insisted that they had to be educated. She carefully described the characteristics of a liberated woman and her relationship with men. She outlined how a society containing liberated women would be ordered.

Montseny believed that the root of the problems of women lay in centuries of economic, physical, and psychological exploitation. Time-honored tradition led to the unquestioned assumption of the innate inferiority of women. Because of this supposed inferiority, it was accepted that women need not, indeed could not, be educated.

Hence, the vast majority of them lived in ignorance and vague, unfocused discontent. As Montseny bitterly described them, they were

> semi-literate, bred for the hearth, to serve the priests, to be sacred ones for God, . . . closed to all innovation with no greater horizon than marriage and the procreation of children. . . . And this, being a slave; and this, maintained in the ignorance of a beast of the field or as an incubation machine for sons. And, as is natural, slaves created slaves, a brutalized person created a brutalized person.[4]

Ironically, she continued, men insisted that these ignorant, inferior, brutalized women were responsible for rearing the children as though that task required only a natural instinct and no education, self-identity, or self-worth. In truth, the child was left with

> an ignorant woman, obtuse, closed to progress; a woman who will . . . transmit to the children all of her prejudices and superstitions: . . . a woman for which there exists no great causes, that will not feel ardor and enthusiasm for ideals; . . . a woman will be, nevertheless, the one who will mold the sons of men.[5]

And men were, of course, only concerned with the production and care of sons.

Anarchist men dreamed dreams and formulated systems for a better society but overlooked the most crucial element of the success of those dreams—emancipated women, capable of being intelligent companions and wise mothers. There could be no hope for social or human progress as long as men continued to entrust the education of each generation to such incompetency and inferiority.[6] Any man who thought otherwise did indeed dream dreams.

Montseny rightly accepted that the existing state of women was one of ignorance, timidity, neurosis, and exploitation.[7] She insisted, however, that it was in no way a natural condition—quite the contrary.

In spite of brutalization and ignorance, women remained "hungry for justice, yearning for majority."[8] Although "semi-literate," women possessed a "muted but profound comprehension" of true human dignity and social justice.[9] Montseny hinted that this almost innate understanding of social justice accounted for the severity of male repression of women. It suggests too, that in women lies the best hope for the ultimate success of the humanistic principles embodied in anarchism, as women naturally carried those principles suppressed within themselves.

As pessimistic as this description of Spanish women is, Montseny remained characteristically optimistic. Once women made up their minds to rectify this dismal situation, Montseny was certain that nothing would stand in their way. Let men of conservative mind take heed.

Sick of suppression, women would instruct the children from their "tenderest infancy to love, to liberty, to progress, and to anarchy; and to despise slavery, authority and tyranny," because they knew that tyranny intimately. By conviction, women would open a "wide breach" in the "bulwark of tyranny" and undermine the entire social structure by "hitting at the first stones of that bulwark, the children."[10] In this statement Montseny implicitly expresses the inextricable relationship between anarchism and her particular interpretation of feminism.

The women leading this assault would be what Montseny described as "future-women" because the desire for reform and the effort to effect it were "implanted only in the restlessness of the non-conforming, . . . those who live poetically, impulsively, beyond any morality, creating marvelous lives of diverse and multiple feelings, sensibilities, and intellect, of intensity and completeness, of insatiable thirst and infinite hungers."[11] Montseny saw herself as a future-woman whose mission was to convince other women that they, too, should have a position in life equal to their talent and of their own making, a life of consciously created richness.

In search of a method for implementing the changes this mission demanded, Montseny considered various alternatives. The ones she scrutinized most closely were political, anarchical, and feminist approaches to the problem.

In the minds of most Spanish women who thought about the issue, political power seemed the logical way to secure equality. To gain political power required gaining the right to vote. Montseny disliked this thinking for two reasons. Observation told her that until women were educated, they simply were not capable of independent judgment about anything, let alone political issues. Secondly, given her conservative propensties, even an educated women would probably vote as priests or demagogic politicians dictated, which certainly would not be to vote for her own emancipation.[12] Clearly, there is more to it than this.

Montseny's objection to this method arose from her anarchist commitments. Her complaint about women in politics really did not lie in their ability to participate in government knowledgeably or to vote intelligently, but rather in Montseny's disapproval of government per se. She thought that it was absurd to think that women would rule better or more humanely than men even though this was an often stated feminist justification for political involvement. "Neither cruelty nor sweetness," she said, was the special possession of either sex. "The woman is equal to the man in intelligence and good will. It is authority and domination that produce the evils in men in government and it will do the same to women. The answer to a better society is not female rulers, but a new society," a libertarian society.[13] Montseny insisted that when "women legislate and administrate, they too will continue injustices, privileges, miseries, and wars" because women in power will be corrupted by that power, becoming as unable as men to change the nature of society.[14] Montseny also feared that political involvement through the extension of suffrage would lead women to an illusion of emancipation, when indeed such power would only perpetuate their social exploitation through the guise of participation. Instead, Montseny insisted that true freedom for women was more likely to be earned through outstanding participation in areas like literature and the arts, where women triumphed clearly and undeniably through the sheer strength of their own individual talent. This would be a "feminine triumph, a thousand times more honorable than triumph in elections."[15]

If Montseny criticized the political road to female liberation, she was not blind to weaknesses in anarchism as well. Her mother had taught her that of all political theories, anarchism offered the best hope for gaining feminine equality, although just how that equality would be achieved was not clear.[16] She implied that anarchists in power would automatically put equality of the sexes into practice: so the theory would suggest. By 1924, when Montseny issued her first major statement about the status of women in Spanish society, she recognized that optimism such as her mother's would not free women.

Montseny considered the failure of the anarchist leadership in this area to be the most disgraceful part of the movement. Theoretically, they had dealt with the problem with "prodigious rapidity, although in practice it represented the point *mas negro*, and the most arduous task of the social question; today [the status of women] is, as Goldman says, a true tragedy."[17] Nor did Montseny think the anarchist revolution would take care of this discrepancy between their theory and practice. And wisely she warned that if the anarchist revolution was to succeed, there would have to be a basic change in men's hearts and minds, a fundamental resolution of the problem between the sexes. Without this there simply would be no libertarian society.[18]

Fearing that the emancipation could not be effected either politically or anarchically, one might suppose that Montseny would have become an outspoken supporter of a strong feminist movement like those in Anglo-Saxon countries and more timidly in the Mediterranean area. This was not the case. Here, too, she found weaknesses of analysis and implementation which defeated the feminists' best intentions.

The decade of the 1920s saw a flurry of activity aimed at women's liberation. These efforts ranged from the "very conservative attempts" exemplified by the International Feminist Congress held in Rome in 1923, to the radical women's movement in Turkey.[19] Montseny thought that on the whole, feminists sought only the privileges and rights held by men with no thought for the future of human society, always her prime concern. They had neither "social transcendency" nor "revolutionary valor." She did think, however, that the movement among the Anglo-Saxons was much "more advanced, more aggressive, and more socially conscious" that its Latin counterpart, which she characterized as "timid and reactionary."[20] Interesting, too, is her evaluation of feminism in Spain: "In reality, no feminism of any kind exists in Spain," and if it did, it would no doubt be "fascist."[21]

As far as Montseny was concerned, none of these feminists

solved the "feminine problem" because they did not solve "the human problem common to both sexes."[22] She condemned them for their too narrow answers. Unfortunately, most women thought only in political and economic terms, never seeking liberation through an understanding of their own internal integrity or through an awareness of their own uniqueness and strength.

Instead, they measured the degree of their liberty by the extent of freedom that they had in acting, speaking, doing, and appearing as men did. Montseny abhorred this notion that freedom and equality had to be measured by standards set by men, for men. Indeed, Montseny thought that nothing was "sillier" than the "scatter-brained" women of the United States who correlated their emancipation with the length of their hair: the shorter the hair, the more liberated they were.[23] Montseny wrote that no women gained equality by cutting her hair, donning pants, painting her face, or smoking.[24] In her evaluation, in no nation was this practice more common than in the United States, where equality was increasingly becoming synonymous with "interchangeability."[25] Interchangeability was not the answer to equality. On the contrary, it produced only uniformity. This was as narrow as thinking that suffrage brought emancipation.

Women also promoted a social tyranny over themselves by conforming to the authority of the current style, or better said, the current fads. For example, Montseny wrote a witty comment that women thought it was especially chic and appealing for men to possess the "fragile, delicate silhouette of Marlene Dietrich or Greta Garbo," even if to do so meant to impair one's health.[26] She scoffed that she would never sacrifice her physical health in an effort to comform to the dictates of the *"mujer-fatal del cine."*[27] Nor did she fear that her noncomformity would leave her unloved. She insisted that the man she wanted and who would want her would be one who would honor the natural expression not only of her mind and spirit which was of course the most important, but also of her physical self. So, if her natural propensity was to rotundity, as indeed it was, then rotund she would be![28] The obvious contradiction between the practice of interchangeability and conformity to a socially imposed image of feminity is a perfect example of the pressure that produced feminine neurosis and perhaps of the ignorance that Montseny felt characterized most modern women.

Above all, Montseny demanded equality and independence for both sexes, but she never thought that equality meant interchangeability or conformity. At all times, a woman must be a woman, as that was her special and humanizing gift to society. In that way alone could a woman hope to find her true and natural quality and contribute that to the enrichment of society. External sameness with men, she feared, seduced women into thinking that they had acquired equality, and as a result, they tended to neglect the more real and permanent development of their own potential. As Montseny said, "to masculinize herself will not gain elevation, liberty, or dignity."[29] Women must have a self-concept higher than the "aspiration and emulation of the other sex. . . . We ought not content ourselves *with all the rights which men have*. We ought to aspire, with an indomitable will, to all the rights he should have."[30] Women should aspire to "absolute liberty, to absolute equality, to absolute right," but in the process she must always aspire to them "as a woman and a human being."[31] The only answer she could accept was

> absolute equality in all aspects for both sexes; independence for the two; . . . an expanded and universally free way for all the species. . . . To propagate feminism is to foment masculinism; is to create an immoral and absurd struggle between the two sexes which no natural law would tolerate. . . . Feminism? Never! Humanism? Always![32]

This total commitment, her anarchist assurance of a better future for all humanity, lay at the heart of her feminism. She called her idea a "rational feminism, humanistic and conscious feminism, serene and balanced feminism, which ought to call itself humanism."[33] This feminism would not separate the sexes, or make men of women. It instead would produce "the most beneficial results for both sexes." It was an emancipation that would allow "unlimited freedom and independence to both sexes."[34] In this liberty, both sexes would be bound together in an essential sense—"through a communication of soul and through mutual respect,"[35]

If Montseny defined the warped and unnatural character of women as women-men and women-feminine, she also clarified the true nature of woman and her role in society. Two characteristics were always a part of this definition of a "woman-woman"—

strength of character and a soul in tune with nature. On one occasion, Montseny synthesized these two aspects by likening a
woman to the Valencian countryside, a countryside with its "soul
flowing in natural richness, in fertile pastures, in its women who
are as fertile as its countryside—women who do not give birth to
children for slavery or war."[36]

Of course, a basic anarchist criticism was precisely that human
society had lost its naturalness and with that loss came the subjugation of women. Yet, for all of her debasement in modern
society, according to Montseny, the woman seemed not to have
escaped so far from the naturalness of things as men had, perhaps
precisely because she had never been allowed full membership in
that society. It was this naturalness that Montseny thought women
would bring back to human affairs with their emancipation. She
insisted that "the women esteem more, a beautiful man, a beautiful
life, a beautiful death, than they do a beautiful automobile."[37]
In women resides "an epic and legendary element, . . . a lyrical and
emotional force necessary in order to convert itself into an invincible
movement of opinion atmosphere, and consciousness."[38] In this
female force lay Montseny's hope for a restoration of naturalness
in human society that would automatically raise women to equality
with men. This kind of idea made Montseny insist that the women's
movement had to be something more than a way to improve the
status of women within the existing society. She felt that women
carried in them a potential to create a better society if they had the
freedom to do so. Montseny defined this free woman as

> a woman-woman, not a woman-man, nor a woman-female . . . a
> woman-woman, not a creature without personality or sex. A woman
> proud and sure of herself, with a clear idea of her destiny and the
> future of the human race; . . . a woman who knows how to represent
> her sex and the species, who possesses a strong appropriate in-
> dividuality, of great moral force . . . of secure and tranquil self-
> concept, of self-confidence, of serenity and dignity.[39]

This definition met with much criticism for being entirely too
idealistic to be achieved unless in some distant future. In a rebuttal
characteristic of Montseny, she said that she surely had written
with "an eye to the future, outside the present." She recognized

that such a woman was a part of a "super-realistic world, a world superior to the contemporary realities," but nevertheless a world certainly possible of creation and attainment through a truly feminine revolution.[40] Flying in the face of her critics, it was according to the standards of this super-real world that Federica Montseny attempted to live. And there she hoped for companionship. But in a beautifully strong comment, she courageously stated: "If no one acompanies me, I will live in it alone, amplified and unlimited."[41]

So Montseny wished for an emancipated humanity, a humanity freed from oppressive, exploitative social organization. That was her goal as an anarchist and a feminist. She thought that all the feminist movements were demanding participation in the *status quo*, which only "liberated" women into a different bondage. However, if women would demand that their own strengths and uniquenesses be valued on a par with those of men, this would help precipitate a social revolution that would lead to the emancipation of all people, not just women. Since she held the anarchist principle that we are only as free as the least free member of our society, even the men that women thought were so free were not if women were not, and women were not if they simply assumed male values and institutions, which obviously had not produced human freedom. Emancipation meant that women would be truly valued for their human strengths. To achieve that goal meant a radically altered society. Truly free women would demand only truly free men and produce a truly free society.

Needless to say, a society peopled by "women-women," or as Montseny sometimes called them "future-women," demanded considerable alteration in the whole character of male-female relationships. The man of her super-real world would have to be of a superiority equal to that which she defined for a woman. He would have to be a man who saw a woman "not as a female, nor an angel, nor a muse, nor even a companion, but simply and surely as a being as free as he, responsible, unique, and the proprietor of her own existence; as an emancipated individual among other individuals," possessing a particular life, ideal, and truth that were appropriate to her and to her alone.[42] She insisted that upon this naturalization of relationships between the sexes depended the future of the species. Humanity was not made up of men and women separately or of women conforming to or imitating men, but of men and women together forging a new society on the anvil of equality.

The absence of this quality of relationship in her day rested in no biological, hence in no natural, difference.[43] Montseny asked why people bound themselves to the present-day concepts that were so unnatural and so highly complex when dealing with questions concerning the relationship between the sexes, when they could as easily follow the ''simple and unified practices of nature.''[44] Reverence for the physical and spiritual beauty of the body and its demands was always an essential part of Montseny's ideas about the naturalness between the sexes. Such reverence represented a natural morality.[45] As Montseny said, there was a morality of nature and the morality that men in their ''preoccupations, ignorance, and prejudices'' tried to impose upon nature. The morality of men could not and should not be allowed when it conflicted with the morality plainly evident in nature. As long as naturalness continued to be thwarted by obscurantism, neither man nor woman would be truly free. Instead, natural morality should be taught because ''those educated to the beautiful and good of the physical body cannot be controlled by false religious morality on this subject.''[46] Clearly Montseny objected to the rigid teachings about sexual relationships that characterized the society in which she lived.

The heart of this humanistic approach, the ingredient necessary for it to work, was love. Montseny remained as critical of what people commonly referred to as love as she was of the general condition of women in society. To describe what she had in mind, one can best begin with what love was not.

Love was not a narcissistic enamoration, which she frequently attributed to men.[47] Nor were women in love ''basically masochistic,'' as many men seemed to think and as women were taught so frequently. They did not ''love to suffer, to be mistreated.'' Their nervous systems were not more delicate than a man's. When making love, women were not ''physically less sensitive than a man, enjoying it in much less intensity.''[48] But ''neither was love that which made of women little more than prostitutes in their sexual activities.''[49] Love was not what allowed men to ''taste of women, abandoning them every two or three months with the triumphant insolence of a seducer."[50]

Nor should a woman allow herself to be seduced by the bait of marriage. Such offers rarely came from conviction, but rather from the male's desire to be free to undertake an affair without reprisal. Marriage, or the promise of marriage, was a method used by men for subordinating the woman's will to their own.[51] Never could love be rooted in the idea of "the conqueror and the conquered."[52] Above all, the "subordination of a woman to a man" did not denote real love or a natural relationship between the two. Montseny insisted that the old standards of love produced "uniformity, vulgarity in love, the death of the amorous illusion and the impossibility of natural selection"; that is, lovers equal to and compatible with each other, two people who could grow together.[53] Here we find Montseny criticizing the custom still in vogue in Spain in the 1920s, that families arranged marriages with little thought to love or compatibility, that engagements were long,that wives were placed on pedestals to be respected, admired, and not enjoyed in a sexual way, that women were surely not to enjoy sex, and that the wife's sole function was to produce heirs for the family. While the husband found his sexual gratification whenever and wherever he wished, the wife was expected to suffer her desires in silence and obedience to the will of her husband and the customs of society.

Real love in Montseny's mind most assuredly was not this. Real love was natural; this was not. "In reality, love is above all an ethic," she wrote. "In love, as in art, no moral exists or can ever exist. Love is instinctive and pure intuition, the expression of the highest wisdom and only absolute before infinite relativity. After life, love is the only categorical imperative."[54] Love is complete spontaneity, "delicious and eternal rashness."[55] Each individual's expression of love has a uniqueness and truth. Each individual searches for and waits for his/her equal.[56]

The basic principle in Montseny's definition of love was her insistence that love had to be between equals. While it could take many expressions, love was at base the same—two individuals equal to each other, bound together in spiritual communion, mutual respect, uniqueness, and independence. To love was to be free, to be in balance between reason and passion. Love was "amorous camaraderie."[57] But before such love could really occur, several conditions had to be satisfied.

One had to love oneself. This was the "basis of life, the most precious of loves."[58] It allowed an individual to form "profound communion" with another person, while at the same time preserving intact one's own uniqueness.[59] More difficult to secure, a woman had to become conscious of her undeniable rights and to insist upon them:

> The right of the free expression of her existence. The right to live her life and to be that which she wished and not that which the man wanted. . . . The right and the duty of looking in the face of life, liberty, health, and happiness, of conquering and suppressing all prejudices, all false moralities, and all unjust and inhuman laws.[60]

The conventional social institution for formalizing love was, of course, marriage. However, for Montseny, nothing could kill the beauty of love more quickly than marriage. "It has been said and repeated that the major adversary of love is matrimony. Matrimony is the tomb of love. Never was anything more truly said, not only because of [marriage's] unsupportable coersion, but because there is no love that survives permanent living together."[61] So Montseny lived with her *compañero*, Germinal Esgleas, with each allowing the other the independence necessary for their separate interests and careers.

Montseny was particularly emphatic on this point, as were most anarchists, because marriage was an institution that in their context stifled the freedom of women more than any other single thing. Marriage led to boredom and the death of love. Marriage legalized the suppression and exploitation of women in the most intimate realm of their lives.

Despite her attitude about marriage, Montseny did believe that a major mission of women "is to create children *and* a world for those children."[62] She praised the woman who "loved whom she wished, when she wished, who had children with the men she desired to have children with, and in a moment in which her being demanded the enjoyments and the responsibilities of happy and free maternity."[63] She insisted that women had a right to choose who would father their children because it gave them some control over the child's "beauty and their future superiority."[64] This she called "the art of maternity, voluntary maternity," of becoming a mother only when and if she chose, a right Spanish women surely did not have.[65] To Montseny, this concept of maternity seemed both natural and justified because with the mother resided the major responsibility for the health, balance, beauty, education, and will of that child and beyond that, the human race. From women came the men of the future: In a most Nietzschean phrase —"men as gods who will replace the men of the present as they replaced the beasts of the past and the present."[66]

When critics condemned that such liberty in love and maternity would lead to libertinism and child neglect or desertion, Montseny denied this. She stressed that above all, parenthood must be a responsible thing and that choice better insured the acceptance of that responsibility. Only when a woman desired a child and when her natural temperament and economic potential were favorable to it should she have one. These factors should also determine how many children she should have.[67] To be more emphatic, Montseny thought that if a woman would approach sex and maternity rationally, there would be no need for unwanted pregnancies or vasectomies. Again one recognizes why Montseny placed such emphasis upon education for women. Through education the woman would learn how her body naturally operated. With this knowledge it became possible for her to practice birth control effectively.

Montseny personally refused to accept the validity of the alternative, the use of vasectomies as a means of birth control. She did not think that vasectomy granted more freedom to men or women. If anything, it produced irresponsibility and promiscuity on the one hand, and on the other, and more importantly, it deprived the male of his basic right and duty—the responsible fathering of children. Instead, she demanded that a woman know her own bodily functions so that the knowledge would alleviate the necessity of that "irremediable operation made upon masculine integrity."[68] While minister of health and public assistance, Montseny strongly supported the *Mujeres Libres'* efforts at this kind of sex education.

Finally, Montseny described the nature of the family created as a product of female emancipation. She turned again to nature. From there, she gathered that the mother was the "natural sustainer of the child."[69] However, if a woman accepted this role in modern society, it often would mean that she had to leave the home in order to provide for the child. This necessitated that the mother had to be educated in order to be able to provide the best for the child.[70] Again, for women with children to leave them to work outside the home was contrary to contemporary Spanish custom. Though strongly criticized, Montseny stood on her commitment that a woman had the right and ability to do other things besides being a mother, things in keeping with her desires, potential, and individuality. But to arrange one's life in this way meant that for the working-class mother, some sort of cooperative effort had to be developed for taking care of the children.[71] One type of organization might be a family unit such as characterized the Montseny household, where the maintenance of the family was divided according to capability, needs, and, let it be stressed, individual preferences and where the returns of all labor were mutually shared. This, of course, was the supreme example that Montseny's system was a workable alternative to that which existed generally in her society.[72] Nowhere is the inextricable blending of anarchism with feminism more visible and understandable than in this arrangement within her own family.

Montseny thought that the emancipation and elevation of women to their natural state of equality with men demanded above all a woman fully aware of her own uniqueness and rights and a woman educated according to her natural potential. She thought that the best way for a woman to win her freedom was through tenacious dedication to a purpose, to a goal, and most importantly, to the fulfillment of herself. Dedication would produce works that would demand recognition of her merit on the basis of her individual capability. Always Montseny stressed the sane, balanced, intelligent, natural woman of strong ethical and physical character. She insisted that the true liberty of a woman must come through her humanity, ability, and uniqueness, not through her sex or class or politics or laws. Such a woman would find companionship with a new man, freed from conventional moralities, ancient tradition, and religious dictates. This new freedom would grant to a man his uniqueness and would also make it possible for him to accept a woman as his equal. However, to say equal was in no way to imply sameness, but rather the ability to recognize individuality and naturalness and to appreciate it as the avenue to greater freedom for both the woman and the man.

This naturalism precluded any need for institutions such as marriage, which forced people into unnatural, exploitative, stifling unions and which forced women into maternity for the wrong reasons. Unwanted maternity deprived the child of his/her right to care and love, which in turn thwarted the development of natural potential. The alternative of free union guaranteed a more permanent, complementary, growing, yet independent relationship between two people, because the union was based on a choice made by those two who wanted sincerely and naturally to be together, two people who had been free and independent enough to seek out their natural complement.

This type of union guaranteed that the couple's child would be the result of the aesthetic of love and the art of maternity. A child raised in such a circumstance would be a future-person, who would in turn lead the way to the anarchist revolution that the feminine revolution had begun. The anarchist revolution would then secure freedom, equality, and uniqueness for each member of society, once and for all. The feminist movement must be included inextricably in the general movement to improve the condition of human society. Montseny insisted that liberated women were essential to the progressive improvement of society and to a successful future for humanity.

Federica Montseny's greatest emotional commitment throughout her life went into this struggle for the emancipation of women. Often loneliness walked with her as she strove to achieve the goals she had set for herself. Nevertheless, Montseny lived according to the principles that she espoused. She was a woman-woman, a future-woman.

NOTES

1. Federica Montseny, *El problema de los sexos* (Toulouse: Ediciones "universo," n.d.), pp. 12, 15. For a novelistic definition of the nature and

rights of women as Montseny interpreted them, see her novels *La Victoria. Novela en la que se narran los problemas de orden moral que se la presentan a una mujer de ideas modernas* (Barcelona: Costa, 1925): idem, *El hijo de Clara* (Barcelona: Costa, 1927); and idem, *Heroinas* (Barcelona: La Revista Blanca, n.d.).

2. Federica Montseny, "Feminismo y humanismo," *La Revista Blanca* 33 (October 1, 1924): 13 [hereafter cited as *RB*]. Also see two essays by Federica's mother, Soledad Gustavo, *El amor libre* (Montevideo: n.p., 1904) and *A los proletarios* (Buenas Aires: Biblioteca de la Questión Social, 1901); an essay by another strong influence on the development of Montseny, the family friend Teresa Claramunt, *La mujer: consideraciones generales sobre su estado ante las prerrogativas del hombre* (Mahon: Imprenta de "El Porvenir del Obrero," 1905); Emma Goldman, "Situación social de la mujer," *Mujeres Libres* (January, 1937): n.p.; and an unsigned editorial, "El problema sexual y la revolución," *Mujeres Libres* (Ocobter, 1936): n.p.

3. Federica Montseny, "La tragedia de la emancipación feminina," *RB* 38 (December 15, 1924): 20.

4. Montseny, *El problema de los sexos*, pp. 15-16.

5. Ibid., p. 11.

6. Ibid., pp. 10-16.

7. Federica Montseny, "Morbosismo," *RB* 353 (October 25, 1935): 1032.

8. Federica Montseny, "Una obra feminina de cultura," *RB* 172 (July 15, 1930): 83.

9. Ibid.

10. Gustavo, *A los proletarios*, p. 8.

11. Montseny, *El problema de los sexos*, p. 14.

12. Ibid., pp. 15-16.

13. Federica Montseny, "La falta de idealidad en el feminismo," *RB* 13 (December 1, 1923): 3-4.

14. Montseny, "Feminismo y humanismo," *RB* 33 (October 1, 1924): 13.

15. Federica Montseny, "Las conquistas sociales de la mujer," *RB* 55 (September 1, 1925): 15-17.

16. Gustavo, *A los proletarios*, p. 14.

17. Montseny, "La tragedia de la emancipación," p. 19; and "Un mitin de 'Mujeres Libres' en Valencia," *Mujeres Libres* (1938): n.p. See also Emma Goldman, "Situación social de las mujeres," and an unsigned article, "Mujeres Libres tiene personalidad," *Mujeres Libres* (September 1, 1936), n.p.

18. Montseny, "La tragedia de la emancipación," p. 20.

19. Federica Montseny, "El movimiento feminino internacional," *RB* 6 (August 15, 1923): 3-5, and idem, "El despertar de la mujer turca," *RB* 11 (November 1, 1925): 5-8.

20. Montseny, "La falta de idealidad en el feminismo," p. 3.

21. Montseny, "Feminismo y humanismo," p. 14.

22. Federica Montseny, "Dos mujeres, dos frases y dos libros," *RB* 59 (November 1, 1925): 13.

23. Federica Montseny, "La mujer, problema del hombre," *RB* 89 (February 1, 1927): 658.

24. Federica Montseny, "La mujer nueva," *RB* 72 (May 15, 1926): 25.

25. Montseny, "La mujer, problema de hombre," p. 658.

26. Montseny Family letters, Federica Montseny to Max Nettlau, December 6, 1933, in Max Nettlau, Nettlau Archives, Instituut voor Internationaal Sociale Geschiedenis, Amsterdam [hereafter cited as F.M. to M.N. with appropriate date].

27. F.M. to M.N., February 15, 1933.

28. Ibid.

29. Montseny, "La mujer nueva," p. 25.

30. Ibid.

31. Ibid.

32. Montseny, "Feminismo y humanismo," p. 14.

33. Montseny, "La tragedia de la emancipación," p. 20.

34. Ibid.

35. Ibid.

36. Federica Montseny, "El alma de España," *RB* 349 (September 27, 1935): 936.

37. Federica Montseny, "El centenario del romanticismo," *RB* 116 (March 15, 1928): 618.

38. Federica Montseny, "Las mujeres de Aragón," *RB* 262 (January 25, 1934): 161-62.

39. Montseny, "La mujer nueva," p. 25. See also her "Lecturas," *RB* 114 (February 15, 1928): 570-72; and idem, "Revista de libros," *RB* 218 (June 15, 1932): 61-64. Montseny wrote in this last article that Alexandra Kollontai's *La mujer y la moral sexual* (Madrid: Ediciones Hoy, 1931), was "one of the better books that I have read on the problem of love and the formation of the feminine personality." Finally, there are striking similarities between Montseny and Goldman, although Montseny also insisted that Goldman had not been an influence in the development of her ideas about women. Federica Montseny to the author, July 27, 1971.

40. Federica Montseny, "Libertad," *RB* 111 (January 1, 1928): 456.

41. Ibid.

42. Ibid.

43. Montseny, *El problema de los sexos*, p. 12.

44. Ibid., p. 14.

45. Federica Montseny, "La moral en las playas," *RB* 337 (July 5, 1935): 648.

46. Ibid.

47. Montseny, "Morbosismo," p. 1032.

48. Ibid.

49. Montseny, *El problema de los sexos*, p. 13.

50. Ibid.

51. Ibid.

52. Federica Montseny, "La derrota de la reacción," *RB* 15 (January 15, 1924): 10.

53. Montseny, *El problema de los sexos*, p. 13.

54. Ibid., pp. 20-21. See also Federica Montseny, "Libros," *RB* 79 (September 1, 1926): 217-18.

55. Montseny, *El problema de los sexos*, p. 21.

56. Ibid.

57. Emile Armand, *Anarchism and Individualism* (Bristol, England: S. E. Parker, 1962).

58. Federica Montseny, "La ruta de los heroes," *RB* 53 (August 1, 1925): 19-21.

59. Montseny, "La tragedia de la emancipación," p. 20. See also Emma Goldman, *Anarchism and Other Essays* (New York: Dover Publciations, 1969), p. 174.

60. Federica Montseny, "España y el problema de los sexos," *RB* 139 (March 1, 1929): 551.

61. Montseny, *El problema de los sexos*, p. 20.

62. Federica Montseny, "Un mitin de 'mujeres libres' en Valencia," *Mujeres libres* (1938): n.p.

63. Federica Montseny, "Una vida de mujer," *RB* 126 (August 15, 1928): 137.

64. Ibid., p. 138.

65. Ibid.

66. Montseny, "La mujer nueva," p. 25.

67. Federica Montseny, "Dos palabras sobre la vasectomia," *RB* 358 (November 29, 1935): 1122.

68. Ibid., pp. 1121-22.

69. Montseny, *El problema de los sexos*, p. 21.

70. Ibid., pp. 21-23.

71. Ibid.

72. Nowhere is this better exemplified than in Montseny's letters to Max Nettlau. See in particular: F. M. to M. N., February 22, 1936, and August 1, 1938, which discuss the family division of labor and the expanded nature of the "family unit"; R. M. to M. N., October 2, 1933, August 1, 1938, and December 24, 1938, which discuss the arrival of children into the family; and of course, the many letters discussing the love and care of those children. Perhaps the most characteristic of F. M. to M. N., October 2, 1934, where María Anguera, a member of the "family," tells Nettlau all about Montseny and her enthusiasm for her first child, a daughter she called Vida.

7.
Margarita Nelken: Women and the Crisis of Spanish Politics

ROBERT KERN

Margarita Nelken is not a well-remembered suffragist or political leader. She was Spanish by birth but a German Jew by parentage, and this cultural contradiction kept her from becoming a respected figure in Spain, while the isolation of Spain itself removed her from the center of the European socialist movement. She clearly belongs to the lesser fringes of women swept into radical politics in the early twentieth century and is a good representative of countries like Spain where the progress of women had been slow and general social crises tended to propel radical women and feminist politics through some strange and difficult times.

Born in 1897, Margarita Nelken y Mausberger, the daughter of a German Jewish family living in Málaga, showed a precocious interest in art and at age thirteen was sent to study in Paris. She soon switched from serious painting to the study of art history and museum curatorship, obtaining a liberal education. During her later life in Madrid, in fact, she helped found the Museum of Modern Art and worked as a curator there and at the Prado. In addition, she frequently wrote on art and artists for a number of Spanish newspapers and presses and also taught painting courses for adults and children.[1]

This connection with children gave her life an unusual turn in 1919. Until then her bohemian life knew only the picturesque poverty of the Left Bank common to student artists in Paris, but friends in Madrid encouraged her to give courses for poor children. Already a political radical in Paris, the opportunity to take up a proletarian cause started Nelken working with children in the working-class barrios of Madrid. It was a stunning experience, she later wrote, to leave her own middle-class world and discover another, "silent" world of malnutrition, ignorance, and neglect, and she reacted by creating a tiny orphanage, *La Casa de los Niños de España*, devoted to the care of working-class children abandoned in the city.[2] The Church, however, quickly objected; orphanages remained under ecclesiastical control along with other charities, and the union of church and state in Spain opposed private philanthropy as a matter of principle.

Outraged, Nelken sought assistance, and she soon met and was helped by a number of socialists who invited her to lecture at the Socialist party's *Casa del Pueblo*, where she became a close associate of such influential young intellectuals as Luis Jimenez de Asúa and Luis Araquistáin, both interested in the development of a feminist program for the party.[3] Nelken joined the Socialist party and the *Unión General de Trabajadores* (UGT) and soon became their feminist leader.

The moment proved advantageous for feminism and for Nelken. A half century's pressure for change in the status of women provided a volatile background in a society where the old saying, *la mujer honrada, la pierna quebrada y en casa* (the only honorable woman is one locked in the house with a broken leg), still represented popular feeling. The 1881 Civil Code had discriminated against women in inheritance matters and denied adultery as grounds for separation if brought by the wife rather than the husband.[4] Spanish justice granted strict marital authority for men and embraced a general philosophy that in marriage women receive protection in return for obedience.[5] Honor and shame, the traditional values of Mediterranean society, represented a male code that buried women's aspirations in fear of competition, equality, or inadequacy. By 1900 only 30 percent of Spanish women were literate, and only fifteen women had earned the *licenciado*, the equivalent of a Ph.D.[6] Most women remained at home, and rural women particularly continued to live in an almost timeless world of male domination.

Those women who did work away from home—22 percent by 1920—found most of their jobs in domestic service, in the cigarette factories, and in mining.[7] Abysmal working conditions influenced the passage of some protective laws, such as the reduction of the workday to eleven hours, but the *Ley de Silla*, passed by the *Cortes* in 1912, typified legislative cynicism by requiring that a chair be placed at each place where a woman worked. As in most European countries of this period, there was a middle-class women's movement more concerned with suffrage than with radical economic and social change. Groups like the *Unión de Mujeres Españoles*, the *Asociación de Mujeres Españolas* and the *Acción Social Femenina* lobbied for the vote in the manner prescribed by Concepción Arenal (1820-1893), Spain's leading female humanist reformer.[8]

Arenal, the first woman to attend lectures at the National University by adopting a George Sand costume to disguise herself in the classroom, is little known outside Spain and Argentina even though she became an active mid-nineteenth-century journalist, social critic, and sociologist. Somewhat ambiguously, she urged women to expand their horizons by fighting for jobs in the male-dominated workplace and seeking the vote to protect the interests of their children, while at the same time advising wives "to meet authority with love" and to allow husbands to have their way at home in order to prevent them from adopting brute force as their only form of household behavior.[9] Her organization, the *Asociación de Señoras de la Caridad*, declined badly after her death and became so impotent that it could not even persuade Premier Dato in December, 1919, to allow an international congress of world feminist groups to meet in Spain.[10]

This low ebb of middle-class feminism, however, came just at the moment when a new generation of women, stirred by the Russian Revolution and the mood of a postwar Spain affected by wage cuts, lockouts, and peasant protest, began entering politics as communists, socialists, or anarchists. The most famous was Dolores Ibarruri *(La Pasionaria)*, wife of an Asturian miner and secretary of the new Communist party, whose political orientation, however, did not include a strong feminist perspective.[11] Federica Montseny, another major radical figure (discussed elsewhere in this book), who did have strong feminist values, belonged to various anarchist groups and thus had little contact with nonrevolutionary forces among women's groups.[12] Still another, Clara Campoamor, came from a poor family and became a brilliant law student who pioneer-

ed new children's laws in 1927, but her concern for reform precluded any left-wing activity.[13] Perhaps the woman most similar to
Nelken was Victoria Kent Siano, the daughter of an English father
and a Spanish mother, who trained in the law with Campoamor
in order to become a penologist, joining the Socialist party somewhat later than Nelkin in protest against the prison conditions she
had encountered.

This wave of new female political leaders obviously encouraged
Nelken to broaden her own interests as well. She proselytized often
for the socialists on suffrage and women's rights and continued to
do so throughout the period of military dictatorship from 1923 to
1931 because the socialists, out of hostility to the liberal parliamentarianism that had been destroyed, rationalized cooperation
with the dictatorship as the opportunity of a lifetime to prepare to
seize power from a regime that could only be temporary. While
Dolores Ibarruri and Federica Montseny faced strong and continual
official pressures, Nelken wrote and spoke without difficulty, even
receiving government patronage in 1926 when Francisco Largo
Caballero, the highest-ranking socialist in the dictator Primo's
civilian cabinet, asked her to investigate conditions among working
women in various industries. There is no evidence, however, that
the government ever published the material she collected.

Even before this, Nelken had written *La condición social de la
mujer en España*, a book much indebted to the previous profeminist arguments of John Stuart Mill and August Bebel.[14] Nelken
argued that women in modern society remained little more than
serfs of religion and of their male relatives, who expected them to
remain passive in all things and at all times. Education, controlled
by ecclesiastical authority, failed to give Spanish women a sense of
reality about the world and its problems; instead, women were sent
to catechism classes after the completion of their basic education.
Modern life, however, demanded that people—particularly oppressed minority groups like women—represent their aims by
force, if necessary, just as trade unions and other agencies of the
working class did.[15] Until women fought for their rights with revolutionary maximalism, Nelken felt they could not expect to form a
feminist force in daily political life or to obtain the rights denied to
them. Emancipation and suffrage were goals that could only be
grasped.

To do so meant putting aside bourgeois beliefs that the wife's major social obligation lay with helping her husband improve his social status or accepting obstacles to advancement in the job market. Nelken insisted that in both areas education prepared women for self-abasement and condemned them to failure because male teachers resented the economic threat of women in education and so denied them full use of school or university opportunities. The government likewise consciously refused to allow women entry into the administrative hierarchy; women employed in commercial offices usually received 60 percent lower salaries than men, got none of the few company or government benefits, and had no access to philanthropic agencies that existed elsewhere (like the British and American YWCAs or the continental hostels).[16] Consequently, many young Spanish women continued to live at home permanently, never achieving any degree of freedom or independence to earn their emancipation and suffrage.

Most tragic, in Nelken's view, was the plight of women workers who, ignored by unions, sometimes became the object of male strikes when hired for new positions. Even the more radical workers feared job losses, reactionary female Catholicism, and a challenge to their *machismo* from women coworkers. Without some kind of independent economic protection, Nelken wrote, "the single woman sacrifices for her father or brothers. Living without youthful joy or equilibrium, the working woman leads a life of submission and absolute passivity alongside men."[17] The situation was equally bleak for working married women, since the law of March 13, 1900, which gave pregnant women three weeks maternity leave, and the short time companies allowed female workers to nurse their children, were considered favors, not rights, and frequently were revoked to force women out of their jobs. Women who worked in Spain's still prevalent cottage industries occupied the bottom of the economic order, receiving no protection whatsoever.[18]

Nelken's book concluded with a general discussion of childbirth, the dangers of sexual ignorance, and the high rate of infant mortality. Because Spain was to her very "artificial" and "hypocritical" about sex education, she stressed the need for new courses and attacked the *Consejo Superior de Protección de la Infancia* for its refusal to exercise secular moral power.[19] The Church ignored all these problems; the police were too corrupt to intervene into the area of prostitution; and the Code of 1881, which gave fathers an absolute right of control over their children, denied abused children the right to protection by the state. The only remedy for all these social ills, Nelken insisted, would come from radical political movements with feminist overtones; not by "just having short hair, a loud voice or the manners of a *marimacho* [lesbian]," but by using the spirit of collectivism and the discipline of a Marxist party.[20]

By traveling and lecturing constantly, Nelken spoke to thousands of Spanish women about socialism and feminism in the 1920s, but like many other radical women, she steadfastly refused to cooperate with the older feminist groups and worked with some success to amalgamate these groups into the Socialist party. Her ideas about women remained vague and general, secondary to her politics, but she was gradually attracted to the problems of peasant women in the South, throughout Andalusia and Estremadura, poor areas where latifundia, absentee landlords, and pauperized, landless agricultural day laborers typified the southern social crisis. Like so many Spanish intellectuals of her time, peasant toughness and self-reliance provided a welcome contrast with bourgeois Spain. Her friendship, too, with Ricardo Zabalez, a young socialist teacher popular with the *Federación Nacional de Trabajadores de la Tierra* (FNTT), a radical peasant union with a chapter in Zabalez's Estremadurian town of Badajoz, led to involvement in peasant strikes during 1930 and 1931, which surprisingly endeared the urban and sophisticated woman to the Badajoz peasantry while at the same time bringing her more attention within the Socialist party.[21]

The fall of the monarchy in April, 1931, brought Nelken back to Madrid to chair the Socialist party's Committee on Women's Affairs. The June elections for the Constituent Cortes elected 117 Socialists, including Victoria Kent and (on another ticket) Clara Campoamor. Nelken herself became a deputy on October 3, 1931, one of the representatives from Badajoz after an expansion of the electoral district.[22] Only after her election, amid accusations of gerrymandering and socialist opportunism, was it discovered that she lacked the citizenship necessary for Cortes membership. The Socialist-Republican majority thus hurriedly had to introduce a bill naturalizing Nelken, much to the amusement of the conservatives.

Even before Nelken's election, the suffrage issue had been a bitter topic, and even many Socialists would go no further than to promise women the vote after clerical influence diminished. The Radicals, much more intransigent, announced in September that they would restrict suffrage to men only, while one deputy even proposed voting ages of twenty-three for men and forty-five for women. The inclusion of women as candidates for the Constituent Cortes, however, predisposed a majority of deputies to accept universal suffrage. Nelken later wrote that she felt torn between the masses of conservative Catholic women who someday might vote against the Second Republic and the real problems that all women would face without legal rights backed up by their right to vote.[23] Because of the problem with her naturalization, she did not vote on the issue, which passed by a forty-vote margin.

Afterwards, Nelken masked her indecision by predicting hopefully that the traditional Catholicism of many Spanish women would vanish as more of them took jobs outside the home.[24] Clara Campoamor, who disagreed completely, felt that suffrage was premature and attributed it to politicians like Largo Caballero and Manual Azaña, the intellectual Republican leader, who "desperately sought to broaden their appeal no matter what the cost."[25] Victoria Kent, however, steadfastly favored enfranchisement, and when one opponent referred to Campoamor and Kent as exceptional women totally unlike the majority of their sex, Kent replied vehemently that the importance of suffrage lay not in the incapacity of women but in the opportunity for the Second Republic to secure a basic human right.[26]

Amid this rancor, Nelken took her seat in the Cortes and actively supported the prohibition of sexual discrimination, equality of men and women in marriage and the family, passage of a divorce bill, and the creation of a constitutional provision to make work a social responsibility covering men and women in a new social security system.[27] She particularly championed divorce and accused ecclesiastical spokesmen of refusing to allow women out of their traditional roles as wives and mothers, "a moral oppression which treats women like real property."[28] Only divorce would lift this old weight and also curb the adulterous *Don Juanismo* of so many Spanish men. Nelken thought divorce proceedings should be determined solely by the women; nothing would more successfully equalize the sexes.[29] This last statement scandalized conservatives and placed her in the forefront of the radical socialists, a position she continued to occupy for a long time.

Almost immediately after the ratification of the Republican constitution in early December, 1931, however, Margarita Nelken put aside her parliamentary campaign for women's rights to rejoin Zabalez in Badajoz, where peasant occupation of large estates to protest the lack of land reform in the constitution had led to calling out the Civil Guard, Spain's national constabulary. On December 26, Nelken by her own account convinced the peasants of her district to confine their activities to peaceful demonstrations, but other observers accused her of making inflammatory speeches that led to the murder of four Civil Guards on December 31, 1931, in Castilblanco.[30] Twelve were charged with murder, but Nelken was not among them, perhaps because of her parliamentary immunity, although both Luis Jiménez de Asúa, lawyer for the defense, and Juan Simeón Vidarte Franco-Romero, the state prosecutor, believed her innocent.[31]

Back in Madrid, Nelken returned to the life of a deputy, strongly backing the Republicans' secular education plan as a means for oppressed, religious women who previously had no other source of information to educate themselves about the modern world.[32] Her concentration never stayed long upon feminist politics, however, and while she became a member of the radical clique around Francisco Largo Caballero, immersed in land reform and labor relations, she was, like many Spanish socialists, confused, ideologically inconsistent, and often ineffective. Moreover, her involvement in Castilblanco made her so suspect that for all her prominence she received only trusteeship on the board of the Prado Museum as her reward from the Cortes.[33] She had no opportunity, despite many requests, to obtain more powerful administrative positions in the government.

This frustration led her back to the suffrage issue. She increasingly insisted that the enfranchisement of women had taken away concern for the "woman question." No new vocational programs or special employment efforts had been created, education lagged, and even the Socialists failed to recruit women members as they once had done. Instead, functionaries like Manuel Cordero propagandized them into believing that female political attitudes had been changed by the grant of universal suffrage.[34] Margarita Nelken profoundly disagreed: "Feminism is, above all," she said in late 1932, "an economic question, of liberty, of dignity and of a place to work."[35] Women, in facing these needs, did not have the opportunity to take the ballot very seriously.

This economic explanation for the failure of Spanish women to join political parties or actively support the Second Republic soon replaced Nelken's anticlericalism as the fundamental causative factor in much of what she later wrote or said. Working women became the key to total emancipation for Spanish women—a process of women leaving the home, encouraged by the government, to emerge into the world through academic or vocational training to take their place in modern society. This may have been a fanciful expectation, but it angered her that the Socialists could not conceive of further female progress beyond emancipation or that other politicians pointed to the short time since the start of the feminist movement. Nelken's impatience, however, stemmed from fear of a growing national conservatism and the series of Republican disasters that in November, 1933, culminated in the Right's victory in the parliamentary elections.

This victory supposedly came on a crest of reactionary votes from religious women, although this allegation subsequently has been proved to be untrue.[36] Women, in fact, tended to vote for women, electing five more than in 1931.[37] Margarita Nelken, though herself reelected, remained unconvinced. The fiery deputy from Badajoz wrote that women were "forced by Jesuit confessors to vote against the Republic."[38] This exaggeration masked her disappointment that new programs to educate or train women for useful jobs were stillborn. The Socialists might have been slow to understand the problems of women, but the Right would cling to tradition without considering any aspect of feminist goals. Not surprisingly, she and Largo Caballero studied Marx and were strongly influenced by Luis Araquistáin, who had just returned from his ambassadorship to Germany and was already a strong antifascist, having witnessed Hitler's rise to power. The three considered themselves "left socialists" and began planning ways to take the offensive against the Right.

The opportunity came in the spring of 1934, after Nelken's old friend, Ricardo Zabalez, was elected president of the FNTT. Together with the left socialists, the peasants' union seized considerable amounts of land in an attack upon the new government. Throughout late April and early May, 1934, peasants refused to plant crops and continued their expropriations. More than 1,563 villages experienced agricultural strikes, with Margarita Nelken quite visible as an organizer of revolutionary dramas, fetes, muralpainting, and speech making. Her call for a national general strike led to premature uprisings on June 5 and 6 in Cáceres, Badajoz, Cuidad Real, Jaén, Granada, Toledo, and Córdoba. Without outside aid, however, the revolt collapsed rapidly, ending in Zabalez' arrest and Nelken a fugitive hiding near Madrid.

Still free several months later, she could only be a spectator to the socialist revolution of "Red October" in Asturias, where miners fought the army for almost two weeks. Later she lavished praises upon this insurrection, comparing it with the Paris Commune or the efforts of Petrograd during the Russian Revolution, but she never speculated what might have happened if the October revolutionaires had been joined by the southern peasantry that had exhausted itself months before. Instead, she called the revolt "a new moral preparation" to create a situation that might "defactionalize" radical politics. There could be "only one order: the insurrection. Only one goal: the struggle to achieve a dictatorship of the proletariat. And only one motto: that of a revolution that integrates all parties."[39]

Presumably this meant development of a popular front, and perhaps this is why she slipped out of the country for a trip to the Soviet Union as a guest of the Association of Soviet Writers. While she seemed only guardedly enthusiastic during her stay, later writing that Russia "lacked popular initiative" and reminded her of Spain under the dictatorship, she was among the first Europeans to learn of the Communist International's popular front strategy.[40] She did not reenter Spain until the summer of 1935, taking advantage of the government's growing weakness and distraction. Back in Madrid, she worked with Largo Caballero as assistant secretary of the Socialist party and with Dolores Ibarruri and Victoria Kent as a cofounder of the *Comité de Auxilio Antifascista*, which sought to unite various women's organizations against fascism.[41] It proved to be the typically ambiguous popular-front type of organization, more useful to Nelken and the others as a vehicle with which to resume their careers than to improve the social or legal position of women in Spanish society.

These three women, plus Campoamor and twelve other female newcomers, won seats in the Popular Front Cortes of February, 1936, some sign of higher esteem for the role of women in politics.[42] Nelken, so far as it can be determined, never acknowledged or discussed the fact that they divided equally between Right and Left, nor did she compare their election with her negative attitude of 1933. Even her former concern with ecclesiastical power in the woman's world now seemed unimportant in a society preparing to fight a civil war over political systems. Margarita Nelken continued her work as assistant secretary of the Socialist party well into the war itself, remaining close to Largo Caballero until his premiership collapsed in the crisis of May, 1937, after which she moved closer to Indalecio Prieto's Communist-leaning branch of the party. She wrote for the Communist-sponsored *Mujeres* throughout the remainder of the war, finally fleeing to Mexico in 1939 where she remained until her death in 1968.

The career of Margarita Nelken, hardly spectacular, nevertheless is interesting. In retrospect, she seems to have had no clear sense of the goals sought by the women's movement elsewhere. She did not (or could not) get the Socialist party to expand its activities beyond the *Agrupación Feminista Socialista* format of a trade union to attract retail clerks and textile workers to the UGT.[43] This very stilted approach prevented a broader-based movement and limited the influence of the Socialists to the relatively weak women's labor movement. Her own old-fashioned anticlericalism fulminated against Catholic politics without clearly getting across the point that women had minds of their own to use in accordance with the facts and information they received. Had she or the Socialists seriously provided women with better adult education programs and periodical material, they might have made a better claim upon their minds.

Margarita Nelken's adventures as a peasant rebel in the South raise other doubts. Her personal attachment to Zabalez aside, the suspicion lurks that Castilblanco may have been Nelken's effort to reach out and gather a following to match the charisma of her rivals, Dolores Ibarruri or Federica Montseny. In fact, the incident robbed her of any influence she had in the Cortes, where she possessed the power to effect greater change than in Castilblanco.

And finally, the ambivalence of Margarita Nelken over the enfranchisement of women presents the greatest puzzle of all. She demanded the vote for women in 1922, seemed paralyzed in 1931, and wished fervently that it had not been given in 1933—a range as extreme as possible. Quite obviously, she wanted women not just to vote, but to vote progressively, with great enlightenment, and immediately, for a totally nontraditional society. It was too much to expect, and too soon, a message that confused Nelken's own followers who too strongly mistrusted the outcome of the 1933 and (to a lesser extent) 1936 elections on the role of women in Spanish politics. Radical women thus entered the Civil War in some state of confusion over their accomplishments, which were not inconsiderable. This and the strain of war forced even Ibarruri to admit in 1938 that "work among women is the weak side of our party activities. . . . We even meet cases of comrades who disapprove of their wives joining the Party or attending meetings."[44] Emma Goldman, the American anarchist who visited Spain in 1936 and 1937, commented that "women still seem cloistered" and wondered if anyone had tried to educated Spanish women on feminist issues before the war had broken out.[45]

Those knowledgeable about Nelken's life have commented that she was subjected to the same quandry that made political choices so difficult for radical women of the late 1960s and 1970s—whether to put feminist issues first or relegate them to a secondary place in the interest of party strength and unity.[46] She seems to have chosen Socialist party politics and thereby slighted her feminist beliefs. It is, however, easy to understand why she made the choice. In an atmosphere of social crisis and imminent civil war, women's issues would have seemed of minor importance; the task at that moment was to save the Republic and preserve and strengthen the forces of leftism in Spain.

Her choice may or may not have been the correct one, but contemporary experience demonstrates some possibility of undertaking revolution and the liberation of women simultaneously. Could it be that the feminist struggle in Spain was weakened not only by women like Nelken but also by refusal of the Socialists to make the greater participation of women a necessary part of the leftist struggle to survive?

This still would not have given the "woman question" an independent existence, but it might have left later Spanish feminists in a stronger position, much more capable of pressing their demands on their socialist colaborators. As it is today, unfortunately, the post-Franco era has yet to produce any legislation affecting women other than the return of the vote.

NOTES

1. There is no autobiography or biography of Nelken. For an outline of her life, see Rosa María Martínez Capel, *El sufragio femenino en la 2ª república española* (Grandad: Universidad de Granada, 1975), pp. 221-27.

2. Margarita Nelken, *La condición social de la mujer en España* (Barcelona: Editorial Minerva, 1922), p. 45. There is a new edition of this book, published in 1975 by CVS Ediciones in Madrid, with an interesting prologue entitled "Un libro polémic sin polémica," written by María Aurelia Capmany.

3. Luis Araquistáin, close friend and advisor of Francisco Largo Caballero, achieved high rank in the Second Republic by becoming the Spanish ambassador to Germany in 1931. He wrote *El comunismo en la guerra civil española* (Carmaux: Travailleurs Reunis, 1939) as an account of his activities. Luis Jiménez de Asúa, a professor of penal law at the University of Madrid, later chaired the committee that drew up the first draft of the 1931 constitution. His writings included *Libertad de amor y derecha a morir* (Madrid: Historia nueva, 1928), which advocated the legalization of free love, sexual education, legalized prostitution, birth control, and euthanasia; and *Al servicio de la nueva generación* (Madrid: J. Morata, 1930), which argued, among other things, that women had a basic right to economic independence.

4. *Código civil* (Madrid: Ministerio de Gracia y Justicia, 1881), pp. 349-99.

5. See Catherine Girard, "La condition de la Femme en Espagne," (Ph.D. diss., University of Paris, 1961), pp. 41-43.

6. Capel, *El sufragio femenino*, p. 97.

7. The Condesa de Campo Alange, *La mujer en España: Cien años de su historia* (Madrid: Aguilar, 1964), p. 357, puts the total female work force at 1,105,443 in 1920, of which half were domestics.

8. See Geraldine Scanlon, *La polémica feminista en la España contemporánea* (Mexico City: Siglo XXI, 1976), pp. 204-12. Also see Temma Kaplan, "Spanish Anarchism and Women's Liberation," *Journal of Contemporary History* 6, no. 2 (1971): 101-10; idem, "Other Scenarios: Women and Spanish Anarchism," in Renate Bridenthal and Claudia Koonz, eds., *Becoming Visible: Women in European History* (Boston: Houghton Mifflin, 1977), pp. 400-421; and idem, "Turmoil in Spain: The Communist Party and the Mass Movement," *Radical America* 11, no. 2 (1977): 53-73.

9. Concepción Arenal, *Cuestión social: Cartas a un obrero y a un señor* (Avila: Impr. de la Propaganda Ibrería, 1880); and *La igualidad y sus relaciones con la libertad* (Madrid: V. Suárez, 1898).

10. *El Sol*, December 11, 1919.

11. Dolores Ibarruri's autobiography, *The Only Road* (New York: International Publishers, 1968) and idem, *Speeches and Articles, 1936-1939* (New York: International Publishers, 1940) contain little on women's rights.

12. See Shirley Fredricks, "Social and Political Thought of Federica Montseny, Spanish Anarchist, 1923-1937," (Ph.D. diss., University of New Mexico, 1972) for a detailed discussion of Montseny.

13. Clara Campoamor Rodríguez, *La Revolution Espagnol vue par une Republicaino* (Paris: Plon, 1937). This memoir of the civil war was her best-known work.

14. These were John Stuart Mill, *The Subjection of Women* (London: Longmans, Green, Reader and Dyer, 1869), and August Bebel, *Woman under Socialism* (1883; reprint ed., New York: Schocken Books, 1971).

15. Nelken, *La condición de la mujer en España*, p. 18.

16. Ibid.

17. Ibid., p. 66.

18. Ibid., p. 124.

19. Ibid., p. 157.

20. Ibid., p. 168.

21. See Nelken's account of the FNTT in *La mujer ante las Cortes constituyentes* (Madrid: Publicaciones Castro, 1931), p. 16 and passim.

22. Consult Amaro del Rosal, *Historia de la UGT en España* (Barcelona: Ediciones Grijalbo, 1977), 1: 381-85.

23. Nelken, *La mujer antes las Cortes constituyentes*, p. 18.

24. Ibid., p. 26.

25. Clara Campoamor Rodríguez, *El voto femenino y yo. Mi pecado moral* (Madrid: Editorial Morales, 1938), p. 91.

26. *Diario de las Sesiones de las Cortes constituyentes*, October 1, 1931.

Also see Luis Jiménez de Asúa, *Anécdotas de las Cortes constituyentes* (Buenos Aires: Patronato Hispano-argentino de Cultura, 1942), which is a good account of the many controversies encountered by the Cortes.

27. Nelken, *La mujer antes las Cortes constituyentes*, p. 47.

28. Ibid., p. 53.

29. Capel, *El sufragio femenino*, p. 225.

30. See Baldomero Díaz de Entresotos, *Seis meses de anarquía en Estramadura* (Cáceres: Editorial Estramadura, 1937), p. 85. The best general work on Castilblanco is Luis Jiménez de Asúa, *Castilblanco* (Madrid: Editorial España, 1933). The chief work on land reform is Edward Malefakis, *Agrarian Reform and Peasant Rebellion in Spain* (New Haven: Yale University Press, 1970).

31. Ibid., p. 4 and passim.

32. *El Sol*, March 13, 1933.

33. Victoria Kent, on the other hand, became director-general of Spanish prisons from December, 1931, to February, 1934. Clara Campoamor rose to become vice president of the Labor Planning Committee and was also a member of the Charities Committee. Capel, *El sufragio femenino*, p. 221.

34. Martine Weiler, *Mujeres activas: Sociología de la mujer trabajadora en España* (Madrid: Ediciones de la Torres, 1977), p. 15.

35. Margarita Nelken, *Por qué hicimos la revolución* (Barcelona: Ediciones Sociales Internacionales, 1936), p. 78.

36. Both Capel, *El sufragio femenino*, p. 242, and Scanlon, *La polémica feminista*, p. 282, refute this charge. Only Nelken and Frank Jellinek, *The Civil War in Spain* (London: Victor Gollancz, 1939) argue to the contrary, although many socialists and anarchists did believe that conservative women had turned the elections in favor of the Right at the time. On the problems besetting the Republican cabinet that led to its loss, see Raymond Carr, *Spain 1808-1939* (Oxford: Clarendon Press, 1966), pp. 516-23.

37. Matilde de la Torre Gutiérrez, Veneranda García Blanco and María Lejarraga y García won as Socialists; Dolores Ibarruri became the first Communist deputy; and Francisca Gavelanes represented the small Agrarian party. Campoamor was reelected, and only Victoria Kent lost her seat.

38. Nelken, *Por qué hicimos*, pp. 126-34.

39. Ibid., p. 157.

40. Margarita Nelken, *Los Torres del Kremlin* (Mexico City: Industrial y Distribuidora, S.A., 1943), p. 103.

41. Capel, *El sufragio femenino*, p. 227.

42. See J. Tusell Gómez, *Las elecciones del Frente Popular en España* (Madrid: Cuadernos para el Diálogo, 1971), vols. 1 & 2, and Joaquín Arrarás, *Historia de la Segunda República Española* (Madrid: Editora

Nacional, 1968), 4: index, for the activities of Aurora Arnaiz, María Luisa Aramburu, Pepita Clavería, Carmen Dorrosoro, María Luisa de Jover, María Lejarraga y García de Martínez Sierra, Carmen Monné de Baroja, María Angela del Olmo, María Casilda Sáenz Lorenzo, Dolores Trena, and Victoria Zárate. All were elected as deputies to the Popular Front Cortes in February, 1936.

43. This group had been one of the earliest women's groups in the CNT, founded in 1917 at the time of Spain's first general strike. See *Solidaridad Obrero*, August 11, 1917.

44. Ibarruri, *Speeches and Articles*, p. 188.

45. Letter of Emma Goldman to Mariano Vázquez, October 11, 1937, Goldman Collection, file 28B, International Institute of Social History, Amsterdam, the Netherlands.

46. My thanks, in particular, to Meredith Dodge, Jane Slaughter, and Elizabeth Kern for comments on this paper.

8.
Communist Women and the Fascist Experience

JOHN M. CAMMETT

The Italian war of resistance against Nazi fascism from 1943 to 1945 saw some 623 women killed in battle or executed by the Germans, while more than 2,750 women partisans were deported to the death camps and 4,600 were arrested, tortured, and tried. There were 35,000 female *partigiane* who actually took up arms, and 70,000 members of the less active but still important women's resistance organizations like the *Gruppi di Difesa della Donna*.[1] Far and away the greatest majority of these women were Communists, although all left-wing women's groups in the Resistance finally did come together to form the Union of Italian Women (UDI), which became a major force in the fight for women's rights after 1945. In addition, meetings of the Women's Congress of the Italian Communist party (PCI) and the profeminist position taken at the time by party leaders like Palmiro Togliatti illustrate the increasing concern of Communists for feminist issues.

These developments, however did not come about without difficulty, especially as many women were still caught in the bind of reconciling traditional female roles (in a country notorious for its *maschilismo*) with this increased public political activity. Moreover, Marxist theory itself, in Italy and everywhere else, was very uncertain on many aspects of the "woman question." Yet women played an activist role throughout the party's history up to the eve of World War II, a remarkable feat originally accomplished by a small handful of women. The sacrifices—especially the prison experiences—of this first generation of Italian Communist women provide an essential contribution to the future character of the PCI. Without their work, we could not account for the fact that the PCI, perhaps unique among modern working-class movements, has been able to assimilate a good part of the content of contemporary feminism.

This is not to say that the early *campagne* were "feminists." With the partial exception of Camilla Ravera (born in 1889 and still very active!), almost none even considered the distinction between the emancipation of women and their liberation. Nonetheless, they helped to create the necessary conditions for a higher level of consciousness among women of the Left in Italy.

The number of women enrolled in a communist party gives no more than a rough indication of the role and importance of the "woman question" in that party. In the case of the PCI, it is difficult even to obtain a rough estimate of female membership, since its founding came in 1921 when the activities of the Fascist *squadristi*, well underway, made party life semiclandestine at best. By late 1926, the party was declared illegal and remained so until the fall of Mussolini in July, 1943. While it is doubtful that any complete membership lists were ever compiled during the period or that any have survived even for a single section, it is estimated from the material available that there were 42,841 members in 1921 and 15,285 in 1926.[2] Party influence, of course, was much higher than party membership, and a military report of 1925 from Trieste states that there were "eighty cells, 800 'enrolled and numbered' Communists, and about 5,000 sympathizers."[3] This last group was a very real part of party strength, and in a relative sense, whatever its actual membership, the PCI had a much greater influence than membership—an influence, moreover, that grew strongly between 1921 and 1926. A lengthy police report in the latter year concluded that the Communist party had become the only organized anti-fascist force in nearly every region and the only one presenting any real danger to the regime.[4]

Whatever the difficulties and uncertainties in determining the general level of membership, everyone seems to agree that the actual membership of women in the party was initially very low. At the time of the Fourth Congress of the Communist International in 1922, there were about 400 members, and women's sections existed

in only 96 of 1,200 sections. More than half of the provincial federations had no women members. Apparently, this number fell to
"little more than a hundred" in the following years, returning to
about 300 in the summer of 1926.[5]

These figures, however, are inadequate as a measure of the
importance of Communist women. First of all, they do not include
the Communist Youth Federation, which had about 10,000 members in 1925, many of whom, at least in certain regions, were
women.[6] The history of the Communist youth movement is closely
related to that of party women, since prior to 1921 the youth movement had emphasized political work among women through a
series of regional meetings. Efforts were made to deal with the
political organization of women as a supplement to the traditional
policy of stressing the right of women to an education.[7] The relative
success of this program played a key role in the founding of the
PCI and also achieved political autonomy and permanent representation for youth at the highest levels of the party. This victory,
which was in many ways unique among communist parties of the
time, undoubtedly facilitated later acceptance of a women's secretariat in each major unit of the party.

The activities of these secretariats often took place outside party
lines and without party identification, attracting many party "sympathizers" among women who for family or practical reasons (no
doubt based on sex-role differentiation) did not join subversive
parties during fascist rule. As the Piedmontese anarchist Francesca
Guasco said, "I never took a party card because my husband said:
'At least you'll stay outside [of jail]'."[8]

There were also "auxiliary," or related, organizations like the
International Red Aid (IRA) in which women figured prominently,
though clandestinely. Police generally assumed that women who
were otherwise "clean" worked in the IRA. It was "an organization
for collecting funds for the support of . . . revolutionary figures
and their families, for protecting them before the courts of the
reactionary bourgeoisie and for taking care of political emigrants
who are obliged to flee from the claws of the White Terror."[9] It
also had the task of "enlightening the working masses as to the
significance of the struggle for which the revolutionaries are thrown
into prison and tortured." It was open to "representatives of all

proletarian political parties, trade unions, cooperatives, youth and women's organizations," but was primarily a "communist front." Ruggiero Grieco's report of 1926 to the party central committee stated that "the forces of the Red Aid are constantly growing and are much larger than those of the party . . . [and claimed that the] women's movement [is] assuming an even greater importance [as the mass of women] have demonstrated a fighting spirit superior to that of the male workers."[10]

A number of so-called "groups of Sympathizing Women" were also organized under the leadership of Antonio Gramsci and Camilla Ravera, but apparently they existed only in Turin and Piedmont.[11] Evidence of a much more extensive presence of communist women than party membership would indicate may be found in the large number of women indicted and sentenced after 1926 and in the relatively large circulation of women's publications, especially *La Compagna*.

Strenuous steps were soon taken to check the spread of communism. On November 2, 1926, the Fascist government approved a series of measures known as the "Special Laws," which outlawed all political parties and instituted a Special Tribunal for the defense of the state, thus destroying what remained of a legal opposition by removing the parliamentary mandates of deputies. The main purpose of the Special Tribunal became the trial, conviction, and sentencing of anyone who continued to belong to the political organizations proscribed by the new law or anyone who attempted to "reconstitute" those organizations or to carry out their propaganda. The court was attached to the Ministry of War, was composed of five judges selected from the fascist voluntary militia, and was presided over by a general officer of the army, navy, air force, or voluntary militia.[12] It began its work in December, 1926, and continued to function until July 20, 1943, five days before the fall of Mussolini. In this span of time it pronounced forty-two death sentences (thirty-one of which were carried out) and condemned 4,956 persons to major sentences.[13]

In addition, an undetermined number of essentially political prisoners were tried and sentenced by the ordinary courts, by the military, or by the special commissions established by the Special Tribunal itself. About 90 percent of those convicted were Communists or alleged Communists. Most, in fact, freely admitted party membership, if little else, during their trials.[14]

As far as can be determined, 124 women faced trial by the Special Tribunal between 1926 and 1943. From 1939 to 1943, 49 others were remanded by the tribunal to ordinary courts for lesser trials.[15] About 175 women were sentenced to *confino* (essentially house arrest in a remote southern village or on an island off the coast), while another 150 or so were placed in confinement by other "judicial" elements of the fascist regime.[16] Rarely if ever in the history of the West has any national group of women been so exposed to the fury of legal authority.

Who were these women? What were their political, class, regional, and age characteristics? It is possible to answer these questions with some precision, at least with regard to the hundred women sentenced by the tribunal through November, 1941, when record keeping was at its most meticulous.[17] Politically, fifty-five were convicted as Communists, three as anarchists, one as a Socialist, four as Jehovah's Witnesses, and twenty-eight as militant antifascists (liberals, socialists, and communists).[18]

Of the ninety-nine women identified by occupation, thirty described as housewives, but a random sample of the cases indicates that use of that term was prompted either by the sexism or indolence of the court clerks, since the great majority of the "housewives" unquestionably were working-class women with considerable work experience.[19] Of the remaining sixty-nine women, twenty-nine were explicitly labeled as workers while nine were classified as clerks or typists, seven as being in service industries, four as small business operators, and nine "intellectuals" (a nurse, a painter, a dancer, two students, five teachers, and one professor). In fact, all but the "intellectuals" and perhaps four or five of the housewives were of the working class.

Since PCI membership in the 1920s was very young, it was not surprising that the imprisoned women, mostly communist, also were young; forty-nine of the ninety-three whose ages were stated were under thirty, while thirty-one were in their thirties, eleven in their forties, and two were more than fifty. And since the PCI was essentially a party of the North and a few regions of central Italy, it also is not surprising that of the ninety-six women identified by province of birth, seventy-seven came from these areas and four were from the South or the islands, while the remaining thirteen were scattered among the other regions.

The profile of a typical female prisoner in fascist Italy in this period indicates that she would be a Communist of working-class origin from northern or north central Italy, in her late twenties, with five children (low for the time and society) and a Communist husband or comrade either also serving a prison term or living in France or the Soviet Union.[20]

Fortunately for the historian, the experiences and attitudes of the women Communist political prisoners are well documented by their individual memoirs as well as in serious histories written by party members.[21] These records indicate the anguish these women suffered as the conflict between their roles as wives and mothers and their devotion to the party took on a very real form through the prison experience.

Since many prisoners were held for a year or more before trial in institutions near the scene of their "crimes," political women were often kept in all the major prisons of the country.[22] In fascist Italy, however, there were just three prisons used for the long-term incarceration of women. Of these, only those at Trani in Apulia and at Perugia in Umbria housed political prisoners, with Perugia having by far the worst reputation.[23]

Long-term imprisonment is difficult for all inmates, but it is particularly agonizing for political prisoners. In some very important respects the political Italian women found it even more onerous than usual. They suffered especially because of their relative isolation, limited opportunities given for reading and study, their stand on the religious question, and the problem of their children and the care they received.

Camilla Ravera, the Turinese Communist who was one of the most important leaders of the party, spent the period from 1930 to 1943 either in prison or in *confino* (close house arrest). She spoke very directly on the problem of isolation.

> The male antifascist prisoners were much more numerous than the women. They could live together in dormitories, talk, discuss and

study together; or, by groups they could continue to some extent a certain political life. Instead, the women, given their much smaller number, were generally isolated and rarely met each other.[24]

Meanwhile, the conditions in which the women lived are worthy of note. Cesira Fiori, a Roman Communist arrested in 1933, spent four months of nearly complete isolation in appalling circumstances.

> "We have reserved for you," [said her guard], "the finest room in our institution—the one they pay for." There wasn't a trace of irony on the lips of Sister Romualda. But what a cell! A humid icebox with a narrow bed like a coffin, a mattress of cornleaves and a niche in the wall to serve as a shelf. I didn't see the window, but when I raised my eyes I discerned the opening in a corner near the high ceiling. That little square was not wider than a foot.[25]

Adele Bei, a Communist from the Marches who had been arrested in 1933, spent one year in complete isolation in a cell similar to Fiori's.[26] The prison in Perugia, she testified, was made "in such a way that the prisoner can see absolutely nothing outside except a tiny section of the sky when looking up. All the cell windows are internal and located on courtyards. Thus for eight years I saw nothing of the outside world except that little piece of sky."[27]

One of the worst spiritual problems for these women was the near impossibility of finding appropriate books to read and study. There were no libraries in the women's prisons save for a few books on the lives of the saints. "What a difference between our libraries and those of the men!" wrote Felicita Ferrero.[28] The reason for this lack of books arose from the fact that before the advent of political prisoners, most women jailed were peasants destroyed by the "idiocy of rural life" and incarcerated for crimes of rage, passion, and madness. The jailers of Trani insisted that previously "no prisoner had ever asked for a book." In fact, they were opposed to *any* books in the prison, "frankly maintain[ing] the position that women ought not learn to read. They thought that the antifascists had rebelled against authority because they *had* learned to read, and had read books which misled and corrupted them."[29]

Through insistent demands, the hesitant cooperation of a few prison officials, and outside aid, the Communist prisoners were partly able to overcome the most barbaric aspects of this attitude. But another aspect of the prison regime was never resolved: the staffing of the prisons almost exclusively with nuns. Except for the director (invariably, so far as I know, a man), the nuns made up the central element in the administration of women's prisons in fascist Italy. Many of the nuns, moreover, were particularly innocent.

> They had lived their whole lives in a convent or in a prison. They all had the same story. As little girls they entered the convent, either because they were orphans or through other circumstances. They grew up there until they were eighteen; then they became nuns and were employed as prison guards, and in the prisons they remained. They never went out and knew nothing of the world outside, its struggles and its problems. . . . They believed the strangest things with the greatest certainty. For them the prison was a kind of nunnery or shelter for women who had committed crimes and who therefore had to accept and submit to penitence. The penitence was handed out by the authorities: it was therefore just and was to be totally accepted with complete submission.[30]

The consequences of this world view obviously made life very difficult for the political prisoners, most of whom were atheists. When Cesira Fiori arrived in Perugia, she was immediately asked to state her religion. " 'Non-professing Catholic,' she replied. After a little gasp of horror, a nun said, 'Of course you politicos all say that when you come in. But you'll see that you too will change like the others.' " Fiori angrily replied that the nuns would not succeed with her. They did not, in fact, but resisting was not easy. After Fiori had asked for a book, or indeed anything to read, a nun responded, "If you will say 'Jesus be praised,' I'll bring you something. But here you must not be in a hurry." It was the same story when the first letters arrived from her family. "If you say to me 'Jesus and Mary be praised,' you'll see what I have to show you. If you don't say it, you'll have to wait."[31]

It is understandable that some women found it difficult to resist pressures of this kind. Such was the case of Felicita Ferrero:

> I rarely saw the sour director but was in daily, even hourly contact with the nuns. I therefore immediately considered the problem of

whether to have them as friends or enemies. . . . I understood that the determining factor for them was whether or not the prisoner accepted religious practices. Although I was well aware that a perfect communist did not go to church, I did not see the political necessity of refusal at any cost.[32]

In short, she began to attend mass, and very soon her transgression became known in party circles as far away as Paris and Moscow.[33] Poor Felicita!! For years after her release and escape from Italy she had to repeat the same "self-criticism" to party functionaries. In those days there was no "historical compromise" with Catholicism that exists as PCI policy today.

Of all the problems faced by these Communist women, the most difficult to convey to a contemporary reader is the sense of anguish which they felt about their children. It is difficult to understand the concurrent existence in these extraordinary women of two such ostensibly contradictory values. On one hand they were wholly dedicated to the class struggle, to antifascism, and to that party which they thought represented the best future for humanity. On the other, they were thoroughly conventional, even traditional mothers who did not find the two roles contradictory, though the long struggle to reconcile them was in some cases overwhelming.

The most revealing treatment of this whole problem can be found in the memoirs of Teresa Noce. "Estella" (her *nom de bataille*) was one of the most remarkable personalities of Italian communism (she died on January 22, 1980). She was born in Turin in a working-class family, began working herself before she was ten, and then participated in the labor movement and the Socialist party. Noce was among the founders of the Communist party in 1921 and quickly won a reputation for herself as an organizer and journalist. In 1926 she traveled to Moscow for further party education, after which she lived in Paris between 1931 and 1934, making several clandestine trips to Italy during this period to organize trade union antifascism. In 1936 she went to Spain as an organizer and journalist with the International Brigades. Returning to France, she worked with the Resistance movement during World War II until 1943, when she was arrested and deported to the death camps of Ravensbruck and Holleischen, which she survived after harrowing experiences. In 1945 she returned to Italy and was elected to the parliament while at the same time working as a trade union leader and a member of the PCI Central Committee from 1933 to 1958 and in the party leadership from 1945 to 1954.

At the same time that she pursued her political career, Noce also had two children with Luigi Longo, now president of the PCI. Luigi (Gigi) was born in 1923 and Giuseppe (Puccio or Putisc) in 1929. Like most other Communist women, she tried to keep her children with her, but her dangerous and frequently unsettled life made this impossible.

For a time Noce sometimes left the children with relatives. Thus Gigi stayed with Longo's parents near Turin in 1927-1928 while she attended school in Moscow.[34] Later on, she found a variety of expedients for "child care." For example, Gigi and Putisc stayed in a boarding school in the Paris suburbs from 1931 to 1934, when she was engaged in periodic trips to Italy and thus constantly subject to arrest. In 1934, after the family had spent some months in Moscow, Gigi was sent to the International Children's House, a special school in Ivanovov for the children of foreign comrades who were victims of fascism and reaction. When Noce went to Spain in 1936, Putisc stayed in Paris with the family of comrades Olga and Ambrogio Donini. Gigi returned to Paris to live with his parents in 1939, but with the German invasion of France in 1940, both children were sent back to Moscow where they remained until the liberation in 1945.

All this represents a terrible odyssey for young children; indeed, they did have some desperate moments. When Noce was about to leave for Italy in 1932, for instance, she told her children that she could return for a few weeks. "Gigi, sad and gloomy, looked at me and then ran almost savagely into my arms. Puccio threw himself on the gate and desperately cried 'Maman Maman!' " Again, in 1934 when Noce was about to leave Gigi in Moscow, the boy said, "You know, Mama, I understand why Puccio is going back to Paris with you. It's not just because he's still little, but also because you couldn't live without at least one child." About to depart for Spain in 1936, Noce felt she had to have Puccio's authorization. After a long discussion in which she tried to explain why she and Longo had to work in Spain, the boy said, "That's all right. You can go to Spain and I'll find another mama.''[35] Apparently the pain that these remarks reveal (and at the same time conceal) was overcome in 1939 when Gigi, then sixteen years old, told his mother that "If I could choose my life, I would choose yours."[36]

Noce's separations from her children were a constant personal torment. After safely crossing the French border on one of her trips to Italy, she muttered to herself, "Puccio, *maman* is coming back."[37] At the same time she never had any doubt that her part in the struggle against fascism was also one to defend the rights of her children and all the other children of Italy. Adele Bei, whose two children also attended the International Children's House, expressed the same sentiment in a statement to the chief justice of the Special Tribunal: "In my activity as a communist, I am also carrying out my duty as a mother."[38] Noce insisted, in fact, that being a mother improved her underground work. "I left for Italy with Puccio's cry ringing in my heart. Every evening for the whole time I stayed inside Italy, I made a kind of self-critical examination of my conspiratorial behavior during the day. I would not be arrested. I wanted to return to Puccio, to my children. Contrary to what some might believe, the thought of my children gave me strength and made me work better by forcing me to be prudent."[39]

The preceding pages can give only the barest indication of these women's tribulations, whether they were in prison, in exile, or in the underground. But their suffering had its rewards, since their careers in the Resistance movement gave "living testimony," as Nilde Jotti expressed it, of "a new type of woman" which had developed in the struggle against fascism.[40] Noce's own remembrance of the change in the life of one of her comrades reveals this same transition.

> Some years ago I went to visit Vera Ciceri Invernizzi in a hospital in Milan where she had had a serious operation. Happy to see me and recalling those meetings a long time ago in Paris, the dear comrade said to me: "Just think! If you hadn't recruited me I'd have stayed a housewife my whole life and thought of nothing but washing floors and cooking for my husband. Thanks to you I became a communist and have had a beautiful and intersting life."

"Beautiful life indeed!" thought Noce, since Ciceri had spent five years in prison and two years in the underground during the Resistance. "It occurred to me that a party with cadres like this working class woman was truly a great party."[41]

The fascist years thus brought many women into active political lives, though the cost was often almost unbearable. After 1945, the struggle for women's liberation still seemed formidable, but the sacrifices and conquests of the past had at least opened the road for future gains.

NOTES

1. Nadia Spano and Fiamma Camarlinghi, *La questione femminile nella politica del PCI* (Rome: Edizioni Donne e Politica, 1972), p. 92. These figures are probably considerably below the real numbers. On this and related points see Anna Maria Bruzzone and Rachele Farina, eds., *La Resistenza taciuta: Dodici vite de partigiane piemontesi* (Milan: La Pietra, 1976), pp. 10-12.

2. For estimates of party membership see Renzo Martinelli, *Il partito comunista italiano, 1921-1926* (Rome: Riuniti, 1977).

3. Archivo Centrale dello Stato (ACS), Rome. Ministero degli Interni. Direzione Pubblica Sicurezza. Divisione Affari Generali e Riservati, Atti Speciali, Busta 102.

4. "I partiti antifascisti," Appendix 1, pp. 593-602, in Pietro Secchia, *L'azione svolta dal partito comunista in Italia durante il Fascismo, 1926-1932* (Milan: Feltrinelli, 1970).

5. Archivio del Parito Comunista (APC), Rome. Fasciolo 87, Fogli 16-45. Foglio 23: "Relazione del PC d'I al IV Congresso dell 'Internazionale." APC 323/2, "C. E./Segretariato femminile" (March 15, 1926); APC 393/30, Morelli (Mauro Scoccimarro) to the Central Committee of the PC d'I (August, 1926); Martinelli, *Il partito comunista*, pp. 172, 287 fn. 52, and Spano and Camarlinghi, *La questione femminile*, p. 17.

6. ACS, Categoria K.1, Busta 102, Circolare no. 14 (April 2, 1925). There were nearly 60,000 members of the Socialist Youth Federation in 1920; the great majority supported the founding of the PC d'I at the beginning of the next year.

7. "La donna nella vita civile," *L'Avanguardia* 14, no. 46 (December 5, 1920), cited in Martinelli, *Il partito comunista*, p. 98 fn. 121.

8. Bianca Giudetti Serra, ed., *Compagne: Testimonianze di partecipa-*

zione politica femminile, 2 vols. (Turin: Einaudi, 1977), 1: 19. Unfortunately, this discretion helped her very little, as she spent four months in prison and two years of house arrest.

9. Israel Amter, "First World Conference of the International Red Relief," *Imprecorr* (July 31, 1925): 557.

10. APC, 393/27 and 393/28.

11. Camilla Ravera, "Come nacque nel PCI una politica per l'emancipazione femminile," *Donne e Politica* 2, no. 5-6 (February, 1971): 6.

12. "La legge 25 novembre 1926, n. 2008," reprinted in Adriano Dal Pont, *Tutti i processi del tribunale speciale fascista*, 2d. ed. (Milan: La Pietra, 1976), pp. 551-53.

13. Berardo Taddei, *Donne processate dal tribunale speciale, 1927-1943*, 4th ed. (Verona: G. Grazia Editore, 1969), p. 12.

14. See Paolo Spriano, *Storia del partito comunista italiano*, vol. 1 (Turin: Einaudi, 1969), and Giorgio Amendola, *Storia del partito comunista italiano, 1921-1943* (Rome: Riuniti, 1978).

15. See Taddei, *Donne processate*, passim.

16. A list of the *confinati* can be found in Celso Ghini and Adriano Dal Pont, *Gli antifascisti al confino* (Rome: Riuniti, 1971). There were also hundreds of women who voluntarily joined their comrades in *confino* that did not appear in the figures. For examples, see Lidia Mancinelli, "Sciopero all'Imola," in Celso Ghini and Adriano Dal Pont, *Gli antifacsiste al confino* (Rome: Riuniti, 1971), pp. 273-75; Giovanna Marturano Grifone, "Al piedi della Maiella," ibid., pp. 281-87; see also Emma Turchi, *La felicità è la lotta* (Venice: Marsilio, 1976).

17. The main sources used here are those previously cited by Taddei, *Donne processate*, and Dal Pont, *Tutti i processi*. A thorough examination of the more than 25,000 individual files of the Fascist period in the *Casellario Politico Centrale* of the ACS would give a more comprehensive answer.

18. Taddei, *Donne processate*, p. 79, observes that beginning in 1936 "the press did not employ the expression Communist Party or other parties regarding the trials of the Special Tribunal." On the Jehovah's Witnesses, many of whom were women who regarded "Hitler, Mussolini and especially the Pope as AntiChrists," see Altiero Spinelli, *Il lungo monologo* (Rome: Edizioni dell'Ateneo, 1968), pp. 97-105.

19. For example, three of the women described as housewives—Iside Viana, Lea Giaccaglia, and Maria Selvatici—were actually working women. Taddei, *Donne processate*, pp. 47, 49, 51; ACS/CPC, "Giaccaglia, Lea," and Melchiorre Vanni, "Ricordo di Lea," *Lo stato operaio* 10, no. 10 1936): 726-28.

20. The last two observations are, I think, accurate; but they are necessarily more impressionistic than statistical.

21. For a good introduction to this literature, see Franco Andreucci and Malcolm Sylvers, "The Italian Communists Write Their Own History," *Science and Society* 40, no. 2 (1976): 28-56. Some of the best available materials are *Lettere di antifascisti dal carcere e dal confino*, vol. 2, 2nd ed. (Rome: Riuniti, 1976); *Enciclopedia dell'antifascismo e della Resistenza*, vol. 1 (Milan: La Pietra, 1966); Cesira Fiori, *Una donna nelle carceri fasciste* (Rome: Riuniti, 1965); Teresa Noce, *Rivoluzionaria professionale* (Milan: La Pietra, 1974); Camilla Ravera, *Vita in carcere e al confino* (Parma: Guando, 1969); Bianca Giudetti Serra, ed., *Compagne: Testimonianze di partecipazione politica femminile*, 2 vols. (Turin: Einaudi, 1977).

22. Felicita Ferrero, *Un nocciolo di verita* (Milan: La Pietra, 1978), pp. 62-63, notes that she spent nine months in the "Nuove" in Turin before being transferred to Rome for her trial by the Special Tribunal.

23. Ibid., pp. 67-68, mentions a prison rumor of the time that "women overwhelmed by the work at Perugia were then sent to die at Trani." Fiori, *Una donna nelle carceri*, p. 70, asserts that "the penitentiary in Perugia which in addition to the regular prison has the section for women lifers, is one of the worst in Italy. In comparison to it, the Mantellate [in Rome] is like a pleasure trip."

24. Camilla Ravera, *Diario di trent'anni, 1913-1943* (Rome: Riuniti, 1973), p. 536. See also her contributions on this and related points in Altiero Spinelli, "Gli antifascisti in galera," in Nino Valeri, ed., *Lezioni sull'antifascismo* (Bari: Laterza, 1960), pp. 156-57, 160-62.

25. Fiori, *Una donna nelle carceri*, p. 66.

26. Bei in *Lettere di antifascisti dal carcere* 2: 43.

27. "Dal carcere di Perugia a Ventotene," in Ghini and Dal Pont, *Gli antifascisti*, p. 210.

28. Ferrero, *Un nocciolo*, p. 75.

29. Ravera, *Diario*, p. 538.

30. Ibid., pp. 536-37.

31. Fiori, *Una donna nelle carceri*, pp. 66, 73, 94.

32. Ferrero, *Un nocciolo*, pp. 72-73.

33. Noce, *Rivoluzionaria professionale*, p. 235. Noce states that both Ravera and Ferrero attended mass at Trani, but there is no other evidence that the former was involved. Cf. Ferrero, *Un nocciolo*, pp. 78, 80, for Ravera's comportment at the time.

34. Noce describes Longo's parents as "petty bourgeois," who heartily disapproved of their son's liaison with a raucous tribune of the people.

Nonetheless, they were happy to keep their grandson. Noce, *Rivoluzionaria professionale*, pp. 113-14.

35. Ibid., pp. 146, 164, 187.

36. Ibid., p. 213. She adds that "luckily for him, he didn't have my life. But anyway I was grateful for his words."

37. Ibid., p. 150.

38. Ibid., p. 149, and Adele Bei, "Con l'attività di comunista si assolve anche il dovere di madre," in Stefano Merli, ed., *Autodifese di militanti operai e democratici italiani davanti ai tribunali* (Milan: Edizioni Avanti!, 1958), p. 234. Bei's letters to her children are included in *Lettere di antifascisti* 2: 43-58.

39. Noce, *Rivoluzionaria professionale*, p. 146.

40. Nilde Jotti, "Da Turati all'elaborazione del PCI," *Rinascita* 18, no. 3 (1961): 219.

41. Noce, *Rivoluzionaria professionale*, p. 128. See also Ciceri's dossier in ACS/CPC.

9.
Humanism versus Feminism in the Socialist Movement: The Life of Angelica Balabanoff

JANE SLAUGHTER

When Angelica Balabanoff died in Rome on November 25, 1965, at the age of eighty-seven, an obituary referred to her as "one of the most striking personalities of the International Socialist Movement."[1] Her life since 1878 was marked by activism in a wide range of radical causes. As a leader of the Italian Socialist party (PSI) and later of the Italian Social Democrats as well as an intransigent antifascist and a dedicated humanist, Balabanoff was a key figure in the history of European radical politics.

Her experience, motivation, and attitude are also highly characteristic of general patterns discerned by scholars currently interested in the particular relationship of women to radical public activism. Sensitivity to others, denial of self-interest, and devotion to an egalitarian ethic provided the form and substance of her life. Marxist socialism furnished a structure through which these values found action. Balabanoff rejected bourgeois female roles and was always concerned with women's problems and condition, but this could be justified only through dedication to a higher ideal. Her world, after all, still preserved the notion of a woman's sphere in which self-sacrifice and female "moral superiority" furnished the only acceptable motivation for activism. Thus devotion to a "higher cause" justified and made her behavior appropriate.[2] This same devotion, however, made it difficult for Balabanoff to resist a party line and insist on women's rights, since this smacked of "self-interest" to her.

Recent study of women in the "old Left" points out "a distinct

culture of personal relations" for those movements.[3] They faced
inevitable conflicts between their personal lives and their commitment to political action, until "all personal doubts and gains got
submerged beneath party language." In essence, personal needs
became "privatized" and personal liberation did not figure prominently as a motive for personal action. Balabanoff recognized
this conflict and stated that

> though I became materialist many, many years ago, and also know
> how frail everything and everybody is, and though I sincerely want
> everybody to enjoy life . . . life taught me to distinguish that feeling
> and sentiment is one thing—reasoning is another.[4]

The guideline for her own life was clear; "there has never been any
conflict between my heart and my brain."[5]

Many women leaders of the early radical movements, "political
career women, without husbands and children . . . to participate [in
political activities], were ready to become freed from emotional
family ties or entanglements."[6] This aptly describes Balabanoff:
"the cause to which her life was devoted absorbed her whole being
to the exclusion of any life outside the political sphere."[7]

It is also important to note that in the span of her life, Balabanoff
saw incredible changes take place in European society and in popular
attitudes toward politics. Particularly after 1945, traditional socialism lost its revolutionary potential. Individuals with their roots in
the "old days" expressed disillusionment and frustration, and
reassessment of goals and values seemed necessary. Balabanoff's
attempts to adjust to change are clear not only in personal expressions and a shift in the focus of her activism, but also in a concern
for "the changes in certain socialist movements in Italy. I don't
speak of exterior defeats; they interest me much less than the psychological attitudes of the leaders as well as the rank and file."[8] One
can only guess at the difficulty she felt in reconciling these new
feelings with the "belief in and opportunity to live for an ideal that
has satisfied all my emotional and intellectual aspirations."[9]

Balabanoff, who entered the Italian socialist movement under
the influence of revolutionary Marxists like Antonio Labriola,
remained critical of reformist pragmatism. As a believer in the

revolutionary potential of the proletariat she found the party politics of Bolshevik Russia unacceptable, resisting any alliance with communist parties both on the international "popular front" level and, after 1947, in internal Italian politics. Her insistence on "questions of principle" and the popular nature of the revolutionary process led others to define her as intransigent, idealistic, and even romantic.[10]

Angelica Balabanoff was born in 1878, the youngest daughter of a wealthy landowning family in the Ukraine. "Her mother was determined to make of this, her last daughter, a 'fine lady.' Surrounded by governesses who taught her many languages and the graces considered proper . . . she was kept away from school and playmates, taught good manners, music, dancing, embroidery and the propriety of charitable deeds."[11] Inquisitiveness and active intelligence made her aware of the contrast between her life of ease and the poverty of family workers, and of the paternal character of her social order. Angelica noticed "the existence of beings who suffered, who had to obey. . . . I began to ask why my mother commanded and others obeyed. . . . Always and above all I wanted to find the 'why' and 'how' of things."[12] Trips to Switzerland and the spas of Europe along with conversations with friends about Western European university life led her to reject her mother's matrimonial plans and insist on an education to enable her to realize the dream of helping others. Balabanoff's mother, worn down by this insistence, eventually gave in, but for a price; Angelica renounced all claim to her father's estate and, accepting a small allowance, set off for the Université Nouvelle in Brussels.

The university exposed her to radical political thought, labor history, and "revolutionary explanations for inequalities she had observed at home."[13] She earned a degree in languages, but her real interest was socialism. She developed strong attachments to a number of Italian radicals and eventually traveled to Rome in 1902 to become a member of the Italian Socialist party. Her first important act, organizing Italian immigrant laborers in the textile mills of St. Gall, Switzerland, lasted until 1906 and carried no salary, a feature that became characteristic of her entire life's work. Like many other young women of her time, Balabanoff, through a series of personal experiences at a relatively young age, found a lifelong career and a cause to which she remained devoted for the rest of her life.

At St. Gall, Balabanoff gave her first public speech and also displayed her facility with languages. These talents brought her to the notice of PSI leaders and provided a basis for the influence she later exercised in party activities. She became increasingly active in socialist politics between 1907 and 1914 on both the national and international levels, attending most national party congresses in these years, working with Benito Mussolini in Milan on the publication of *Avanti!*, the party paper, and in 1912 won election to the party executive for the first time. She also maintained contact with the Russian revolutionary movement in exile and attended meetings of the Second International, first as an observer and translator but eventually as an official delegate to the 1912 meetings in Basel. Balabanoff was tied ideologically to the "Left" or revolutionary faction within Italian socialism of the time. On the international level her zealous commitment to the brotherhood of the working class made it hard for her to accept national party differences and political infighting.[14]

At the time that Balabanoff joined the PSI, concern for the emancipation of women was already a stated party goal largely through the work of Anna Kuliscioff.[15] Party congresses debated the issues of woman suffrage and the organization and recruitment of women as well as questions relating to "moral life" and the family. The latter issues, unfortunately, never received a serious, in-depth analysis, with the party always seeking to distinguish its concern for women's condition from that of bourgeois feminism. Kuliscioff, Maria Gioia, Carlotta Clerici, and others ultimately succeeded in founding a Union of Women Socialists; Balabanoff soon served on its executive committee.

She also attended the 1907 meeting of the International at Stuttgart to witness Clara Zetkin's efforts to create an International Women's Secretariat. In 1910 and 1912 Balabanoff represented Italy at the women's congresses in Copenhagen and worked with Zetkin to arrange a meeting at Bern, Switzerland, for March, 1915, to present a unified front against the war that had been raging for eight months.[16] It is clear from her own writings and the records of these meetings that she was concerned about the experiences of women as workers, mothers, and political activists during this period.[17]

At the same time, while many other socialist women faced the contradictions in the relation of socialist theory to women (denying, for instance, that feminism could be subsumed simply within socialism, or challenging the inevitability of women's emancipation under socialism), Balabanoff did not confront these difficulties.[18] She worked with Maria Giudice on a women's periodical, *Su, Compagne*, but for her feminism was a concept linked with the bourgeoisie, and women's rights were only a segment of the broader struggle. She believed socialism meant "absolute social equality. That note from which I derive my constant intransigence has always been the dominant one. . . . Thus I don't believe it necessary to dedicate myself in a special way, that is, separately, to antimilitarist, anticlerical questions, to that of women's emancipation."[19]

Meanwhile, the European socialists in 1912 debated what positions the national parties would take if a war began. For some, this sort of controversy seemed symbolic of the inability of the Second International to foster revolutionary proletarian unity. Balabanoff remained steadfast in support of peace and neutrality, regarding the International as the only organization that could effectively mobilize working-class opposition. She worked tirelessly in the socialist peace movement, supporting the PSI's adoption of a neutrality resolution; and along with the Swiss socialist, Robert Grimm, helping to organize the International meetings at Zimmerwald and Kienthal in 1915-1916.[20]

Balabanoff hoped that these meetings could present a solid front of socialist antiwar opposition, but though an International Socialist Commission was chosen to act in an executive capacity, unity never materialized. On one hand, some socialists, including several Italian representatives, felt that signing a resolution against the war was imprudent if they came from warring countries; on the other hand, Lenin and his supporters hoped for a denunciation of the Second International and organization of a countermovement. Balabanoff adhered to a center position, supporting Lenin's analysis of the war as imperialist, but she remained unwilling to abandon the Second International altogether because, as she put it, the International remained the only organization adequately expressing "the unity of the international proletariat."[21]

Balabanoff's disillusionment with the outcome of these efforts soon was reinforced by her reaction to the Bern conference of women in March, 1915. Bolshevik representatives, including Inessa Armand and Nadezhda Krupskaya, proposed a resolution denouncing the socialist parties of belligerent nations and calling for a break with the International. Although the resolution did not pass, it divided the conference and caused Balabanoff to criticize Lenin for encouraging an action that disrupted the unanimity of the women's group.[22]

Balabanoff stayed with the International Commission through most of the war, but her disappointment grew as European socialists became more and more divided over the issue of neutrality. At "home" in the women's sections of the PSI the division became evident as various factions favored entry into the war on the side of the *Entente*, but Balabanoff held to her Bern position.[23] While she once said she would never focus upon a single issue like antimilitarism, in fact she did just that, justifying this position on the grounds of proletarian unity. Perhaps it was fortunate for her that the Russian Revolution began in the spring of 1917. Fading hope for international socialist unity now could be replaced by another "higher cause"—that of the egalitarian revolution in Russia. Her humanistic ideals seized upon the hope that her old homeland might be drastically changed, but the reality of these changes was very different from what she imagined in 1917.

Balabanoff arrived in Russia shortly after the Bolshevik triumph and soon was working actively to win support for the revolution among various European socialist parties. For a brief period she served as commissar for foreign affairs in Kiev, but in 1919, as preparations began for the First Congress of the Third International (Comintern), she was recalled to Moscow. Lenin appointed her secretary of the International, and although she refused the post at first in order to continue propaganda activity among the masses, she finally did serve in the post from May to October, 1919.

While she was thus involved, women like Alexandra Kollontai and Inessa Armand organized Bolshevik women and created a Women's Union. Balabanoff supported the organizing of working-

class women and wrote several pamphlets on women's liberation—
among them a denunciation of the *Baryshnyas*, "young ladies from
petty-bourgeois families accustomed to idleness and being kept by
men of wealth and position."[24] She also maintained that when
asked to assume leadership responsibilities in the Women's Union,
she refused because she claimed to have neither the interest nor the
talent for such work.[25]

As secretary of the International she began to feel real disen-
chantment with party politics and intrigue, particularly on the part
of G. E. Zinoviev, a man she detested even though they worked
together on international affairs sucessfully for a time. Victor
Serge describes her as secretary: "Perpetually active, she hoped for
an International that was unconfined, open-hearted and rather
romantic."[26] She became sadly disappointed, however, on a number
of counts, continuing to feel that her most effective role was in
propagandizing the people. Reports of terrorism by the Bolsheviks
also appalled her; she considered this "organized systematic violence" of the type "inherent in capitalism" and not related to the
revolutionary goals of liberty, equality, and justice.[27] Her personal
dislike for Zinoviev was compounded by the fact that she felt a
sense of being used to gain adherents to the new Comintern. In the
spring of 1920 she helped organize and prepare for the meeting of
the Second Congress, but by July her faith in the revolution seemed
badly shaken. When ordered on a propaganda mission to Turkestan
(for which she felt entirely unsuited, since she did not know the
language or culture), she refused to go. This meant her eventual
dismissal from the party executive, but by then she realized she
could not stay in Russia.

During meetings of the Second Congress (July-August, 1920)
Balabanoff's resistance to Bolshevik tactics deepened as she witnessed pressure put on her PSI colleagues to adhere to the ideology
and platform of the Third International and to expel its reformist
faction. The issue of dissent from established doctrine was clearly
in her mind when she wrote: "You have to choose between what
you conceive to be your duty, between your personal dignity and
honesty, and your collaboration with this institution. . . . You can't
expect a revolutionist to remain indifferent when methods he considers damaging are applied to the movement he is supposed to

serve."[28] She requested permission to leave Russia, and Lenin eventually complied with the request late in 1921. Even though deeply disappointed in the revolution's tactics. Balabanoff never openly condemned Lenin and always retained a certain respect for him. Her account of their last meeting indicates a mutual sadness at their estrangement.[29] During this period, she had not wavered in what she believed to be the true work of socialists; that is, the education of the masses toward a consciousness of their human and social rights resulting in a spontaneous mass movement that would inevitably lead to an egalitarian society.

Balabanoff's return to Europe and subsequent reintegration into Italian socialist activities coincided with the rise of Italian fascism. After 1925, she found it expedient, like most other radical political leaders, to take up French and Swiss residence as an exile. These circumstances meant that for the next two decades her energies would be focused on antifascism.

Balabanoff began this exile period by assuming the editorship of the Paris *Avanti!* in 1928; two years later she became the Socialist party secretary. Ideological divisions, however, already had badly fragmented the PSI. One group withdrew in 1921 to form the Italian Communist party (PCI), and in 1922 the remaining majority Socialists voted to expel the reformist faction led by Filippo Turati. Italian socialists hereafter struggled with little success to recreate a unified front essential to any sort of effective opposition to fascism. For Balabanoff, there could be no compromise with the PCI or with the reformists, since she considered them on the left or right of the "true" workers' movement.[30] This position provoked a harsh statement by Turati that when distinguishing between Left and Right, Balabanoff had "the brain of a chicken."[31] Other socialists like Pietro Nenni criticized her lack of a critical assessment of events since 1919 and insisted that pragmatic necessity called for unity. By 1934 a majority of Italian socialists reunited to sign a pact of unity with the PCI, but Balabanoff and a small group remained outside this union, maintaining an independent organization and continuing to publish *Avanti!*

Disagreement with her socialist colleagues in these years did not alter Balabanoff's commitment to educating the masses to socialism and to turning them against fascism. She produced numerous essays, pamphlets, and newspaper articles intended to provide in simple language basic instruction for the working class to the goals, promises, and hopes of socialism. She also continued to publish exposés about fascist politics and to report on the experiences of its victims.[32] In 1935 she traveled on a speaking tour to the United States to raise funds to fight fascism, and although she continued to communicate with her socialist comrades in Europe and to write for *Avanti!*, she remained in the U.S.A. until the end of the war.

Living in New York, she discovered support for Mussolini in some Italian-American and conservative circles before the United States entered World War II, and so she edited and wrote a small periodical, *Il Traditore*, which between January, 1942, and May, 1943, contained a series of articles describing Mussolini's early years, his persecution of socialists, and the fascist record of assassinations and brutality in Italy.[33] She also, more generally, attacked Stalin and international communism as betrayers of the workers' movement, calling Nenni and the PSI tools of the Comintern.[34] Throughout the war she called out again and again for the improvement of working-class conditions, social justice, and the creation of a humane society to replace that being destroyed by the war. Not surprisingly, however, the practicalities of a transition to socialist society remained nebulous in her writings and were overshadowed by her ethical humanism. This became evident in several interviews with American journalists. One writer noted that "her single most remarkable trait [is] her total integrity, which is why she fail[ed] in the game of power politics"; while another wrote that "to listen to her soft, compassionate voice, telling of the suffering of the people of Italy and all over Europe . . . is to understand that revolutionary faith can be synonymous with humanitarianism."[35]

During the war, of course, feminism within the socialist and communist parties remained almost nonexistent. The Left concentrated on antifascism wherever possible and wrestled with numerous theoretical and tactical differences that needed to be reconciled in order to present a united front. Clearly antifascism superseded all other concerns, and emphasis on feminism no longer played a part in practical politics. Mainstream socialist leaders and organizations, even before 1918, considered the "woman question" important but clearly secondary to political and economic issues. Now, with war and fascism dominating European politics, it was almost impossible to mention feminist issues. Women party members, highly visible in antifascist activism, mobilized as workers against fascism. Balabanoff's position was characteristic of the general movement and in keeping with her previous view that women's rights issues were secondary to the question of the workers' struggle. She sought to make proletarian women and men aware of capitalistic society as their common enemy, but she was most sympathetic to women, since they often bore the burdens of class oppression as well as the brunt of fascism and war. Balabanoff became highly emotional when describing their suffering and hoped to rouse women from their passivity.[36]

After 1945 Balabanoff resumed her commitment to activism in Italian working-class politics and was able to return to her adopted home in time for the national meeting of the socialists at Palazzo Barberini in January, 1947. Her role at that meeting resembled the one she played earlier. Though the socialists had managed to maintain a tentative unity and cooperation with the PCI during the Resistance and postwar reorganization of Italian politics, another split occurred in 1947. A minority group led by Giuseppe Saragat, encouraged and supported by Dalabanoff, joined with other small splinter groups to form the Italian Social Democratic party (SD), and a year later entered a new four-party "center" cabinet dominated by the Christian Democrats. The major point of disagreement became the traditional problem of cooperation with other parties. Balabanoff's intransigence once again took concrete form in refusing to affiliate with the PCI because "the communist movement does not represent a party, since a party must represent the views and interest of a given country, and not be led by Moscow's agents."[37]

As a member of the SD executive, Balabanoff participated in national party congresses and often attended meetings of the Second International, with which the SD affiliated. Her primary commitment to educating the working class was realized through speaking engagements, informal contacts with working-class groups, and publication of articles dealing with varied aspects of socialism. But the general economic and social problems of postwar Italy, as well as the ineffectiveness of the SD and socialism in general, took their toll. Balabanoff became increasingly hard-pressed to maintain the optimistic idealism of years past. After the 1952 meeting of the International, at which she spoke, her disillusionment plainly showed when she said, "As far as the International is concerned, you can imagine how my old Marxist heart bled in comparing what is with what *was*; but because I am a Marxist, I understand that now it could not be otherwise, and I was not disappointed at all and tried to make my contribution."[38]

Nevertheless, her sense of disappointment grew worse and worse. Forced to live in very modest circumstances in Rome with only a small allowance from the party for support, she wrote in 1961 that

> the situation is getting worse from day to day. . . . I am surrounded by optimists . . . and wishful thinking, in circumstances like the present one this irritates me, . . . [and a year later wrote] my work does not satisfy me as it used to. I don't want to be misunderstood, my comment does not imply that I am less satisfied with socialism as a philosophy or as a vision of the future. I wanted only to say that in former times when the sufferings of underprivileged were more evident and the political atmosphere was not so corrupt and selfish, we had more evidence of the immediate result of our work.[39]

Her ethical belief in the goodness and humility of the poor and downtrodden now seemed tarnished as she saw "the working class, the theoretical redeemer of itself and of society, dissolving into private persons, each concerned with his job, his wages, his family." As her old friend Bertram Wolfe observed, "she is too honest with herself not to realize that her dream has failed to come true."[40]

Even on the issue of cooperation with other socialist groups she seemed to bow to the inevitable, noting that "even if we could stop this drive we should not: experiments are unavoidable—and maybe useful in a mass movement; besides, since we are democrats we should not decide against the aspiration of a great majority of our members."[41] She struggled to deal with the realities of contemporary society, but her heart was not really in it.

Interestingly enough, however, a little of her old enthusiasm and zeal continued to shine through in one area of socialist activity, that of organizing working-class women. While socialist and communist parties had, for a long time, organized women's sections, real emphasis on this aspect of the party program flourished only during the Resistance and after 1945 primarily because of interest in a socialist electoral victory. The Women's Committee of the Socialist International, which met irregularly during the 1920s and 1930s, revived after 1945, holding regular meetings first as the International Socialist Women's Secretariat and then as the International Council of Social Democratic Women.[42] When the SD executive asked Balabanoff to assume responsibility for organizing women in 1953, she first refused, as she had "never 'specialized' in this realm of socialist activity. . . . Of course the problem is of great importance. Here as elsewhere the greatest part of the voters are women, for obvious reasons—unless we influence them and induce them to *think*—they vote clerical or communist."[43]

As she began this work, she realized the difficulty of her task, not only because of traditional pressures on women, but also because the party itself seemed to have little comprehension of the problem and gave her minimal encouragement.[44] Nevertheless, working with other SD women like Lina Merlin, Tina Lazzari, and Lina Aliquo, Balabanoff helped organize the first nationwide conference of SD women at Bolgona in November, 1958. The key proposal of this meeting was a request that the party's executive and federations provide active material support for the development of women's sections. Balabanoff served as the chairperson of the Social Democratic movement and often presided over national conferences. Most efforts at this point sought to get women to vote for the party and to have the party give increased support to their work at all levels.[45]

Balabanoff also became a highly visible figure at the international meetings of the Council of Social Democratic Women from 1956 to 1961 as a member of the conference presidium. She often made opening speeches at their meetings and debated such issues as "Women and the Second Industrial Revolution" or "What Democratic Socialism Means to Women Today."[46] She maintained her old position that women's emancipation was an aspect of human freedom best achieved through socialism. Like many other Social Democratic women, she did not examine specifically how Marxist theory related to women, and her approach still remained quite reductionist or economistic when it came to the "woman question." Nevertheless, she showed increasing interest in the crucial role women could play in creating a socialist society and clearly seemed aware of specific problems women faced in the postwar world.

Prior to the Fifth Congress of the Socialist International in 1957, the Women's Council held a special meeting in Vienna to commemorate the founding of the Women's Secretariat in 1907. Balabanoff was a principal speaker at this meeting, since she was one of the two women present who had attended the Stuttgart conference fifty years before. Her speech reviewed the grand successes and painful failures of socialism and emphasized the sense of responsibility and the hopes each socialist had held. When she returned to Rome after the meeting, she wrote to friends that the International's general gathering had been "neither exciting nor interesting, the women's section was better—on a higher level than the other one."[47]

Balabanoff's health began to fail in 1964, and she spent much of her last year confined to bed under the care of physicians. Her death in 1965 was an occasion of sorrow and mourning for socialist leaders and rank and file alike. Throughout her life, in letters and other personal expressions, Balabanoff consistently emphasized her sense of duty to alleviate the sufferings of others. While she recognized that society and nature contained no perfect justice, she believed that self-denial and moral humility provided the only real guidelines for the realization of her ideal "to share the sufferings and deprivations of the poorest among the poor."[48] In the sense that the party had remained her family and the workers her children, the obituary in the *Corriere della sera* correctly pointed out "the only monogamy to which she felt morally pledged was to that of her own ideology."[49] Peace, equality, social welfare, and justice were her values.

In the postwar years, such ideals were difficult to sustain. The unfulfilled revolution seemed remote, and socialist parties turned to the pragmatic aspects of electoral politics. Society itself altered, so that clear definitions of separate spheres for men and women blurred, while materialism and individual self-fulfillment replaced the ideal of collective welfare. Even so, Balabanoff stubbornly held on to her earlier ideals as long as she could. Invited to Israel in

1962 to address several women's groups, she noted that Israeli men and women worked together without distinction but that the women bore arms. This latter fact disturbed her because "perhaps [the Israeli women] were destined to kill the sons of other women."[50] She could accept this situation only because the women "in defending their own liberty were defending the greater good of all"—a fitting final judgment for Balabanoff, the revolutionary humanist.

NOTES

1. *Bulletin* of the International Council of Social Democratic Women 11, no. 11-12 (1965): 106.

2. The impact of the idea of a "higher cause" is discussed by Veronica Geng, "Requiem for the Women's Movement," *Harpers*, November, 1976, pp. 49-68.

3. Ellen Kay Trimberger, "Women in the Old and New Left: The Evolution of a Politics of Personal Life," *Feminist Studies* 5, no. 3 (1979): 433, 441.

4. Hoover Institution Archives, Bertram D. Wolfe Collection (hereafter HIA, Wolfe): Balabanoff, Correspondence, letter of January 16, 1950.

5. Angelica Balabanoff, *My Life as a Rebel* (London: Hamilton, 1938), p. 253.

6. Robert Shaffer, "Women and the Communist Party, U.S.A., 1930-40," *Socialist Review*, no. 45 (1979): 92.

7. *Bulletin* of the International Council, p. 106.

8. HIA, Wolfe: Balabanoff, Correspondence, letter of October 7, 1964.

9. Angelica Balabanoff, *Tears* (New York: E. Laub Pub. Co., 1943), "Introduction."

10. Balabanoff's early politics are discussed in detail by Nancy G. Eshelman, "Forging a Socialist Women's Movement: Angelica Balabanoff in Switzerland," in Betty Boyd Caroli, Robert F. Harney, and Lydio Tomasi, eds., *The Italian Immigrant Woman in North America* (Toronto: The Multicultural History Society of Ontario, 1978), pp. 44-75.

11. Bertram D. Wolfe, *Strange Communists I Have Known* (New York: Stein and Day, 1965), p. 82.

12. Alessandro Schiavi, *I buoni artieri* (Rome: Editore Opere Nuove, 1957), p. 9.

13. Ronald Florence, *Marx's Daughters* (New York: Dial Press, 1975), p. 163.

14. Angelica Balabanoff, *Ricordi di una socialista* (Rome: Donatello di Luigi, 1946), p. 51.

15. For discussion of the early women's movement in Italian socialism, see Franca Pieroni Bortolotti, *Alle origini dell'movimento femminile in Italia, 1848-92* (Turin: Einaudi, 1963), and idem, *Socialismo e questione femminile in Italia, 1892-1922* (Milan: Mazzotta, 1974). Also see Mirella Alloisio and Marta Ajo, *La donna nel socialismo italiano tra cronaca e storia, 1892-1978* (Cosenza: Lerici, 1978), pp. 26-27.

16. Franca Pieroni Bortolotti, "Femminismo e socialismo dal 1900 al primo dopoguerra," *Critica Storica* 8 (January 31, 1969): 42; Alfred E. Senn, *The Russian Revolution in Switzerland* (Madison, Wisc.: University of Wisconsin Press, 1971), p. 41; and Balabanoff, *My Life*, p. 145.

17. Georges Haupt, ed., *Bureau Socialiste International, 1900-1907*, 2 vols. (Paris: Mouton & Co., 1969), 2: 272, 276, 285; and idem, *Le Deuxieme Internationale, 1889-1914* (Paris: Mouton & Co., 1964), pp. 346-48.

18. See Jane Slaughter, "Feminism and Socialism: Theoretical Debates in Historical Perspective," *Marxist Perspectives* 7 (1979): 32-49; and specifically for Italy, see Nilde Jotti, "Da Turati all'elaborazione del PCI," *Rinascita* 18, no. 3 (1961): 209-20.

19. Balabanoff, *Ricordi*, p. 49.

20. Balabanoff, *My Life*, p. 141; Edoardo and Duilio Susmel, eds., *Opera Omnia di Benito Mussolini*, 36 vols. (Florence: La Fenice, 1951-1963), 6: 405; and Senn, *The Russian Revolution*, p. 82.

21. Senn, *The Russian Revolution*; pp. 97, 100; and for detailed account of all the meetings, see Robert Grimm, *Zimmerwald und Kienthal* (Bern: n.p., 1917).

22. Senn, *The Russian Revolution*, p. 41; Balabanoff, *My Life*, pp. 151-52.

23. Pieroni Bortolotti, "Femminismo e socialismo," pp. 51-52; and *Socialismo e questione femminile*, pp. 131-35.

24. Richard Stites, *The Women's Liberation Movement in Russia* (Princeton, N.J.: Princeton University Press, 1978), p. 316; Louise Bryant, *Mirrors of Moscow* (New York: Thomas Seltzer, 1923), p. 124.

25. Stites, *Women's Liberation*, p. 334.

26. Victor Serge, *Memoirs of a Revolutionary, 1901-1941* (Clarendon: Oxford University Press, 1967), p. 105.

27. Balabanoff, *Ricordi*, p. 157.

28. Angelica Balabanoff, "John Reed's Last Days," *The Modern Monthly*, January, 1937, p. 4.

29. Angelica Balabanoff, *Impressions of Lenin* (Ann Arbor, Mich.: University of Michigan Press, 1964), p. 151.

30. Simona Colarizi, "Il partito socialista italiano in esilio," *Storia contemporanea* 5, no. 1 (1974): 73-74. This article discusses the whole sequence of events surrounding the debates on unity.

31. Filippo Turati and Anna Kuluscioff, *Carteggio, 1923-25*, 6 vols. (Rome: Einaudi, 1959), 6: 503.

32. Among her political essays are *Erzeihung der Massen zum Marxismus* (Berlin: n.p., 1927); *Sozialismus als Weltanschauung* (Jena: n.p., n.d.); *To the Victims of Fascism* (n.p., n.d.) probably written after 1934, proceeds from which were to aid the victims of fascism; *Almanacco Socialista*, 1931 (Paris), pp. 11-13; *Avanti!*, June 15, 1934 (Paris), p. 1.

33. *Il traditore: Benito Mussolini e la sua "conquista" del potere* 1, nos. 1-8 (June, 1942,-May, 1943).

34. See, for example, *La Contracorrente*, May, 1943, 1:3-4; and ibid., June, 1946, 4:4.

35. Terese Pol, "Angelica Balabanoff: 1878-1965," *Nation*, December 13, 1965, p. 482 (from a 1942 interview); HIA, Wolfe: Balabanoff, Topical, copy of article, *Herald Tribune*, January, 1945.

36. Balabanoff, *Tears*, "Introduction."

37. HIA, Wolfe: Balabanoff, Correspondence, letter, 1947.

38. Ibid., letter of October 30, 1952.

39. Ibid., letters, 1961 and February, 1962.

40. Wolfe, *Strange Communists*, p. 97.

41. HIA, Wolfe: Balabanoff, Correspondence, letter, May (? but after 1956).

42. See, for example, Labour and Socialist International, International Women's Committee, International Study Week, August 22-29, 1936, Brussels.

43. HIA, Wolfe: Balabanoff, Correspondence, letter, 1953.

44. Ibid., letter of May 27, 1955.

45. *Bulletin* of the International Council 4, no. 12 (December, 1958): 81; ibid. 7, no. 3 (March, 1961): 21; and ibid. 8, no. 4 (April, 1962): 22.

46. Ibid. 3, no. 7-8 (July-August, 1957); and ibid. 5, no. 7-8 (July-August, 1959), passim.

47. HIA, Wolfe: Balabanoff, Topical, Report of the 1957 Vienna speech; and Balabanoff, Correspondence, letter, August, 1957.

48. Ibid., letter of February 10, 1961.

49. *Corriere della sera*, November 26, 1965, p. 3.

50. HIA, Wolfe: Balabanoff, Topical, copy of article, *Cronaca di Roma*, July 3, 1962.

10.
Ulrike Meinhof:
An Emancipated
Terrorist?

DAVID KRAMER

Who was Ulrike Marie Meinhof? The question has become increasingly difficult to answer as legend, rumor, and prejudice have grown. Many Americans regard her as a sort of teutonic Ma Barker, violent and pathological. Fredrick J. Hacker's laconic description of her as a "sociology teacher" is both factually incorrect and devoid of analytical value.[1] On the other hand, the statement by the German writer Erich Fried, that she was "the most important woman in German politics since Rosa Luxemburg," has probably contributed more to public perplexity than to general enlightenment.[2]

Despite the confusion, one thing is clear: She was an unusual woman. While more than one half of the Western German population today is female, very few women are actively involved in any way in politics. Of these, only a small number are involved in radical politics and even fewer in terrorism. Most of the latter have made little personal impact on the public mind, but Ulrike Meinhof was different. Her name has gone into history as part of a generic designation: "Baader-Meinhof," as in gang, terror, and so on.

This notoriety alone would be reason enough to investigate her life to determine who she was and why she turned to political terrorism. But there is more at stake here than simply a flamboyant biography or a paradigm of aberrant development. The women's movement in its broadest form is one of the most important social and political issues facing advanced industrial societies. Thus the question of Meinhof's relationship to this movement is of much more than merely biographical significance. This brief essay is an attempt to address the question, but it would be presumptuous to pretend that a completely satisfactory answer can be provided at the present time. The issues are too complex, the documentary basis is fragmentary, and the political atmosphere is still highly charged. Above all, we are not far enough removed from the events described. Many of the same forces that shaped Ulrike Meinhof's life and determined the sexual division of labor and life in the advanced capitalist world remain undisturbed. Perhaps several generations from now the terrorists of recent years will be regarded as the Founding Fathers (and/or Mothers!) of something or other, or they may have been entirely forgotten.[3]

This essay does not purport to be a treatise on terrorism or a manual for combatting it. It is an effort to understand the tragic development of one German woman and her relationship to the movement toward the emancipation of women in general. After a sketch of Meinhof's life, a second section will consider the historical forces that helped to mold her as a German woman, the unfolding of her consciousness as a feminist, and the meaning of her terrorist activities with respect to the emancipation of women. My own conclusions, which may disappoint those who thrive on the bombast that characterizes much of the discussion of terrorism, form the final section.

Ulrike Marie Meinhof was born on October 7, 1934, in the second year of the Reich that lasted only 988 years short of a thousand years. She was the second daughter of the art historian Dr. Werner Meinhof and his wife Ingeborg. In 1936 Werner Meinhof became director of the city museum of Jena, in what is now the German Democratic Republic, while he also lectured at the Academy of Art in Weimar. The family moved from Oldenburg, where Ulrike had been born, to Jena and took up residence in a bourgeois section of town.

Ulrike's early childhood appears to have been comfortable and unexceptional. Her family was typical of the non-Nazi, intellectual middle class of the period—pious, serious, orderly, and relatively nonpolitical. The year 1939 brought crisis for both the German Reich and the Meinhof family. On September 1 German troops marched into Poland, beginning the European phase of World War II. At about the same time Dr. Meinhof became seriously ill with a disease that could not immediately be diagnosed. He died in early 1940 from cancer of the pancreas.[4]

Although Ulrike, five years old at the time, appeared to take her father's death in stride, the family was not left in an enviable position. Ingeborg Meinhof was now a widow in her early thirties with two children to support and no higher education or job experience. She was not eligible for a state pension because her husband had been only a municipal employee. Moreover, her chances of finding another spouse were greatly reduced by the war, which drew more and more men into the armed forces. Their only good fortune was an offer by the Jena municipal government to pay Ingeborg's way through the university. Here she may have benefited indirectly from a relaxation of quotas on the admission of women to universities after 1939.[5]

Ingeborg Meinhof enrolled in the University of Jena and, like her deceased husband, studied art history. Soon she met a young student named Renate Riemek, who shared her dislike of the Nazi system and her skepticism about the eventual outcome of the war. Renate was especially charmed by Ulrike, who insisted that she should come live with the Meinhofs, urging her mother's friend to "move in with us, there you'll get something to eat."[6]

This was arranged, and the two older women continued their studies while Ingeborg's two daughters, Ulrike and Wienke, attended school. In order to have a little time alone with her mother, Ulrike met Ingeborg daily at the university so they could walk home together.[7] Both Ingeborg and Renate finished their studies in 1943 and completed the preliminary state examinations for teacher certification the following year, but by then the collapse of Nazi Germany was not far off.[8]

Jena, though originally taken by American troops, belonged to the Soviet zone of occupation. The Meinhof-Riemek "family" decided to move west. In early 1946 they settled in the staid city of Oldenburg, birthplace of both Meinhof daughters, in what was then the British zone. Ingeborg and Renate began teaching; Wienke was enrolled in public school, but eleven-year-old Ulrike attended a Catholic institution because the public system was overcrowded. In 1948, just as the worst of the postwar ordeal seemed to be coming to an end, it was discovered that Ingeborg Meinhof had cancer of the breast. After an unsuccessful operation she died in March, 1949.[9]

Renate Riemek took the Meinhof girls to live with her. She continued to play the role of both mother and friend to the sisters while writing books and laying the foundation of a distinguished academic career. In 1951 she was named to a professorship, thus becoming as a woman the youngest professor in Germany. Ulrike Meinhof spent her late teenage years living between the contradictions of Riemek's leftist, academic life-style and the West Germany of the "economic miracle." During the cold war Ulrike must have felt a certain distance from her larger political environment, especially since her foster mother Renate Riemek agreed with Thomas Mann that anticommunism represented the "fundamental foolishness of the twentieth century" and was vehemently opposed to the rearmament of West Germany.[10]

Just as Ulrike turned eighteen in October, 1952, she moved with Renate Riemek to the Hessian town of Weilburg. Here she finished her secondary education in 1955 and received a prestigious scholarship from the *Studienstiftung des Deutschen Volkes*. Enrolling in the University of Marburg to study pedagogy and psychology, Ulrike seemed more interested in religion than in politics. She joined a Christian group associated with the *Berneuchener Kreis* current of Lutheranism.[11]

In 1957 Ulrike transferred to the University of Münster, where she first became deeply involved in politics. Together with a political science student named Jürgen Seifert she actively participated in the protest movement against atomic weapons, issuing a series of pamphlets entitled "Das Argument."[12] Ulrike was ultimately elected speaker of the Münster Committee against Atomic Armament.[13]

In connection with her political activities Ulrike met her future husband, Klaus Rainer Röhl, the publisher of the leftist magazine *Konkret*. Röhl was a secret member of the illegal Communist party, and his publication was financed in part by subsidies from East Germany,[14] leading some observers to imply that the cloak-and-dagger aspects of *Konkret*'s early history had something to do with a continuing East German sponsorship of Western European terrorism.[15] Röhl claims that although the East Germans supplied money for the publication of his magazine, his editorial decisions were never subordinated to the party line.[16] And in fact *Konkret* did take a number of independent positions and over the years featured writers who criticized the policies of the Communist party.

Ulrike Meinhof began her career at *Konkret* in September, 1959. That winter she went to Jena to do research on a dissertation that she planned to write on a rather obscure seventeenth-century pedagogue. However, she failed to complete the dissertation and returned to Hamburg in 1960 to resume her work as an editor/journalist for *Konkret*. On September 13, 1960, she and Röhl announced their engagement, and they were married in late 1961.[17] According to Röhl, Meinhof also joined the illegal Communist party and sometimes accompanied him to East Berlin for conspiratorial and recreational rendezvous with *Konkret*'s East German patrons.[18]

Even before her marriage, Meinhof had become editor-in-chief of *Konkret*, and her tenure was soon marked with controversy. In one of her own articles she wrote that "just as we question our parents about Hitler, so will we be questioned one day about Mr. Strauss."[19] Franz Joseph Strauss, the conservative Bavarian politician, promptly filed suit, and Meinhof was defended by Gustav Heinemann, who later became president of the Federal Republic. Through the publicity surrounding the case, which was eventually thrown out of court, Ulrike Meinhof became a media celebrity.[20]

During this period, it is impossible to determine the true nature of Meinhof's private life and its meaning for her later development. From Röhl's point of view,

> what had not begun as a love affair became a harmonious marriage. We thought of ourselves as equal partners and, in fact, that is what we were. . . . The marriage to Ulrike, or respectively, our common life and work, remained unclouded from 1959 until 1967—a long connection that withstood all political and economic changes.[21]

Röhl measures the success of the relationship largely against the standard of professional cooperation, yet it may well be that Meinhof sought more in marriage than mere collaboration. Although Röhl maintains that the marriage was characterized by "complete monogamy,''[22] he has been described by friends as "the sort of man who has two affairs a week.''[23] One well-informed writer has concluded that the Röhl-Meinhof relationship "was not a happy marriage even to start with.''[24]

The year 1962 was a trying time for Ulrike Meinhof. Conflicts between *Konkret* and the East German Communists convinced her that the end of cooperation was near even before Röhl had grasped the gravity of the situation.[25] Moreover, about the same time Meinhof became pregnant. In her last month she suffered terrible headaches, so that after giving birth to twin girls by Caesarean section, she underwent an operation to remove a suspected brain tumor, a difficult procedure which revealed an expanded blood vessel in the brain. Despite the lesser problem, her recuperation was marked by excruciating pain and several other disabilities, and she recovered very slowly.[26] Although Ulrike wrote regularly for *Konkret* during her convalescence, Röhl indicates that not until 1964 was she able to resume her full editorial duties. By then the long-simmering dispute with the East German Communists had come to a boil, and the party ordered the magazine closed, canceling its subsidies, Rather than bow to the pressure, Röhl made *Konkret* independent. There was no issue in July, 1964, but in August the magazine reappeared with the appeal "SOS *Konkret*", which called for increased reader support and new subscriptions. Ironically, the editors stated: "We are not Communists. We don't want to become ones either." The statement was true, but only as far as it went, since both Röhl and Meinhof had quit the party in May, 1964, and presumably had no desire to rejoin in August.[27]

Ulrike Meinhof was still featured in the masthead of August, 1964, as editor-in-chief. However, there was a noticeable change in the September issue. Both Röhl and Meinhof were listed as legally responsible publishers, but Meinhof's name was followed by an inscrutable parenthesis: "(presently on vacation)." Röhl writes that the August, 1964, issue was the first that he produced alone, but he gives no indication as to the nature of Meinhof's "vacation."[28] It is impossible to determine just when the "vacation" ended, for that matter, because in November, 1964, Meinhof disappeared from the masthead entirely, although her columns were featured prominently in the issues thereafter.

About this time, *Konkret* adopted cheap sex as part of its sales strategy. The first naked woman appeared on the cover in October, 1964, and if scant remnants of modesty were preserved by a strategically placed headline ("Does a view of the naked body endanger youth?"), this only reflected prevailing standards of newsstand morality at the time. Henceforth, there was scarcely a cover of *Konkret* that did not feature either a suggestive picture of a woman in some state of undress or the promise of a sex story, or both.

It may be, as Röhl insists, that Meinhof was not offended by *Konkret*'s sexual sensationalism until after their divorce.[29] It is, of course, also possible that she was offended but said nothing earlier. But in any case she continued to write her column and care for the children while becoming, during the mid-1960s, the darling of Hamburg's liberal high society. Hamburg is the mecca of West German media, and many powerful publishers and journalists seemed fascinated by Meinhof's intensity and radicalism. Röhl's marketing strategy for *Konkret* successfully increased circulation from 50,000 to 140,000, but Meinhof's fame rose even more rapidly as she began contributing to the established press and became a familiar radio and television personality as well.[30] She cultivated a circle of chic friends and even insisted on buying a house in the fashionable Blankenese district of Hamburg.[31]

At the time, Ulrike Meinhof was acutely aware of the contradictions in her life. She wrote in a letter,

> sometimes I have the feeling that I could flip out. The relationship with Klaus, being accepted into the establishment, working together with students—three things that seem incompatible—pull me, tear me.[32]

These pressures finally proved too much for the marriage. In late 1967 Meinhof took the children and moved to West Berlin, the center of student revolt in West Germany. Peter Rühmkorf has described the West Berlin of that time as "a locality where one can perceive no real outlet, no normal communication, no positive perspective and where ruling force and anti-authoritarian impetus paralyze each other."[33] In this atmosphere the distance grew between Meinhof and the stylish, liberal world she had left behind in

Hamburg. She still wrote for *Konkret*, and she still contributed often to radio and television programs, but her interests and the tone of her articles were changing.

A crucial moment came in October, 1968, when she observed the trial of four young people charged with setting fire to two department stores in Frankfurt. Two of the accused, the student Gudrun Ensslin and Andreas Baader, a ne'er-do-well from the fringes of the student Left in Berlin, later became Meinhof's most important accomplices in terrorism. At the time, however, she seemed ambivalent toward the act of political arson. In a *Konkret* article, she noted that the possible injury of innocent people rules out the use of arson, although "the burning of a department store has this progressive aspect, that it breaks laws which protect crime."[34] It was the start of an emotional identification with Baader and Ensslin.

Meinhof had become deeply dissatisfied with the editorial policies of her former husband and was involved in sundry conspiracies either to force Röhl to change *Konkret*'s policy or else weaken his control over the publication. These intrigues culminated in May, 1969, when Meinhof and a group of supporters from Berlin attempted to force Röhl to accept their "demands" by occupying the offices of *Konkret*. The purpose of the operation was to prevent production of the magazine, but Röhl's staff had received word of the plan in time to organize their work at other locations, thus reducing the "invasion" to little more than a farce. The Berliners vented their frustration by vandalizing Röhl's house in Blankenese —the same house that Meinhof had coaxed him into buying a mere two years earlier. In the midst of the rampage, while one of her friends was urinating in the bed that she had previously shared with Röhl, another participant turned to Ulrike with the not inappropriate remark: "It must be a thought-provoking moment for you."[35]

The break with *Konkret* and with almost all remnants of her former life was now final. Back in Berlin, Meinhof became even more deeply involved in the radical politics and bohemian lifestyle that were characteristic of the leftist "scene." She continued writing and even lectured part-time at the Free University of Berlin, but her projects now included direct agitation of marginal social groups widely thought by student radicals at the time to have revolutionary potential.

In the spring of 1970, Ensslin and Baader, who had jumped bail, returned to Berlin.[36] Baader, never one to hide his candle under a bushel, was soon rearrested, and Meinhof was persuaded to join in a scheme to free him from jail. The plan began to unfold when West Berlin penal authorities granted Baader permission to do research for a book on "the organization of marginal youths" at the *Deutsches Institut für soziale Fragen* in the Dahlem district of Berlin. On May 14, 1970, Meinhof showed up at the institute, as she explained, to help Baader in his work. Several other armed associates of Meinhof's gained entry to the institute after Baader had been escorted into the building, catching his guards by surprise and shooting wildly in all directions while Baader and Meinhof jumped out a window. In the confusion, the entire group quickly disappeared in a stolen car.

Such was the birth of the "Baader-Meinhof gang." It had no systematic ideology, no real infrastructure, no clear goals. Röhl even claims that Ulrike Meinhof had no plans to join Baader in the underground and only jumped out the window when she saw that an employee of the institute had been shot.[37] The Baader-Meinhof group, pursued by the police and in need of an identity, fled to East Berlin, where the reception was cool; to Jordan, where the bohemianism of the Germans led to differences with their Palestinian hosts; and finally back to West Germany, where a process of terror and political self-isolation began that has not yet completely run its course. Banks were robbed, papers were stolen or forged, "political analyses" were issued, and people were killed.[38] And yet, although these activities generated a small number of sympathizers and emulators, the terrorists failed to establish themselves as a viable alternative to the political status quo.

The *Rote Armee Fraktion* (RAF), as the Baader-Meinhof group called itself, proved to be unequal to the state that it had set out to destroy. Of course, this was not merely a failure of the RAF itself, since, as Walter Laqueur has pointed out, "there is in modern history no known instance in which a small terroristic group has taken power."[39] Horst Mahler, one of the early leaders of the RAF, was captured by the police as early as 1970. Baader, Ensslin, and Meinhof, all arrested in the summer of 1972, left a political legacy of severely eroded civil liberties in the federal republic and a high degree of demoralization and confusion throughout the German Left.

On May 9, 1976, after nearly four years of confinement, Ulrike Marie Meinhof's lifeless body was found hanging from the bars on her prison window. Officials quickly arrived at the conclusion that her death was self-inflicted, but the suspicion has often been expressed since then that Meinhof may actually have been a victim of foul play.[40] The charge of murder—both in Meinhof's case and in connection with the deaths of other incarcerated West German terrorists—is so far-reaching in its implications that every reasonable investigative effort is called for whenever uncertainties or irregularities are found to exist. However, even though a recent report by an international investigative commission has raised a number of disturbing questions with respect to the circumstances surrounding Meinhof's death and autopsy, nothing thus far adduced justifies the assumption that she was murdered.[41]

Surprisingly little comprehensive research is available about the impact of recent history upon the female majority of the German population. Impressionistic opinions of the type offered by Talcott Parsons, that German women have been relatively "submissive" in comparison to American women, are clearly not a satisfactory substitute for neglected investigation.[42] Although a brief essay on one German woman terrorist is certainly not the place to attempt an assessment of the history of women in Germany, it may be appropriate to call attention to a few of the little known historical circumstances that do not seem to be compatible with the theory of the relatively submissive, backward German woman:

> the fact that during World War I more women than men were employed in the German economy;[43]
>
> the fact that many women participated actively in the German revolution of 1918-1919;[44]

the fact that at the beginning of 1933 almost twice as many
women were employed in Germany as in the United States,
even though the German population was only half as large.[45]

Of course, it cannot be ignored that German women were subjected for twelve years to the dubious solicitude of National Socialism. When the Nazis came to power in 1933, they brought with
them an antiemancipatory ideology that was consonant with their
generally regressive social views. Ideally, the Nazis wished to restrict women to the traditional "three Ks": *Kinder, Kirche, Küche*
(children, church, kitchen). In reality, however, even though the
Nazis actively promoted discrimination in most areas, the employment of women in the German economy did not decrease during
the "Third Reich," but rather increased substantially.[46] A techno-
crat like Albert Speer might complain that Nazi Germany did not
make optimal use of its women's potential for labor,[47] but the fact
remains that German women made many contributions to the
German war effort beyond praying, having babies, and darning
socks.[48] It is also true, however, as the biographies of Ingeborg
Meinhof and Renate Riemek illustrate, that not all German women
fell prey to the tawdry blandishments of Nazi propaganda and the
pseudo-eroticism of the *Führer* cult.

In any case, the "repressive protection" of women in Nazi
Germany did little to prepare them for the harsh realities they
faced in 1945.[49] The collapse of the German state and the occupation of German territory by the Allied armies subjected German
women to an ordeal whose many horrors can only be suggested
here. Sexual assault was not the least of the dangers confronting
the women of the defeated nation. As Alexander Solzhenitsyn
remarked from the perspective of a Russian soldier: "all of us knew
very well that if the girls were German they could be raped and then
shot."[50] By all indications large numbers of German women were
abused.[51]

At the end of the war millions of German men were either dead
or in captivity, leaving their female dependents to fend for themselves in an economy that was severely stricken.[52] The French
political scientist Alfred Grosser describes the situation as follows:

The [German] population seemed to consist only of women and children and old men, and even boys of fifteen had been given rifles. 1,650,000 men had been killed in action, 2 million were prisoners, and 1,600,000 were missing. Food supplies and transport had completely broken down; there were no mails or newspapers; administration had collapsed, and chaos was unchallenged.[53]

Whereas the Nazis had generally tried to discourage women from working, the Allied Control Council in October, 1945, declared it a duty of all women between the ages of fifteen and fifty to work.[54] The enormous contribution of women in digging Germany out from under the rubble of defeat was quickly forgotten in the delirious prosperity of subsequent years.

The economic pressures of the postwar period had other, less savory effects as well. Many German women were impelled across "the murky line that divides wartime rape from wartime prostitution."[55] As late as 1949, 15,000 prostitutes were still reported in Cologne, as compared to 1,500 before the war.[56] Material needs appears to have been a common motive behind liaisons between Allied soldiers and German women. Of the 67,753 children sired by Allied soldiers in Germany, more than half, some 37,000, had American fathers.[57] One of these unfortunate "by-products" of the American occupation of Germany, Irene Goergens, was later "adopted" by Ulrike Meinhof in Berlin and went on to join her in the terrorist underground.[58]

All indications are that Ulrike Meinhof lived a relatively sheltered life during this period; yet, common sense suggests that her consciousness could not remain unaffected by the general conditions of the time. For example, Klaus Rainer Röhl thought that the shortage of food in postwar Germany contributed to the early death of Ingeborg Meinhof, and more importantly, Ulrike may have felt the same way.[59] Obviously such considerations alone provide no explanation of why Ulrike Meinhof later turned to political terrorism; millions of women suffered similar or even worse tribulations without becoming terrorists. But this is precisely the point, that all German women, including Ulrike Meinhof, were marked by the postwar experience in ways not yet understood.

In 1949 a new political era was inaugurated in the British, French,

and American zones of Germany with the adoption of a constitution *(Grundgesetz)*. But a constitutional provision of equaltiy
between men and women did not change social reality overnight.
Until April, 1953, West German law still required a woman to
support her husband in his career. Moreover, if a woman "neglected" her familial and household duties, her husband could get a
court order empowering him to terminate her employment against
her will.[60] Despite steps toward formal, legal equality, women in
West Germany have remained among the economically disad-
vantaged. For most of the history of the federal republic, women
have comprised slightly more than one-third of all jobholders.[61]
Although special wage categories for women were declared illegal
in 1956, low-wage categories that in reality apply primarily to
women (so-called *Leichtlohngruppen*) are still in effect.[62] Women
in West Germany still earn substantially less on the average than
men.[63]

Discrimination against women is not, of course, restricted to
wage differentials. Women in the federal republic are the victims
of a broad spectrum of social disadvantages, most of which are by
no means uniquely German. The "double burden" of job and
household work, limited educational opportunities, insufficient
supportive institutions, such as preschools, and restrictive abortion
laws are only a few of the many problems that could be mentioned.
As is also the case in other countries, many West German men have
little sympathy for emancipatory initiatives.

Such restrictions affected Ulrike Meinhof in her development
less than most West German women. Her adolescent years were
spent in a secure, nonrepressive environment, without male domination. She received a fine formal education, and she soon enjoyed
a professional success that most men would envy. Perhaps the
vantage point of such a relatively privileged position enabled her
to develop an incisive critique of the role of women in West German
society.

Former terrorist Astrid Proll noted in a recent interview: "Ulrike
Meinhof had written for years about the oppression of women in
the Federal Republic."[64] This aspect of Meinhof's career, though
largely overshadowed by her later terrorist exploits, began even
before radical feminism had achieved a high public visibility in

West Germany. In the first issue of *Konkret* in 1968 she wrote an article on the social significance of the sex-murderer Jürgen Bartsch, in which she disapproved of a society that

> still has not come to grips with the fact that it has ten million working women, and far more than one million working mothers with children under fourteen, all of whom must help themselves more or less with emergency solutions for their children, all of whom must bear the burden of job and family alone, even though their jobs are socially necessary; but the places in Kindergartens are rare, full-day schools a utopia, half-time jobs hard to get.[65]

The connection that she makes in this article between the disadvantages of women and the resultant neglect and abuse of children seems characteristic of her thinking during her final years of "legality." She returned to this theme in a long article on the situation of women in the July, 1968, issue of *Konkret*, concluding that "it is not at all possible to honestly discuss whether taking a job can be reconciled with raising of children—it cannot." Women, she complained, are "blackmailed" because of their children, "and this comprises their humanity, that they allow themselves to be blackmailed with their children. . . ."[66]

Later the same year the radical feminism that arose in many countries around the world as part of the broad movement of political dissent during the 1960s also made a spectacular appearance in West Germany. Helke Sander delivered a strongly feminist speech before the 23rd Conference of Delegates of the West German SDS in Frankfurt and then hurled a barrage of tomatoes at the organization's (male) steering committee.[67] Many other actions—some theatrical, some not—soon followed.[68]

Ulrike Meinhof's reaction to the tomato-throwing episode was published in *Konkret*:

> The tomatoes that flew at the SDS Conference of Delegates had no symbolic character. The men whose suits were spotted (women will clean them), should be forced to think about things, about which they have not yet thought.[69]

Her analysis corresponded closely to that of the insurgent women in the SDS; however, she also denounced the way the incident had been reported in the press, including *Konkret*. Meinhof's discontent, seen in hindsight, is understandable, since even *Konkret*'s report on the conference had focused on the sensation of flying tomatoes without conveying any of the important substantive arguments that Sander presented.[70] Male radicals in West Germany were not yet prepared to discuss feminist issues.

Meinhof, by publicly justifying a militant feminist action based on the theory that men "in the private sphere are objectively the functionaries of the capitalist society for the oppression of women," probably became increasingly uneasy about her affiliation with a magazine that trafficked openly in sleazy images of female sexuality.[71] A letter in the issue of *Konkret* for November 14, 1968, protesting against the use of women as sex objects on the cover of the magazine, may well be typical of the kind of critique that Meinhof encountered among her friends in Berlin.[72] In any event, Meinhof wrote an article in December, 1968, disassociating herself from Röhl's "internalization of the dictates of the market."[73]

This criticism left Röhl cold. He wrote:

> Ach, Ulrike demands something beautiful, exciting, but impossible: pure doctrine and exact research, the up-to-dateness of *Spiegel* and the conscientiousness of *Kursbuch*, no naked girls on the cover and no concessions to the market, but more money for the editors and punctual payment of honoraria. I am certain: if such a magazine were possible, it would already exist.[74]

Meinhof's reaction was not surprising: she embraced radical feminism even more actively, giving public speeches on women's problems and working with groups of women and institutionalized girls in Berlin.[75] Even her personal relationships reflected an increasingly greater degree of feminist consciousness, which caused her to describe her friendship with Gudrun Ensslin as something different from the eternal "man-shit."[76] The curious attack Meinhof instigated against the *Konkret* offices and Röhl's house came soon afterwards, severing her remaining ties to the magazine and her former husband and leaving her even more emotionally dependent upon her friends in Berlin.

During the year between the attempted takeover of *Konkret* and the freeing of Baader, Meinhof seemed largely absorbed with the problems of institutionalized girls, whom she now regarded as an important "revolutionary subject." Not only did she criticize conditions in juvenile institutions in several radio broadcasts, but she also completed a television play called "Bambule" on this theme.[77]

The play had strong documentary overtones, portraying the boredom and oppression experienced by the wards of juvenile institutions. "Bambule" was based upon tape-recorded interviews; the girls whose experiences formed the substance of the drama played themselves in the film, while the roles of the institutional personnel were taken by actors. The story brings to light a number of problems often encountered in juvenile institutions: violence, purposelessness, and lesbianism—a topic that later led to speculation about Meinhof's own latent homosexuality.[78]

The filming of "Bambule" in April, 1970, was surrounded by strong differences of opinion between television editor Eberhard Itzenplitz and Ulrike Meinhof.[79] The play was nevertheless scheduled to be broadcast on May 24, 1970, during prime evening time. But the escape of Andreas Baader came ten days before the drama could be shown, and "Bambule" was promptly removed from the schedule. Meinhof's state of mind at the time she wrote "Bambule," shortly before her disappearance into the underground, is probably best reflected in the words she assigned to one of the characters in the play:

> Whoever is good is forgotten, he will rot in here. Whoever goes along with things will be destroyed. Do you understand . . .? If you go along, they will be happy that they have destroyed you. And then they are nice to you because they have destroyed you. No, . . . No![80]

In the years 1968 to 1970 Ulrike Meinhof was one of the most important popularizers of the new feminist consciousness in the Federal Republic of Germany. Thus the question is certainly relevant: What became of her feminism during her final phase as a terrorist? The evidence is contradictory and only partially reliable.

A well-known terrorist, Michael "Bommi" Baumann, described the relationship between the sexes in another terrorist organization during the early 1970s as follows:

> The problem was, the group was actually a terrible male sect, really, we were just plain male chauvinists, you can't say it any other way, and it is in this connection that the problem of betrayal appears.[81]

The extent to which this description may have applied to the situation in the RAF is uncertain, but it is interesting to note that there have been reports for years that Mahler was betrayed to the police by a woman, and one rather questionable source even suggests that Meinhof, jealous of Mahler's attempts to seduce some of her girl-friends, among them Irene Goergans, may well have been the informant.[82]

Reports of tensions between Meinhof and Baader are so numerous that they can scarcely be doubted. Former RAF member Beate Sturm related one such conflict. Once when Meinhof demanded a discussion of the group's activities, Baader responded by shouting: "You cunts,[83] your emancipation consists of yelling at your men."[84] What Meinhof thought about this blatantly sexist outburst is not known.

Another, more serious conflict between the two allegedly concerned the question of the Röhl-Meinhof twins. At the time Meinhof fled with Baader, she had made no permanent provision for the care of her own children, who had been sent to spend a few days with friends in Bremen. The prospect of a protracted period of illegality raised the question of what was to become of them. Baader reportedly thought that Meinhof should separate herself forever from the twins as relics of her "bourgeois past."[85] After much argument, it was decided to send the children to a Palestinian orphans' camp, where they would be raised as "soldiers" in the struggle against Israel. A more radical violation of the rights and interests of the girls is difficult to imagine. Even the representatives of the *Fatah* are said to have reacted icily and were quoted as asking, "Would you like to make little monsters of them?"[86]

The twins, after receiving new identities from the Palestinians, would never be seen by their mother again. But while arrangements were being made to transfer them to the Middle East, a former employee of *Konkret* received a tip as to their location and the codeword that would allow him to take them away. Thus the children were returned to their father and rescued from their designated career as adopted Palestinians. Röhl wrote, "I am convinced that Ulrike herself spared the children from their uncertain fate in Jordan and played a role in bringing them back to me. I am likewise convinced that Baader was able even later to blackmail Ulrike with the children."[87] Such speculation certainly is as believable as the notion that Meinhof, the journalistic champion of women and neglected children, would abandon her own children to an existence much worse than what she had so recently portrayed in "Bambule."

Was the conflict between Meinhof and Baader merely a clash of personalities, or was it symptomatic of a more general sexual rivalry within the RAF? Beate Sturm has indicated that female members of the group were conscious of their strength as women: "One thing was really great, that we women were really emancipated, that we could simply do many things better than the men. We simply felt ourselves stronger."[88] Whether Ulrike Meinhof shared this view cannot be determined, but the fundamental assumption that personal emancipation can be achieved through terrorist violence has caused some sharp controversy among European women. The French feminist Françoise d'Eaubonne, for example, has posed the rhetorical question: "From which oppressor, which rapist, impregnator or attacker did the female fighter in the Baader-Meinhof group have to fear assault as she transported dynamite and forged documents?"[89] D'Eaubonne's own position is clearly implied in the way the question is formulated. On the other hand, Margarete Fabricius-Brand, accepting a definition of emancipation based on the realization of the objective interests of women and the achievement of full equality between men and women in society, has accused the female terrorists of the RAF of having in fact practiced a radical denial of women's specific interests, thereby internalizing the very psychological mechanisms that help to perpetuate inequality between the sexes.[90]

If the women of the RAF indeed had a coherent strategy for the general emancipation of women, it found no realistic expression in the theoretical statements attributed to the group. The incisive analyses of women's concrete problems that characterized Meinhof's writings from 1968 to 1970 are absent from the turgid pronouncements of the RAF. The world as seen through the eyes of the West German terrorists was not filled with real women and men struggling under burdens imposed upon them by antagonistic social relationships but rather with manichean political abstractions. Ulrike Meinhof's abandonment of a sober feminist critique for the romantic delusions of terrorism isolated her from the real movement of West German women toward emancipation—a movement to which she herself had made major contributions as a journalist.

In November, 1978, the West German Federal Criminal Office *(Bundeskriminalamt)* issued a wanted poster that bore the pictures of twelve suspected terrorists, ten of whom are women. The poster is symbolic of the prominence of women in recent terrorism, a fact that has commanded a good deal of attention from West German media.[91]

Of all women terrorists of the 1970s Ulrike Meinhof was (with the possible exception of Patty Hearst) the best known. Yet she was in some ways atypical of the female terrorists; she was, for example, both older and more famous in her own right than most of the others. There is no simple answer to the question of why Ulrike Meinhof turned to political terror. Any answer that purports to contribute to a clarification must be as complex and even contradictory as her life and the times in which she lived.

Ulrike Meinhof, like millions of other women in the Federal Republic of Germany and around the world, was seeking a path to emancipation. But there is certainly very little to be learned from statements like that made by Günther Nollau, former head of the West German political police *(Verfassungsschutz)*, that perhaps female terrorism is an "excess of the emancipation of women."[92] Can this possibly be any more or less true than that male terrorism is an excess of the emancipation of men? Even an Edmund Burke would likely blush at such a suggestion. Iring Fetscher comes closer to the point when he writes, "If there is a connection between the emancipation of women and female terrorism, then [it is] a backwards one: not because of too much emancipation and equality does many a woman turn in despair and confusion along with young men to senseless terror, but because of too little.''[93] But there is no guarantee that increasing emancipation will provide a quick remedy for female terrorism, any more than the liberalization of Spain since the death of Franco has brought an end to the violence of Basque separatists.

Richard Clutterbuck's suggestion that one learn to live with terrorism will probably have to do until we all learn somehow to live without it. Until then Meinhof's biography provides one more tragic example of terrorism's essentially negative impact on modern society. Ulrike Meinhof was not emancipated by terrorism; she was destroyed by it.

NOTES

1. Fredrick J. Hacker, *Crusaders, Criminals, Crazies* (New York: Bantam Books, 1978), p. 69.

2. *Frankfurter Allgemeine Zeitung*, May 17, 1976, p. 2. Jillian Becker, *Hitler's Children* (London: Granada Publishing, 1978), p. 331, attributes this statement to the German theologian Helmut Gollwitzer; however, in the German edition of her book, *Hitlers Kinder* (Frankfurt/M: Fischer, 1978), p. 238, the quotation is correctly attributed to Fried.

3. Horst Harold, the president of the West German Bundeskriminalamt, seemed to be thinking along these lines when he stated that ''terroristic phenomena possess a signal effect, [they] are predecessors of other social changes that substantially involve the mass of the population both vertically and horizontally.'' *Frankfurter Rundschau*, May 3, 1979, p. 11.

4. Becker, *Hitler's Children*, p. 136.

5. David Schoenbaum, *Hitler's Social Revolution* (Garden City, N.Y.: Anchor Books, 1967), pp. 188-89; cf. Dörte Winkler, *Frauenarbeit im 'Dritten Reich'* (Hamburg: Hoffmann und Campe Verlag, 1977), p. 196.

6. Renate Riemek, ''Gib auf Ulrike!'' *Konkret*, November 18, 1971, p. 8.

7. Klaus Rainer Röhl, *Fünf Finger sind keine Faust* (Cologne: Kiepenheuer und Witsch, 1974), p. 120.

8. Becker, *Hitler's Children*, p. 138.

9. Upon hearing that her mother had died, Ulrike asked Riemek to read from the Bible. After Riemek had read John 3:16, Ulrike said: ''That's mother's verse for the burial ceremony,'' and then she cried, but only briefly. See Becker, *Hitler's Children*, pp. 140-41.

10. Ibid., pp. 140, 143-45.

11. Ibid., pp. 154-55.

12. These pamphlets had nothing to do with the Berlin publication *Das Argument*, which developed into one of the rallying points of the early student movement. Becker's statement (*Hitler's Children*, p. 361 fn. 1) that *Das Argument* developed from pacifism to support of the ideology of violence is, in a book about terrorism, at least misleading.

13. Röhl, *Fünf Finger*, p. 124.

14. Ibid., p. 9.

15. For example, Claire Sterling, "The Terrorist Network," *The Atlantic* (November, 1978): 46. Such authors choose to ignore masses of evidence to the contrary, one example of which is contained in Chancellor Helmut Schmidt's speech of October 20, 1977, thanking those who had been helpful during the Mogadischu action: "The willingness of the Soviet Union to intervene with the government of South Yemen in our behalf counts among the positive experiences. That the GDR was also ready to do this is a heartening confirmation of the progress in our relations"; *Zum Gedenken an die Opfer des Terrorismus* (Bonn: Presse und Informationszentrum des Deutschen Bundestag, 1978), p. 29.

16. Röhl, *Fünf Finger*, passim.

17. Becker, *Hitler's Children*, pp. 169-70.

18. Röhl, *Fünf Finger*, pp. 10-11, 166, 174.

19. Ibid., p. 159.

20. Ibid., pp. 159-60.

21. Ibid., p. 173.

22. Ibid., p. 234.

23. Becker, *Hitler's Children*, p. 182.

24. Ibid., p. 172.

25. Röhl, *Fünf Finger*, p. 172.

26. Ibid., pp. 181, 234.

27. Ibid., pp. 11-12, 185-97.

28. Ibid., p. 199.

29. Ibid., p. 288.

30. Becker, *Hitler's Children*, p. 181.

31. Peter Rühmkorf, *Die Jahre, die ihr kennt* (Reinbek: Rowohlt, 1972), p. 224; cf. Röhl, *Fünf Finger*, p. 272.

32. Ibid., p. 285. Becker, *Hitler's Children*, p. 184, attributes part of this quotation to "diary notes" without explaining the contradiction to Röhl's published account.

33. *Konkret*, May 19, 1969, p. 3; reproduced in Rühmkorf, *Die Jahre*, pp. 229-31.

34. *Konkret*, November 4, 1968, p. 5.

35. Bernward Vesper, *Die Reise* (Frankfurt/M: März Verlag bei Zwei-tausendeins, 1979), p. 184. Vesper, a former boyfriend of Gudrun Ensslin, was a participant in the events described.

36. Becker, *Hitler's Children*, p. 213.

37. Röhl, *Fünf Finger*, pp. 417-18.

38. There is a general tendency to overestimate greatly the level of violence of West German terrorism. In fact, according to a report by the West German Ministry of Justice, as of September 8, 1977, only twenty-two persons had been killed over the years in the federal republic through terrorist violence. In addition, 102 attempted murders, 90 injuries due to bombings and shootings, and 14 hostage takings were also reported; *Frankfurter Allgemeine Zeitung*, September 9, 1977, p. 3. A CIA research study attributes five acts of international or transnational terrorism (all bombings) between January 1, 1969, and December 31, 1975 to the "Baader-Meinhof Gang." See CIA Research Study, *International and Transnational Terrorism: Diagnosis and Prognosis* (Washington, D.C.: Library of Congress, April, 1976), appendix C. The disparity between the relatively low level of violence and the relatively high level of publicity and public insecurity generated by recent West German terrorism requires much more research and analysis than it has thus far received.

39. Walter Laqueur, *Terrorismus* (Kronberg/Ts.: Athenäum, 1977), p. 218.

40. See, for example, Jürgen Saupe, "Fakten zum Vorwurf 'Mord'," *Konkret*, September, 1976, pp. 9-10. Röhl no longer has anything to do with the magazine Konkret.

41. See Commission internationale d'enquete, *La Mort d'Ulrike Meinhof* (Paris: François Maspero, 1979); (German ed.), Internationale Untersuch-ungskommission, *Der Tod Ulrike Meinhofs* (Tübingen: iva-Verlag bernd polke, 1979).

42. Talcott Parsons, *Beiträge zur soziologischen Theorie* (Neuwied/Berlin: Luchterhand, 1968). p. 267.

43. Winkler, *Frauenarbeit*, p. 16.

44. Gertrud Pinkus, "Gegen den Krieg—für die Räterepublik," *Emma* (November, 1978): 28-35; cf. Ernst Toller, *Eine Jugend in Deutschland* (Reinbek: Rowohlt, 1978), pp. 79, 106.

45. Schoenbaum, *Hitler's Social Revolution*, pp. 180-81.

46. Hans Peter Bleuel, *Sex and Society in Nazi Germany* (New York: Bantam Books, 1974), p. 85.

47. Albert Speer, *Erinnerungen* (Frankfurt/M: Ullstein, 1975), p. 234.

48. Some of the more bizarre aspects of Nazi population policy, such as

the "Lebensborn" organization and other campaigns to encourage illegitimate births, may have had some influence on the consciousness of women and on sexual attitudes in general, but it is impossible, given the present state of research, to estimate reliably what this influence may have been. Cf. Bleuel, *Sex and Society*, pp. 224-34; Heinz Höhne, *Der Orden unter dem Totenkopf*, 2 vols. (Frankfurt/M: Fischer, 1969), 1: 156; Eberhard Aleff, *Das Dritte Reich* (Hannover: Verlag für Literatur und Zeitgeschehen, 1963), p. 112.

49. Tim Mason, "Zur Lage der Frauen in Deutschland 1930 bis 1940: Wohlfahrt, Arbeit und Familie," in *Gesellschaft, Beiträge zur Marxschen Theorie* 6 (1976): 119.

50. Alexander Solzhenitsyn, *The Gulag Archipelago* (Glasgow: Collins/Fontana, 1974), 1: 21; cf. Lew Kopelew, *Aufbewahren für alle Zeit!* (Munich: dtv-Verlag, 1979), pp. 13-277.

51. That rape was not unknown even among U.S. soldiers is shown in the fact that the U.S. army conducted 971 courts-martial on rape charges between January, 1942, and June, 1947, (how many of these were related to Germany, however, is unknown); Susan Brownmiller, *Against Our Will* (New York: Bantam Books, 1976), pp. 76-77. Most accounts indicate that the Russian army was by far the most undisciplined of the occupying forces. See Cornelius Ryan, *The Last Battle* (New York: Pocket Books, 1967), pp. 445-63. Even Leon Uris' epos of political corn, *Armageddon* (New York: Dell, 1977) seems fairly believable in this respect.

52. The city of Berlin provides a particularly drastic example. An East German history text estimates that among the more than 2 million people left in Berlin at the end of the war, there were almost twice as many women as men; see Gerhard Keiderling and Percy Stulz, *Berlin 1945-1968* (Berlin: Dietz Verlag, 1970), pp. 16, 57. Ryan cites unnamed "military authorities," who estimated Berlin's population at the end of the war at about 2.7 million, of which more than 2 million were women; see idem, *Last Battle*, p. 15.

53. Alfred Grosser, *Germany in Our Time* (Harmondsworth, England: Penguin Books, 1974), p. 57.

54. Manfred Rexin, "Die Jahre 1945-1949," in Herbert Lilge, ed., *Deutschland 1945-1963* (Hannover: Verlag für Literatur und Zeitgeschehen, 1967), p. 21.

55. Brownmiller, *Against Our Will*, p. 75.

56. Grosser, *Germany*, p. 83.

57. Harold Zink, *The United States in Germany 1944-1955* (Princeton, N.J.: Van Nostrand, 1957), p. 138.

58. Becker, *Hitler's Children*, pp. 125, 210, 381; Margarete Fabricius-

Brand, "Frauen in der Isolation," in Susanne von Paczensky, ed., *Frauen und Terror* (Reinbek: Rowohlt, 1978), p. 102 fn. 8.

59. Röhl, *Fünf Finger*, p. 120.

60. Herta Däubler-Gmelin, *Frauenarbeitslosigkeit* (Reinbek: Rowohlt, 1977), p. 35.

61. Karin Jurczik, *Frauenarbeit und Frauenrolle* (Frankfurt/M: Campus Verlag, 1977), pp. 4, 85, 89, 110.

62. Däubler-Gmelin, *Frauenarbeitslosigkeit*, p. 37.

63. A recent study by the West German Statistisches Bundesamt indicates that women in the federal republic still earn, on the average, approximately one-third less than men; see *Der Tagesspiegel* (West Berlin), June 8, 1979, p. 20.

64. *Stern*, November 23, 1978, p. 26.

65. Peter Bruckner, *Ulrike Marie Meinhof und die deutschen Verhältnisse* (Berlin: Verlag Klaus Wagenbach, 1978), p. 44.

66. *Konkret*, July, 1968, p. 27.

67. Peter Mosler, *Was wir wollten, was wir wurden* (Reinbek: Rowohlt, 1977), p. 160; cf. Tilman Fichter and Siegward Lönnendonker, *Kleine Geschichte des SDS* (Berlin: Rotbuch Verlag, 1977), pp. 142-43. The substance of Sander's speech is documented in *Konkret*, October 7, 1968, p. 6.

68. See Ursula Linnhoff, *Die neue Frauenbewegung* (Cologne: Kiepenheuer und Witsch, 1974), p. 38 ff.

69. *Konkret*, October 7, 1968, p. 5.

70. Ibid., September 23, 1968, p. 7.

71. Ibid., October 7, 1968, p. 7.

72. Ibid., November 14, 1968, p. 54.

73. Ibid., January 13, 1969, p. 2.

74. Ibid., p. 6.

75. See *Konkret*, March 24, 1969, p. 54.

76. Röhl, *Fünf Finger*, p. 416.

77. Klaus Wagenbach, "Nachwort," in Ulrike Meinhof, *Bambule* (Berlin: Verlag Klaus Wagenbach, 1978), p. 95.

78. Becker professes to see "hints of lesbianism" and "sadomasochism" in Meinhof's adolescence, traits that allegedly persisted into her later life and emanated from her play "Bambule"; see Becker, *Hitler's Children*, p. 148. The scurrilous *Baader-Meinhof Report* (Mainz: Hase und Koehler, 1972), went even further, noting fastidiously in one place that Meinhof, like Gudrun Ensslin, was "inclined toward those of her own sex" (p. 33) and proclaiming more bluntly in another that "the majority of

the female members of the political terrorist group" was "lesbian or bi-sexual" (p. 17).

79. Becker, *Hitler's Children*, p. 209.

80. Meinhof, *Bambule*, p. 94.

81. Michael Baumann, *Wie alles anfing* (Frankfurt/M: Sozialistische Verlagsauslieferung, 1976), pp. 87-88.

82. See *Berlin Extra-Dienst*, October 10, 1970; cited in *Baader-Meinhof Report*, p. 230.

83. The translation of the German word "Votzen" as "bitches" in Jon Bradshaw's article in *Esquire*, July 18, 1978, p. 39, appears to be an unwarranted bit of delicacy; my translation here corresponds more nearly to the original.

84. *Der Spiegel*, August 8, 1977, p. 25.

85. Röhl, *Fünf Finger*, p. 400.

86. Ibid., p. 401.

87. Ibid., p. 402.

88. *Der Spiegel*, August 8, 1977, p. 25.

89. Evelyne Le Garrec, "Nachwort," in Françoise d'Eaubonne, *Feminismus und Terror* (Munich: Trikont, 1978), p. 142.

90. Margarete Fabricius-Brand in Paczensky, *Frauen und Terror*, p. 62 ff.

91. See the cover story of *Der Spiegel*, August 8, 1977, p. 22 ff. For further contributions and bibliographical references to the discussion of women in terrorism see Paczensky, *Frauen und Terror*, and the essay by Hermann Glaser, "Die Diskussion über den Terrorismus," in *Aus Politik und Zeitgeschichte. Beilage zur Wochenzeitung Das Parlament*, June 24, 1978, pp. 8-10.

92. *Der Spiegel*, August 8, 1977, p. 23. Nollau's phrase seems to be making its way around the world. One of the (many) things about which Françoise d'Eaubonne is quite angry is the headline "Excess of Emancipation?" in *France-Soir*, October 25, 1977; quoted by Françoise d'Eaubonne, *Feminismus*, p. 44.

93. Iring Fetscher, *Terrorismus und Reaktion* (Cologne: EVA, 1978), p. 24.

Selected Bibliography

GENERAL WORKS ON THE LEFT

The works listed below are some of the major works available in English-language editions on the history of the European Left from the late nineteenth century to the present. North American, Latin American, and Asian studies have not been included. Biographical material on Karl Marx and other early socialists also lie outside the range of this bibliography.

BOOKS

Bookchin, Murray. *The Spanish Anarchists: The Heroic Years, 1868-1936.* New York: Free Life Editions, 1976.

Borkenau, Franz. *Socialism, National or International:* London: Routledge, 1942.

_____. *European Communism.* London: Faber and Faber, 1953.

Braunthal, Julius. *History of the International, 1914-1943.* New York: Praeger, 1967.

Buttinger, Joseph. *In the Twilight of Socialism. A History of the Revolutionary Socialists of Austria.* New York: Praeger, 1953.

Cammett, John. *Antonio Gramsci and the Origins of Italian Communism.* Stanford, Cal.: Stanford University Press, 1967.

Carr, Edward Hallet. *The Bolshevik Revolution, 1917-1923.* London: Penguin Books, 1966. 3 vols.

Cattell, David T. *Communism and the Spanish Civil War.* Berkeley, Cal.: University of California Press, 1955.

_____. *Soviet Diplomacy and the Spanish Civil War.* Berkeley, Cal.: University of California Press, 1957.

Caute, David. *Communism and the French Intellectuals, 1914-1960*. New York: Macmillan, 1964.

———. *The Left in Europe since 1789*. New York: McGraw-Hill, 1966.

Cole, G. D. H. *A History of Socialist Thought, 1789-1939*. 5 vols. New York: St. Martin's Press, 1953-1960.

Cole, Margaret. *The Story of Fabian Socialism*. London: Heinemann, 1961.

Colton, Joel. *Léon Blum: Humanist in Politics*. New York: Knopf, 1966.

Conquest, Robert. *V. I. Lenin*. New York: Viking Press, 1972.

Deutscher, Issaac. *Stalin. A Political Biography*. London and New York: Oxford University Press, 1949.

———. *The Prophet Armed: Trotsky, 1879-1921*. New York: Vintage, 1965.

———. *The Prophet Unarmed: Trotsky, 1921-1929*. New York: Vintage, 1965.

———. *The Prophet Outcast: Trotsky, 1929-1940*. New York: Vintage, 1965.

Drachkovitch, Milorad M. *The Revolutionary Internationals*. Stanford, Cal.: Stanford University Press, 1966.

Fischer, Ruth. *Stalin and German Communism. A Study in the Origins of the State Party*. Cambridge, Mass.: Harvard University Press, 1948.

Gay, Peter. *The Dilemma of Democratic Socialism*. New York: Columbia University Press, 1952.

Gouldner, Alvin. *The Two Marxisms: Contradictions and Anomalies in the Development of Theory*. New York: Seabury Press, 1980.

Haimson, Leopold H. *The Russian Marxists and the Origins of Bolshevism*. Cambridge, Mass.: Harvard University Press, 1955.

Hobsbawm, Eric. *Revolutionaries*. London: Weidenfeld & Nicolson, 1973.

Hunt, Richard. *German Social Democracy, 1918-1933*. Chicago: Quadrangle, 1970.

Joll, James. *The Anarchists*. New York: Grosset & Dunlap, 1966.

———. *The Second International, 1889-1914*. New York: Harper & Row, 1966.

Kern, Robert. *Red Years/Black Years: A Political History of the Spanish Anarchists, 1911-1937*. Philadelphia: ISHI, 1978.

Landauer, Carl. *European Socialism: A History of Ideas and Movements*. Berkeley, Cal.: University of California Press, 1959.

La Palombara, Joseph. *The Italian Labor Movement: Problems and Prospects*. Ithaca, N.Y.: Cornell University Press, 1957.

Lichtheim, George. *Marxism in Modern France*. New York: Columbia University Press, 1966.

_____. *A Short History of Socialism*. New York: Praeger, 1973.

Lorwin, Val. *The French Labor Movement*. Cambridge, Mass.: Harvard University Press, 1954.

McInnes, Norman. *Communist Parties of Western Europe*. Oxford: Clarenden Press, 1975.

Micaud, Charles A. *Communism and the French Left*. New York: Praeger, 1963.

Napolitano, Giorgio. *The Italian Road to Socialism*. Westport, Conn.: Greenwood Press, 1972.

Orwell, George. *Homage to Catalonia*. New York: Harcourt & Brace, 1952.

Pelling, Henry. *The British Communist Party. A Historical Profile*. London: A. and C. Black, 1975.

Schapiro, Leonard. *The Communist Party of the Soviet Union*. New York: Random House, 1970.

Schorske, Carl. *German Social Democracy, 1907-1917*. Cambridge, Mass.: Harvard University Press, 1955.

Tucker, Robert. *Stalin as Revolutionary, 1879-1929. A Study in History and Personality*. New York: Norton, 1973.

_____, ed. *Stalinism: Essays in Historical Interpretation*. New York: Norton, 1977.

Ulam, Adam. *Stalin: The Man and His Era*. New York: Viking Press, 1973.

_____. *The Unfinished Revolution: An Essay on the Sources of Marxism and Communism*. New York: Random House, 1960.

Wohl, Robert. *French Communism in the Making, 1914-1924*. Stanford, Cal.: Stanford University Press, 1966.

Woodcock, George. *Anarchism*. Cleveland, Ohio: Meridian Books, 1962.

ARTICLES

Bell, Daniel. "Socialism." *International Encyclopedia of the Social Sciences*. Vol. 15 (1968).

Crosland, C. A. R. "The Future of the Left." *Encounter* 14 (1960).

Gordon, Max. "Italian Communism Today." *Marxist Perspectives* 3 (1978).

Heilbroner, Robert L. "Socialism and the Future." *Commentary* 48 (December 1969).

Lipset, Seymour Martin. "The Changing Class Structure and Contemporary European Politics." *Daedalus* 21 (1964).

Lyman, Richard W. "The British Labour Party: The Conflict Between

Socialist Ideals and Practical Politics Between the Wars." *The Journal of British Studies* 5 (1965).

Mander, John. "The Future of Social Democracy." *Commentary* 50 (1970).

BACKGROUND FOR WOMEN'S HISTORY AND EUROPEAN FEMINIST MOVEMENTS

Because the nature and extent of women's involvement in radical politics is tied to more general aspects of social, economic, and political history, an understanding of such topics as family history, women and work, social attitudes, and stereotypes provides an essential background. Additionally, since traditional radical parties are often influenced by the existence of autonomous movements for women's rights, these also must be considered. The following, though highly selective, provide a general context for discussing women's experiences in Europe.

BOOKS

Atkinson, Dorothy; Dallin, Alexander; and Lapidius, Gail, eds. *Women in Russia*. Stanford, Cal.: Stanford University Press, 1977.

Banks, J. A.; and Banks, Olive. *Feminism and Family Planning*. Liverpool: Liverpool University Press, 1964.

Branca, Patricia. *Women in Modern Europe since 1750*. New York: St. Martin's Press, 1970.

Bridenthal, Renata, and Koonz, Claudia, eds. *Becoming Visible: Women in European History*. Boston: Houghton Mifflin, 1977.

Carroll, Berenice, ed. *Liberating Women's History*. Urbana, Ill.: University of Illinois press, 1976.

Evans, Richard. *The Feminist Movement in Germany, 1894-1933*. London: Sage, 1976.

———. *The Feminists. Women's Emancipation Movements in Europe, America and Australasia, 1840-1900*. New York: Harper & Row, 1979.

Friedman, Barbara; Greenstein, Emily; Pollack, Fannette; and Williamson, Jane. *Women's Work and Women's Studies*. New York: Barnard College Women's Center, 1975.

Harrison, Brian. *Separate Spheres: The Opposition to Women's Suffrage in Britain*. New York: Holmes and Meier, 1978.

Holcombe, Lee. *Victorian Ladies at Work: Middle Class Working Women in England and Wales, 1850-1914*. Hamden, Conn.: Archon, 1973.

Hollis, Patricia, ed. *Women in Public: The Women's Movement, 1850-1900*. London: Allen and Unwin, 1979.

Lapidus, Gail. *Women in Soviet Society: Equality, Development and Social Change*. Berkeley, Cal.: University of California Press, 1978.

Mitchell, Juliet; and Oakley, Ann, eds. *The Rights and Wrongs of Women*. New York: Penguin Books, 1976.

Norris, Jill, and Liddington, Jill. *One Hand Tied Behind Us: The Rise of the Women's Suffrage Movement*. London: Virago, 1978.

Rover, Constance. *Women's Suffrage and Party Politics, 1866-1914*. London: Routledge and Kegan Paul, 1967.

Tilly, Louise, and Scott, Joan. *Women, Work and Family*. New York: Holt, Rinehart & Winston, 1978.

Vicinus, Martha, ed. *A Widening Sphere*. Bloomington, Ind.: University of Indiana Press, 1977.

_____, ed. *Suffer and Be Still*. Bloomington, Ind.: University of Indiana Press, 1972.

Wheaton, Robert, and Hareven, Tamara, ed. *Family and Sexuality in French History*. Philadelphia: University of Pennsylvania Press, 1980.

RADICAL THEORETICAL RESPONSES TO THE "WOMAN QUESTION"

Starting with the fundamental definition of the "woman question" by Karl Marx and Friedrich Engels, a variety of individuals in the socialist and communist parties have elaborated on certain of the themes relating to women's emancipation. In this section, we have included non-European theoretical statements, because in the area of theory there has been a great deal of cross-national stimulation. In addition, we have made a chronological division at the end of World War II because in the last several decades of radical pluralism, Marxist-feminism increasingly has helped to alter general radical political theory by emphasizing the primacy of the "Woman Question" and family relations in understanding the mechanism of social and economic development.

BOOKS BEFORE 1945

Bebel, August. *Woman under Socialism*. 1883; reprint ed., New York: Schocken Books, 1971.

Engels, Friedrich. *Origins of the Family, Private Property and the State*. 1884, reprint ed., New York: International Publishers, 1972.

Ford, Isabella. *Women and Socialism*. London: Independent Labour Party, 1904.

Inman, Mary. *In Woman's Defense*. Los Angeles: The Committee to Organize the Advancement of Women, 1940.

Lenin, Vladimir Ilich. *On the Emancipation of Women*. Moscow: Progress Publishers, 1968.

Snowden, Ethel. *The Woman Socialist*. London: George Allen, 1907.

Trotsky, Leon. *Their Morals and Ours: Marxist versus Liberal Views on Morality*. New York: Pathfinder Press, 1973.

_____. *Women and the Family*. New York: Pathfinder Press, 1970.

The Woman Question: Selections from the Writings of Karl Marx, Friedrich Engels, V. I. Lenin and Joseph Stalin. 1951; reprint ed., New York: International Publishers, 1970.

Women and Communism: Selections from the Writings of Marx, Engels, Lenin and Stalin. Westport, Conn.: Greenwood Press, 1973.

Zetkin, Clara. *Lenin on the Woman Question*. New York: International Publishers, 1934.

ARTICLES BEFORE 1945

"A Feminist Symposium." *The New Review* 8, no. 8 (1914).

Draper, Hal. "Marx and Engels on Women's Liberation." *International Socialist*, no. 57 (1970).

Marx, Eleanor, and Aveling, Edward. "The Woman Question." 1885; reprinted in *Marxism Today* 16, no. 3 (1972).

BOOKS SINCE 1945

Beauvoir, Simone de. *The Second Sex*. New York: Alfred A. Knopf, 1969.

_____, and Sartre, Jean Paul. *Poets and Players*. Santa Barbara, Cal.: Harvest Publications, 1979.

Castro, Fidel. *Women's Liberation: The Revolution within the Revolution. The Santa Clara Speech, December 9, 1966*. New York: Merit Pamphlet, 1970.

Dalla Costa, Mariarosa. *Women and the Subversion of the Community*. Bristol, Conn.: Falling Wall Press, 1972.

Dunayevskaya, Raya. *Philosophy and Revolution*. New York: Dell, 1973.

Eisenstein, Zillah, ed. *Capitalist Patriarchy and the Case for Socialist Feminism*. New York: Monthly Review Press, 1979.

Foreman, Ann. *Femininity as Alienation: Women and the Family in Marxism and Psychoanalysis*. London: Pluto Press, 1977.

Guettell, Charnie. *Marxism and Feminism*. Toronto: The Women's Press, 1974.

Inman, Mary. *The Two Forms of Production under Capitalism*. Long Beach, Cal.: by the author, 1964.

Jenness, Linda, ed. *Feminism and Socialism*. New York: Pathfinder Press, 1972.

Kuhn, Annette, and Wolpe, Ann Marie. *Feminism and Materialism*. London: Routledge and Kegan Paul, 1978.

Mitchell, Juliet. *Woman's Estate*. London: Penguin Books, 1971.

Smith, Dorothy. *Feminism and Marxism*. Vancouver, B.C.: New Star Books, 1977.

Weinbaum, Batya. *The Curious Courtship of Women's Liberation and Socialism*. London: South End Press, 1978.

ARTICLES SINCE 1945

Bridenthal, Renate. "The Dialectics of Production and Reproduction in History." *Radical America* 10, no. 2 (1976).

Ehrenreich, Barbara. "Toward Socialist Feminism." *Heresies* (1977).

Gimenez, Martha E. "Marxism and Feminism." *Frontiers* 1, no. 1 (1975).

Prokop, Ulrike, "Production and the Context of Women's Daily Life." *New German Critique*. No. 13 (1978).

Rowbotham, Sheila. "The Women's Movement and Organising for Socialism." *Radical America* 13, no. 5 (1979).

Slaughter, Jane. "Feminism and Socialism: Theoretical Debates in Historical Perspective." *Marxist Perspectives* 2, no. 3 (1979).

Waters, Mary-Alice. "Feminism and the Marxist Movement." *International Socialist Review* 59 (1972).

"Women and Class Struggle." *Latin American Perspectives* 4, nos. 1-2 (1977).

"Women in the Fight Against Capital: International Marxist Discussion." *World Marxist Review* 16, no. 6 (1973).

"Women and Contemporary Capitalism: Some Theoretical Questions." *Science and Society* 42, no. 3 (1978).

CASE STUDIES OF WOMEN IN RADICAL POLITICAL PARTIES

BOOKS

Berkin, Carol, and Lovett, Clara, eds. *Women, War and Revolution*. New York: Holmes & Meier, 1979.

Boxer, Marilyn, and Quataert, Jean, eds. *Socialist Women: European Socialist Feminism in the Nineteenth and Twentieth Centuries*. New York: Elsevier, 1978.

Marks, Elaine, and Courtivron, Isabelle de, eds. *New French Feminisms: An Anthology.* Amherst, Mass.: University of Massachusetts Press, 1979.

Quataert, Jean. *Reluctant Feminists in German Social Democracy, 1885-1917.* Princeton, N.J.: Princeton University Press, 1979.

Rowbotham, Sheila. *Hidden From History.* New York: Pantheon, 1974.

_____. *Women, Resistance and Revolution.* New York: Vintage, 1974.

Stites, Richard. *The Women's Liberation Movement in Russia: Feminism, Nihilism and Bolshevism, 1860-1930.* Princeton, N.J.: Princeton University Press, 1978.

Thomas, Edith. *The Women Incendiaries.* New York: George Braziller, 1966.

Thönnessen, Werner. *The Emancipation of Women: The Rise and Decline of the Women's Movement in German Social Democracy, 1863-1933.* London: Pluto Press, 1973.

ARTICLES

Burke, Carolyn Greenstein. "Report from Paris: Women's Writing and the Women's Movement." *Signs* 3, no. 4 (1978).

Bobroff, Anne. "Alexandra Kollontai: Feminism, Worker's Democracy and Internationalism." *Radical America* 13, no. 6 (1979).

Engel, Barbara Alpern. "The Emergence of Women Revolutionaries in Russia." *Frontiers* 2, no. 1 (1977).

Hamai, Thomas Lewis. "Beyond Feminism: The Women's Movement in Austrian Social Democracy, 1890-1920." Ph.D. diss., Ohio State University, 1973.

Hayden, Carol Eubanks. "The Zhenotdel and the Bolshevik Party." *Russian History* 3, no. 2 (1976).

Honeycut, Karen. "Socialism and Feminism in Imperial Germany." *Signs* 5, no. 1 (1979).

Kaplan, Temma. "Spanish Anarchism and Women's Liberation." *Journal of Contemporary History* 6, no. 2 (1971).

Kern, Robert W. "Anarchist Principles and Spanish Reality: Emma Goldman as a Participant in the Civil War, 1936-1939," *Journal of Contemporary History* 11, no. 1 (1976).

Kline, Rayna, "Partisans, Godmothers, Bicyclists and Other Terrorists: Women in the French Resistance and Under Vichy." *Proceedings of the Annual Meeting of the Western Society for French History.* No. 5 (1977).

Knight, Amy. "The Fritschi: A Study of Female Radicals in the Russian Revolution." *Canadian-American Slavic Studies* 9, no. 1 (1975).

Lafleur, Ingrun. "Adelheid Popp and Working Class Feminism in Austria." *Frontiers* 1, no. 1 (1975).

McNeal, Robert H. "Women in the Russian Radical Movement." *Journal of Social History* 5, no. 2 (1971-1972).

Peterson, Brian. "The Politics of Working Class Women in the Weimar Republic." *Central European History* 10, no. 2 (1977).

Rowbotham, Sheila. "Women and Radical Politics in Britain, 1830-1914." *Radical History Review* 19 (1978-1979).

Stanton, Donna. "Activism and the Academy: A Report from Europe." *Signs* 5, no. 1 (1979).

Stites, Richard. "Zhenotdel: Bolshevism and Russian Women," 1917-1930." *Russian History* 3, no. 2 (1976).

Sowerwine, Charles. "Women and Socialism in France, 1871-1921." Ph.D. diss., University of Wisconsin, 1973.

_____. The Organization of French Socialist Women, 1880-1814." *Historical Reflections* 3, no. 2 (1976).

Ventura, Angelo. "Anna Kuliscioff, Filippo Turati and Italian Socialism during the Postwar Crisis, 1919-1925." *The Journal of Italian History* 1, no. 1 (1978).

Wolfe, Bertram. "Lenin and Inessa Armand." *Slavic Review* 22 (1963).

Wheeler, Robert F. "German Women and the Communist International: The Case of the Independent Social Democrats." *Central European History* 8, no. 2 (1975).

BIOGRAPHY AND AUTOBIOGRAPHY

The works in this section cover biographies and autobiographies of European women, some of whom are not directly discussed in the articles in this collection, but whose lives are important for a good understanding of the period and the struggle.

BOOKS

Broido, Vera. *Apostles into Terrorists: Women in the Russian Revolutionary Movement of Alexander II*. New York: Viking, 1977.

Clements, Barbara Evans. *Bolshevik Feminist: The Life of Alexandra Kollontai*. Bloomington, Ind.: University of Indiana Press, 1978.

Drinnon, Richard. *Rebel in Paradise: A Biography of Emma Goldman*. Chicago: University of Chicago Press, 1961.

Figner, Vera. *Memoirs of a Revolutionist*. New York: International Publishers, 1927.

Florence, Ronald. *Marx's Daughters*. New York: Dial Press, 1975.

Goldman, Emma. *Living My Life*. New York: Scribner, 1932.

Goldsmith, Margaret. *Seven Women Against the World*. London: Methuen, 1935.

Holt, Alix, ed. *Alexandra Kollontai: Selected Writings*. Bristol, Conn.: Lawrence Hill, 1978.

Ibarruri, Dolores. *They Shall Not Pass: The Autobiography of La Pasionaria*. New York: International Publishers, 1966.

Kollontai, Alexandra. *The Autobiography of a Sexuallly Emancipated Woman*. New York: Schocken Books, 1975.

McNeal, Robert H. *Bride of the Revolution: Krupskaya and Lenin*. Ann Arbor, Mich.: University of Michigan, 1972.

Mitchell, David. *The Fighting Pankhursts: A Study in Tenacity*. London: Jonathan Cape, 1967.

Mitchell, Geoffrey, ed. *The Hard Way Up: The Autobiography of Hannah Mitchell*. London: Faber & Faber, 1968.

Montefiore, Dora. *From a Victorian to a Modern*. London: E. Archer, 1927.

Nettl, John. *Rosa Luxemburg*. 2 vols. Oxford: Clarenden Press, 1966.

Popp, Adelheid. *The Autobiography of a Working Woman*. Chicago: F. G. Browne, 1913.

Strachey, Rachel. *Millicent Garrett Fawcett*. London: John Murray, 1931.

Webb, Beatrice. *My Apprenticeship*. New York: Longmans Green, 1926.

ARTICLES

Felstiner, Mary Lowenthal. "Seeing *The Second Sex* Through the Second Wave." *Feminist Studies* 6, no. 2 (1980).

Jardine, Alice. "Interview with Simone de Beauvoir." *Signs* 5, no. 2 (1979).

Widgery, David. "Sylvia Pankhurst: Pioneer of Working Class Feminism." *Radical America* 13, no. 3 (1979).

COMPARATIVE WORKS

In this final section, we have chosen works relating to the radical tradition in the United States and in those nations currently defined as socialist. Women's history has a strong comparative tradition, and by looking at other areas of the world, we are better equipped to understand both the objective factors of women's historical experience and the varieties of methodology that can be applied to a study of women's relation to radical politics.

AMERICAN RADICALISM

BOOKS

Avrich, Paul. *An American Anarchist: The Life of Voltairine de Cleye.* Princeton, N.J.: Princeton University Press, 1978.

Cook, Blanche Wiesen, ed. *Toward the Great Change: Crystal and Max Eastman on Feminism, Antimilitarism and Revolution.* New York: Garland, 1976.

Dennis, Peggy. *The Autobiography of an American Communist: A Personal View of a Political Life, 1925-1975.* Berkeley: Lawrence Hall, 1977.

Flynn, Elizabeth Gurley. *The Rebel Girl.* 1955; reprint ed. New York: International Publishers, 1973.

Howe, Bertha Washburn. *An American Century: The Recollections of Bertha Washburn Howe, 1866-1966.* New York: Humanities Press, 1966.

Weisbord, Vera Buch. *A Radical Life.* Bloomington, Ind.: University of Indiana Press, 1977.

ARTICLES

Dancis, Bruce. "Socialism and Women in the U.S., 1900-1917." *Socialist Revolution* 6, no. 1 (1976).

Dixler, Elsa. "The Woman Question: Women and the American Communist Party, 1929-41." Ph.D. diss., Yale University, 1974.

Loader, Jayne. "Women in the Left, 1906-1941: A Bibliography of Primary Sources." *University of Michigan Papers in Women's Studies* 2, no. 1 (1975).

Shaffer, Robert. "Women and the CPUSA, 1930-1940." *Socialist Review.* No. 45 (1979).

Trimberger, Ellen Kay. "Women in the Old and New Left: The Evolution of a Politics of Personal Life." *Feminist Studies* 5, no. 3 (1979).

Wiener, Jon. "The Communist Party Today and Yesterday: An Interview with Dorothy Healey." *Radical America* 11, no. 3 (1977).

THE SOCIALIST EXPERIENCE

BOOKS

Croll, Elizabeth. *Feminism and Socialism in China.* Boston: Routledge and Kegan Paul, 1978.

Davin, Delia. *Women-Work: Women and the Party in Revolutionary China.* Oxford: Clarenden Press, 1979.

Grace, Paul, ed. *Vietnamese Women in Society and Revolution*. Cambridge, Mass.: Vietnam Resource Center, 1974.

Heitlinger, Alena. *Women and State Socialism: Sex Inequality in the Soviet Union and Czechoslovakia*. Montreal: McGill-Queens University Press, 1979.

Randall, Margaret. *Cuban Women Today: Interviews with Cuban Women*. Toronto: Women's Press, 1974.

Scott, Hilda. *Does Socialism Liberate Women?* Boston: Beacon Press, 1974.

ARTICLES

Davin, Delia. "The Implications of Some Aspects of C.C.P. Policy Toward Urban Women in the 1950s." *Modern China* 1, no. 4 (1975).

Chan, Anita. "Rural Chinese Women and the Socialist Revolution: An Inquiry into the Economics of Sexism." *Journal of Contemporary Asia* 4, no. 2 (1974).

Curtin, Katie. "Women and the Chinese Revolution." *International Socialist Review* 35, no. 3 (1974).

Kuei-fang, Ying. "The Current Women's Movement on the Chinese Mainland." *Issues and Studies* 10, no. 10 (1974).

Scott, Hilda. "Women's Place in Socialist Society: The Case of Eastern Europe." *Social Policy* 7, no. 5 (1977).

Weinbaum, Batya. "Women in the Transition to Socialism: Perspectives on the Chinese Case." *Review of Radical Political Economy* 8, no. 1 (1976).

Index

About the Editors
and Contributors

Marilyn J. Boxer received her Ph.D. in history from the University of California, Davis; since 1974 she has served as Chair of the Department of Women's Studies at San Diego State University. She is coauthor of *Socialist Women: European Socialist Feminism in the 19th and Early 20th Centuries* (Elsevier, 1978) and is currently preparing a monograph on women who worked in home industry in Paris in the early twentieth century.

John M. Cammett received his Ph.D. in history from Columbia University and is currently Professor of History at the John Jay College of Criminal Justice (City University of New York). He is the author of *Antonio Gramsci and the Origins of Italian Communism* (Stanford, 1967) and other studies of Italian communism and fascism and is editor of *Science and Society*.

Linda Edmondson has worked as a research assistant at University College, London, and recently completed a doctoral dissertation on feminism in Russia before the Revolution. She is currently working on civil rights in Russia before and after 1917.

Shirley Fredricks received her Ph.D. in history from the University of New Mexico and currently teaches history and acts as Affirmative Action Officer at Adams State College, Alamosa, Colorado, where from 1978 to 1980 she also served as Acting Vice-President for Academic and Student Affairs. A previous article on Federica

Montseny appeared in *Frontiers* (Winter 1976), and Fredricks' on-going research project is a biography of this Spanish anarchist-feminist.

Karen Honeycut received her Ph.D. in history from Columbia University. She has held editorial-research positions in German literature at the Modern Language Association and in early American history at the University of Connecticut. She is currently Coordinator of Special Projects in the Office of the Chancellor at the City University of New York and also a scholarship student at New York Law School. Among her publications is a recent article on "Socialism and Feminism in Imperial Germany," appearing in *Signs* (Fall 1979).

Robert Kern received his Ph.D. from the University of Chicago and is currently Professor of History at the University of New Mexico. Author of *Red Years, Black Years* (ISHI, 1978) and two earlier books, he is now working on the history of northern Spain during the Civil War.

David Kramer studied at the University of Redlands and Tulane University and in 1970 moved to Berlin. He taught at the Free University of Berlin and the University of Maryland in Europe and is presently Professor of Social Policy and Prorektor of the Fach-hochschule für Sozialarbeit und Sozialpadagogik in Berlin.

Jane Slaughter received her Ph.D. from the University of New Mexico and in 1975 returned to that institution as an Assistant Professor of History and a member of the Women Studies Program. She has published previous articles on feminism and socialism in the *Social Science Journal* and *Marxist Perspectives* and is currently preparing a monograph on women and the Italian Resistance, 1943-1945.

Beverly Tanner Springer is Associate Professor of International Studies at the American Graduate School of International Manage-ment in Glendale, Arizona. She received her Ph.D. in political science from the University of Colorado and has done field research in Italy and the United Kingdom. She is a contributor to *Women in the World*, edited by Lynn B. Iglitzin and Ruth Ross.

Richard Stites is Assistant Professor of Russian and East European History at Georgetown University. He is the author of *The Women's Liberation Movement in Russia: Nihilism, Feminism and Bolshevism, 1860-1930* and various articles on women in Russian history. He has recently translated, edited, and introduced Paul Miliukov, *The Russian Revolution*, 3 vols. (Academic International Press, 1978) and is currently working on a book dealing with utopianism and experiment in the Russian Revolution, 1917-1930.